Lars Levi Læstadius

Fragments of Lapp Mythology

Part 1: Doctrine of the Gods

Nils Magne Knutsen and Per Posti

Translated by John Weinstock

Agarita Press

Copyright © 2017 Agarita Press
Dripping Springs, Texas
ISBN-978-0998472300

Set in Minion Pro and Bodoni 72

The original of this book was published as

Lars Levi Læstadius

Fragmenter i Lappska Mythologien

Gudalära

Angelica Forlag AS, Tromsø 2003

Cover Design by John Weinstock and Beth Brotherton

Ollu giitu dáid olbmuide hui buori veahki ovddas:
Nils Magne Knutsen, Per Posti,
Harald Gaski, Robert Rovinsky

This translation has been published with
the financial support of NORLA.

Doctrine of the Gods

Contents

Foreword

Per Posti:
Lars Levi Læstadius' Sámi mythology –
the manuscript's birth and its strange history 9

Sources 49

Lars Levi Læstadius:
*Fragments of Lapp Mythology – Part 1,
Doctrine of the Gods (Gudalära)* ,,,,,,,,,,,,,,,,,,,,,,,,,,,,,,,,,,,, 55

Index of Sámi gods, objects and concepts
mentioned in *Doctrine of the Gods (Gudalära)* 175

Index of authors cited or discussed in
Doctrine of the Gods (Gudalära) 191

Roald E. Kristiansen:
Doctrine of the Gods (Gudelæren) in L. L.
Læstadius' *Fragmenter i Lappska Mythologien* 193

Literary references 201

Foreword

In September of 2002 the undersigned published the book *La Recherche – En ekspedisjon mot nord – Une expédition vers le Nord* (An expedition to the north). Here a thorough account is given of the large-scale French Recherche expedition that went to northern Scandinavia and Svalbard (Spitzbergen) in the years 1838-40. One of the most well-known participants was the Swedish pastor and botanist Lars Levi Læstadius who accompanied the expedition on the journey from Hammerfest to Karesuando in the fall of 1838.

During the years 1839-45 Læstadius wrote an important monograph on Sámi mythology that was going to be included in the Recherche expedition's official publication series. But the monograph that bore the title *Fragments of Lapp Mythology* was never printed, and the manuscript disappeared, apparently without a trace.

The monograph's fate has interested a number of Scandinavian investigators since the manuscript went astray more than 150 years ago. After some extensive and exciting detective work in archives and libraries however the manuscript was found again piece by piece. Part 1 was found in the little French town Pontarlier in 1933, and the next parts turned up in 1946 at Yale University in the USA. The investigators then believed that the entire monograph had been found, but 55 years later, in the fall of 2001, while working on *La Recherche – An expedition to the north*, another part of the manuscript turned up in Pontarlier. This new part, which comprises 108 copy book pages, turned out to be a continuation of the monograph's first part, *Gudalära*. Thanks to this discovery, we can present the first complete printed version of this part of Læstadius' monograph.

The introductory article considers the background as to why the monograph was written and Læstadius' laborious effort to get it published. Here too is explained the extensive effort leading to all parts of the manuscript finally being found again.

The book concludes with an article where the historian of religion and Læstadius scholar, associate professor Roald E. Kristiansen at the University of Tromsø puts this last discovered part of *Fragments of Lapp Mythology* into a scholarly perspective.

Læstadius is not always linguistically consistent in his manuscript for *Gudalära*. Therefore, in this printed version we have had to make certain choices on a number of points. First of all, we have begun all sentences with capital letters as well as using them for proper names. With common nouns, we have followed Læstadius' own usage of initial capital letters, though with certain adjustments. In addition, we have allowed ourselves a careful adjustment of the punctuation. As for italics and underlining there were certain problems of interpretation, but we have to the best of our ability followed Læstadius' manuscript. Inconsistencies in the orthography we have largely retained, while we have corrected a few small omissions or slips of Læstadius' pen. Where errors or missing letters affect understanding of the text or something is not clear, we have suggested additions in square brackets [ ]. The usual parentheses are Læstadius' own.

In the previously printed portion of *Gudalära*, which goes to the middle of §111, there are some proof errors and misinterpretations of Læstadius' handwriting, especially in the 1997 edition. These errors we have corrected, to the extent possible.

A large thanks is extended to Musée de Pontarlier and its curator Joël Guiraud who most willingly put the newly discovered manuscript at our disposal. Likewise, a large thanks to the institutions and private persons who have made books, letters, diaries, illustrated material, etc. available to us. A special thanks to Universitetsbiblioteket i Tromsø (HSJ), to librarians Per Morten Bryn at Bibliothèque Nordique in Paris, research assistant Marja-Leena Hänninen at Museiverket in Helsinki, archivist Anne Wiktorsson at Kungl. Vetenskapsakademien in Stockholm and librarian Magne Rundberg at Universitetsbiblioteket i Tromsø, div. Tromsø Museum for much good will and helpfulness. Thanks also to the printers, Lundblad Media AS in Tromsø, who with their technical competence and attitude to service have been important partners cooperating on the project. A special thanks is extended to TotalFinaElf Exploration Norge AS who with its generous support made possible the discovery of the manuscript in question.

The first part of the manuscript was rediscovered by a Finn, the next parts were discovered by a Swede. With the thought of the great importance Lars Levi Læstadius has also had in Norway, we now from the Norwegian side can put the last piece of the puzzle in place, and in that way contribute to the prolonged Nordic effort to solve the mystery of the lost manuscript.

Tromsø, June 2003

Nils M. Knutsen and Per Posti

Lars Levi Læstadius' Sámi mythology – the manuscript's birth and its strange history

By Per Posti

Lars Levi Læstadius was born in January of 1800 in Jäckvik along the large lake Hornavan in Arjeplog Lappmark in Sweden. The little family lived there as settlers under extremely modest circumstances.

Both Lars Levi and his two-year younger brother, Petrus, received their first education at home. About this the latter writes: *In all their poverty, in all their striving for life's bare necessities, our parents did not forget and ignore teaching us to read.*

The spoken language at home was Swedish, while the dominant language in the small villages where the Læstadius brothers grew up, was Sámi. They must already early on have become familiar with Sámi belief and superstition and history, and at the gymnasium in Härnösand and during college days in Uppsala this knowledge was undoubtedly strengthened and broadened. Lars Levi himself says about this: *I have never made mythology a main study. As a child, I heard quite a lot belonging to Lapp [mythology], and as a student I did excerpts of Leem.*

In an undated manuscript, the pastor Kristian Nissen writes about the mythologist and folklorist and how during his wanderings through forests and over mountains, as a naturalist, missionary and pastor, he got to see and hear much about old Sámi mythology:

To be sure, it was already a couple centuries since the Lapps in the Swedish Lappmarks had been baptized Christian, organized into congregations with their own pastors. But even a hundred years or so before Læstadius began his service as a pastor in Pite Lappmark in 1825, the magic drum was in use in many places. And sacrifices at old ritual sites could probably still occur. Only through extensive internal and external reforms in the Swedish church's work in the Lappmarks, which in part was inspired by Thomas von Westen's influence in Norway (1714-27), were these remnants of old Lapp paganism essentially defeated. But this stage in the Lappmarks' history of conversion thus lay in Læstadius' time as a missionary and first years as a pastor just one hundred years back in time. And it goes without saying that for someone like Læstadius who was so conversant with the Lapps' language and mode of thought and whole culture there was an entire world of living traditions to draw upon.

Lars Levi Læstadius began as a parish pastor in Karesuando in 1826. Together with his wife Brita Katarina (Kajsa) and a steadily growing flock of children he remained here for more than 20 years.

Læstadius was an able pastor, investigator and author, with a very large range. In Karesuando many important religious and botanical writings were composed, several thousand plants were collected, pressed and distributed to museums and collections in Scandinavia and France; it was here the famous Læstadian revival started, and it was here the monograph on Sámi mythology was written.

Early on, Læstadius had thoughts of using his knowledge of Sámi mythology and history in one way or other. As early as 1830, in a letter to the zoologist Gabriel Marklin in Uppsala, he wrote:

My Historia lapponum is not yet planned, even less begun. Nevertheless, I really want information about everything concering the Lappmarks. A list of all authors who have written anything about Lappland, would for a start be welcome to me.

Whether Læstadius was sent a synopsis of the literature is not known. Four years later, however, he made probably his first attempt at creating a sort of outline of Sámi mythology. The background was that during the period 1832-34 he had written a series of articles in "Tidskrift för jägare och naturforskere" [Magazine for hunters and natural scientists]. In April of 1834 he sent some material to the periodical, and in an enclosed letter to one of the editors, the zoologist Bengt Fredrik Fries, he wrote that in addition he had

/.../ inserted a brief token of a prospective Mythologia Lapponica, a work I have long had in mind, but have not had time to begin.

But Læstadius was lacking decent literature on the subject and says further in the letter:

The worst is that in the Lappmarks one finds oneself without ready literary help, and must be without the means to procure the most necessary books. This is in part the reason why so many Lapp pastors fall into inactivity and are finally forgotten by the rest of the world.

Three years later, the fall of 1837, Læstadius was visited by the zoologist Sven Lovén who was overwhelmed by Læstadius' knowledge about Sámi history. Lovén wrote in his diary:

His knowledge of the Lapps' customs, practices and tales is unusual, and it would be a great loss if they disappeared without being made public. He related much about that, more tales, and informed me as well, that the Lapps in days of yore lived in caves of which there are still traces in the southern Lappmarks.

That same autumn, navy doctor and zoologist Paul Gaimard was sitting in Paris putting the finishing touches on the planning of a scientific expedition to the northern parts of Scandinavia. A thorough account of the background and execution of this expedition is found in Nils M. Knutsen and Per Posti: *La Recherche – An expedition to the north*, that appeared in 2002.

On March 29, 1838 Paul Gaimard sent a letter to the secretary of Kungliga Vetenskapsakademien [Royal Academy of Science] in Stockholm, Baron Jøns Jacob Berzelius, where the plan for the expedition was sketched. A printed copy of the

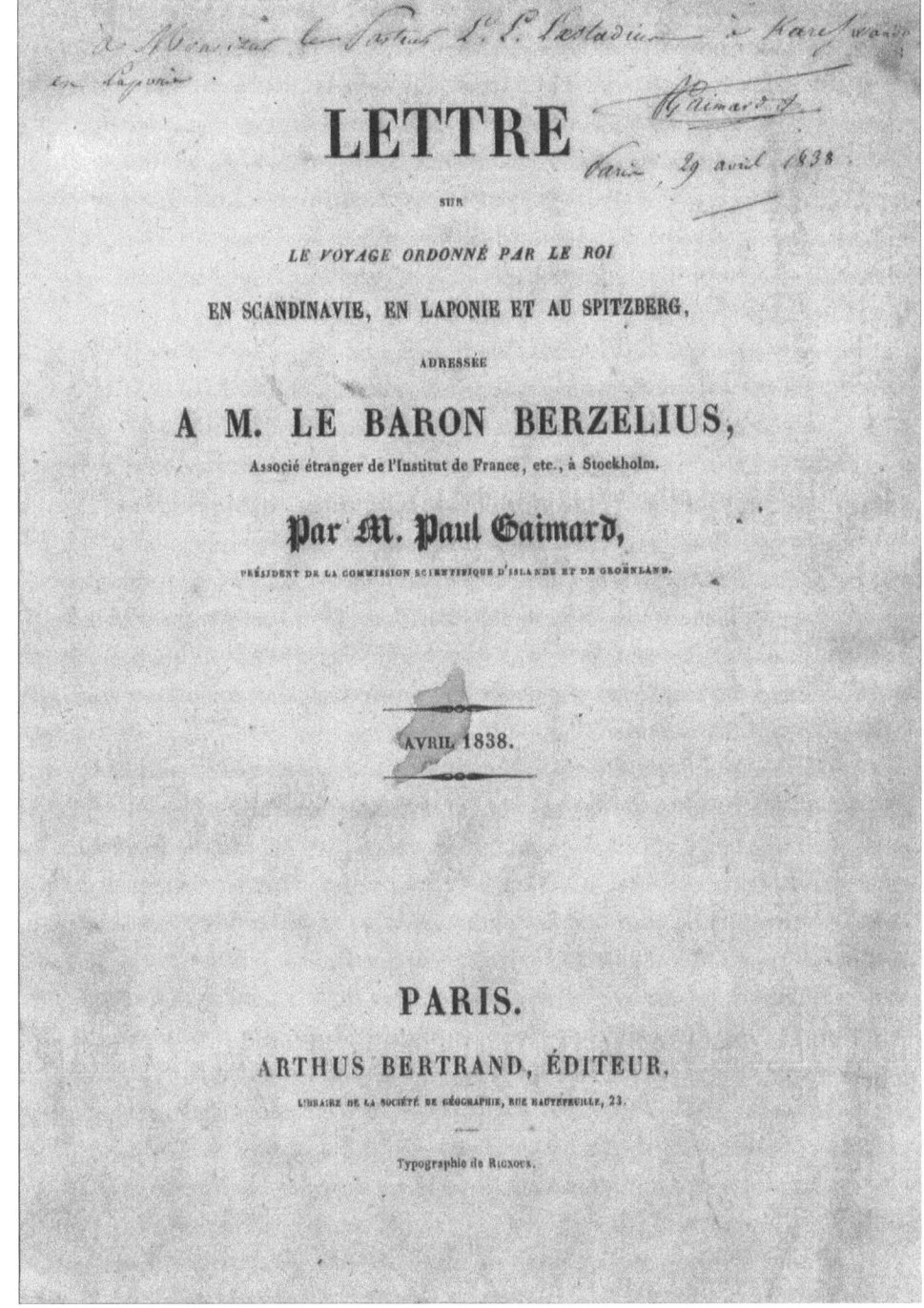

On March 29, 1838 Paul Gaimard sent a letter to the secretary of Kungliga Vetenskapsakademien [Royal Academy of Science] in Stockholm, Baron J. J. Berzelius in which the program for the Recherche expedition was sketched. A printed copy of the letter was sent to a number of prominent European scientists.

The illustration shows the front of Lars Levi Læstadius' copy, dated April 29, 1838. Privately owned.

letter was sent to a number of prominent European researchers, including Lars Levi Læstadius. The Academy of Science in Stockholm though had earlier in the winter contacted Gaimard in Paris concerning the expedition, and had already in a letter of March 16 asked Læstadius whether he wanted to participate. The letter was signed by natural scientist and professor Peter Fredrik Wahlberg, and Læstadius replied in a letter dated April 11:

If the intention with the scientific expedition is that I should go along to Spitzbergen, then I must refrain, since to begin with I get seasick, and secondly as father of a rather large family I have much hesitation about such a trip, which is often dangerous, if one doesn't have a trustworthy skipper. /…/ But if I were to be able to restrict myself to the boundaries of northern Scandinavia, then I could certainly accept the offer.

Læstadius now got a leave of absence from his position as parish pastor in Karesuando, and in May he started his journey toward the Gulf of Bothnia where he thought he would join the expedition. But he had gotten poor information about the expedition's itinerary; the official invitation from Gaimard did not get to Karesuando until August 21.

When Læstadius got to Piteå at the turn of the month May-June, he could read in the newspaper the disheartening news that the corvette *La Recherche* was going to sail northward along the Norwegian coast without calling at any Swedish ports. He thereby had to turn around and start a roughly 1000 km long journey to the north, with Hammerfest as the ultimate goal. In the middle of the summer he was in Happaranda, and in the first half of July he arrived at Muonioniska. Here he met the Finnish philologist and ethnographer Mathias Alexander Castrén who in a letter writes about Læstadius:

His intended Lapp mythology and bent for speculative matters led us to discussions that usually stretched into the morning. We separated as brothers and friends; – but with me he left a memory that will never fade.

From the letter, it is seen that Læstadius at this point in time was already thinking about writing a Sámi mythology.

Læstadius continued his journey to the north, and at the beginning of August he had come to Norway. On the 12th of August, he could be found in the newly built church in Kåfjord in Alta. In the church register for Talvik, the pastor Andreas Jørgen Fleischer had written for this day:

Sunday the 12th of August, 9d Trinit. services were held in Kaafjord for an abundant congregation and preached on the Gospel Luke 16. Pastor Læstadius from Karesuando officiated at confession for about 100 Kven communicants, for which I myself then administered the sacrament. The confession was held in the Kven language.

Læstadius then traveled to Hammerfest where he joined the expedition, which had just returned from Svalbard [Spitzbergen]. The corvette *La Recherche* now returned to France, while some of the participants in the expedition traveled to Kåfjord with the steamer *Prinds Gustav*, which just that spring had started its regular route between Trondheim and northern Norway.

In Kåfjord there followed some hectic days of taking on supplies, checking clothing and equipment, renting horses and porters, in addition to carrying on scientific collecting. The 29th of August everything was ready, and they could leave Kåfjord – an impressive caravan of 23 people and 20 horses. This is likely the largest party of travelers ever to have crossed Lapland. At the head went the travel guide, the old Sámi nomad Mikkel Johansen Kemi, who was from Kautokeino, where he earlier had also been sheriff. After the travel guide came 12 pack horses with porters, and last, eight riders all of whom were members of the Recherche expedition. Four of these were Frenchmen: the expedition leader, doctor and zoologist Paul Gaimard, geologist Eugène Robert, author and man of letters Xavier Marmier plus Gaimard's personal valet François, who also was cook on this Lapland journey. Besides there were the Norwegian Emanuel Meyer and the Swedish count Ulric Wilhelm Gyldenstolpe along as attachés, and the Swede Carl Jacob Sundevall as zoologist. The eighth person in the group was pastor and botanist Lars Levi Læstadius.

Later in the evening on August 30th they had come up onto the actual mountain plateau, and they came to a halt in a little birch grove where a brook ran quietly past. Sundevall says in his diary that the place was called Gurpmotvuopmi. Here the tents were put up and a bonfire made, and, Marmier writes:

/…/ soon the nice warmth gave some life to our stiff limbs. We doled out a ration of brandy, and everyone was immediately in a better mood. While there was moaning and groaning under the heavy loads, now only shouts of joy were heard. After the evening meal, Mr. Læstadius sat down on a reindeer hide beside the fire, lit his pipe and said he was going to tell us Sámi folktales. We were quick to sit down in a circle around him, and then he told us about Stallo.

The Frenchmen were very fascinated by the stories, and Marmier wrote further about this memorable evening:

It was completely quiet around us. All we heard was the sound of a horse bell a way off and the wind whispering in the birch branches. At the sight of the crackling embers in the bonfire, the tent which stood there in the shade, the dark forest, and all of us who were sitting there on the hill in front of the storyteller, then it reminded one most of all of a group of arabs listening to one of the stories about Antara(h).

Sámi mythology did not belong to the original plans for the Recherche expedition's publications. Læstadius was now however requested to write about Sámi mythology and history for publication in the expedition's publication series. This fit well with his own plans for this material, and he most likely accepted the offer.

On the 5th of September the fellow travelers arrived in Karesuando where they were lodged with the family Læstadius. Here there were relatively cramped quarters from before, but the hospitality was great, Marmier writes:

By putting mattresses and straw around the floor it was possible to house all of us, and we found the situation most confortable after our fatiguing journey through Lappland. Then for the first time in several weeks we could sit down at the table and eat on plates, drink from glasses – and no porcelain from Sèvres, no utensils of silver could have delighted us more than the coarse earthen vessels and iron forks in Karesuando parsonage.

Participants from the Recherche expedition stop at Lupsäkoppi between Kåfjord and Kautokeino, September 8, 1839. Here one can perceive some of the same atmosphere around the open fire as when Læstadius was telling his Stallo tales to the Frenchmen one year earlier.

Sketched by Charles Giraud and printed as a lithograph. Plate nr. 160 in the Recherche expedition's *Atlas historique et pittoresque*. Norsk Polarinstitutt, Tromsø. Photo: Mari Hildung, Tromsø.

In Karesuando the caravan was dispersed. Horses and drivers returned to Norway, while the expedition now continued in river boats down the Muonio River. Læstadius followed along to Muonioniska where he took leave of his traveling companions on September 11th.

The practical portion of Læstadius' participation in the Recherche expedition was thereby over. Now remained his contribution to the official publications, which to begin with was going to comprise meteorology, botany and Sámi mythology and history. But, as we shall see, his contribution came to be significantly reduced.

In February and March of 1839 Læstadius was visited by the Danish botanist Jens Moestue Vahl who also had been on the Recherche expedition. He had stayed in Tromsø after the expedition concluded in the fall of 1838. In January Læstadius sent a tempting invitation to his botanist colleague where among other things it says:

My Lapp herbarium is the result of nearly 20 years of excursions in almost all parts of northernmost Sweden and Norway, and accordingly contains more plant varieties than anyone else's collections from these northern districts.

Vahl let himself be tempted, and the 5th of February he left Tromsø to set to work on his own private Lappland journey via Lyngen to Karesuando. He stayed with Læstadius almost 14 days, and upon his departure on March 2nd was given a letter and 50 riksdaler to be delivered to P. F. Wahlberg in Stockholm. An enclosure in the letter contained a list of the books Læstadius wanted purchased and sent on to Karesuando. The list included several books of travel from the northern areas, botanical and zoological literature, a history of the bible and J. G. Gruber's handbook on the old classical mythology. Four of these books are among the sources Læstadius mentioned in the introduction to his Sámi mythology, namely by the authors Johan W. Zetterstedt, Jon Engström, Petrus Læstadius and Johann G. Gruber. Vahl himself got the task of providing the Danish linguist Rasmus Rask's *Lappske Grammatik* from 1832. From this it is evident that Læstadius, in addition to collecting literature in religion and natural science, was also in the process of building up a library on the theme of Lappland's history and mythology.

Now Læstadius worked more determined on mythology. Right after Vahl had left Karesuando, Læstadous wrote a long letter to the Finnish philologist Carl Axel Gottlund, dated the 5th and 6th of March. He wrote among other things a bit on the Recherche expedition:

Under way over the mountain ridge from Alta to Karesuando I happened to tell some Lapp stories about Stallo, which in certain respects resemble novels, and these stories brought such pleasure to the Frenchmen's ears, that I got no peace from them until I had to promise to write a Lapp mythology, which will be intertwined in their forthcoming large work, which beforehand is expected to cost between 700 to 900 francs.

Here Læstadius pretended he had to be urged several times, but in reality he had, as previously mentioned, long planned to write a monograph on Sámi mythology, and he saw this as a golden opportunity to get the material published. He says also further in the letter to C. A. Gottlund that he has much material on this subject, but still lacks a library. He lacks especially books on Finnish Sámi mythology, and now comes his real errand:

You who are presumably initiated in the old Finns' secrets, could undoubtedly assist me with some important information. Such as for example whether the Finns in paganism were convinced of the soul's immortality, about punishment and reward in another world, which gods they actually worshiped, with what sacrifices they wanted to appease the angry gods etc.

C. A. Gottlund wrote back the 4th of August the same year, but Læstadius did not get extensive answers to his questions nor very much help from what Gottlund wrote; they were namely not in agreement on the definition of the word mythology.

Spring of 1839 had been a difficult time for Læstadius. On April 1st his son Levi died, and in a letter to the botanist Carl Johan Hartman from May 11th Læstadius wrote:

My children have been suffering from measles, and the hideous guest carried off one of the most beautiful plants I owned, a little fellow of 2 years and 8 months, and that loss has made me more and more fed up with the world and the natural plants; if I don't get into a better mood, then I probably won't have the patience to go through the duplicates for a long time.

In his deep sorrow at having lost the apple of his eye, as is evident here, Læstadius was set back somewhat in his work on botany. In all likelihood, he didn't get much written on his Sámi mythology either. In any case, he hadn't gotten very far in this work when the members of this year's Recherche expedition passed by in September. First came a little vanguard, namely the artist François Biard and his 19-year-old partner Léonie d'Aunet. They had been on the expedition to Svalbard and were actually supposed to go with the others through Lappland. But for unknown reasons they started a week earlier from Kåfjord and arrived in Karesuando on September 12th. Léonie had been ill and confined to bed in Kautokeino, and furthermore they had had poor weather conditions on the trip to Karesuando, where the parsonage was the natural place to spend the night. Whether it was her self-pity that caused it, or whether it was Læstadius' continual sorrow over the loss of his son, shall remain unsaid; in any case, it was not a very pleasant meeting between the two, and Léonie was crass in her characterization:

This pastor was not a very pleasant acquaintance. In spite of our letter of recommendation and our miserable plight after the strenuous journey, he received us with a superior expression. With his cap on his head and pipe in his mouth he showed us to our room and didn't bother any more with us. I felt deeply offended.

From all conversations at this time with Læstadius and from all reports about staying at the parsonage in Karesuando, this one stands apart. Læstadius is mentioned otherwise exclusively in positive turns of speech. One example is the German printer and globetrotter, called Lavirer-Anders, who just this year, 1839, started his journeys through a number of countries in Europe, Asia and Africa. In the fall of 1847 he arrived in Karesuando, and in his diary, he writes about his meeting with Læstadius:

During the Lappland journey of 1839 the painter François Biard made a number of sketches of Sámi, and in Karesuando he made studies of Lars Levi Læstadius. One of the results became a large oil painting with the title: *Le pasteur Laestadius instruisant des Lapons – Pastor Læstadius preaches to the Sámi*. The picture was exhibited at the Salon in Paris in 1841.

Biard's somewhat imaginative surroundings rest on the fact that he did not experience snow on his

Lappland journey in September of 1839. On Svalbard, though he saw plenty of snow and ice formations. In his studio in Paris he then combined the elements: Sámi from Lappland, ice from Svalbard. It is not likely he experienced such a situation as the picture shows during the few days he stayed with Læstadius in Karesuando. It is though reasonable to believe he could have noticed both top hat and fur coat in Læstadius' "garderobe," and thereby he also included these elements in the picture. O.p.l. 131x163 cm, Nordnorsk Kunstmuseum, Tromsø. Photo: Hazlitt, Gooden & Fox, London.

Herr Læstadius is a big Latinist and an excellent botanist, especially very intimately familiar with the Lapland Flora. With his diligence, he benefits science a great deal just as his noble mentality and heart ardently work for the people's happiness. I lodged in his study, where his library, which mostly consisted of botanical works, and his plant collection was found. The herbarium lay, systematically organized and inserted in blotting paper, on shelves on the wall. In his chamber, it looks very simple, a painted table, a cabinet and wooden chair are its furniture. On the whole Læstadius seems to be a great foe of luxury; nevertheless, as a guest I found in his house comfort and what was necessary for a good life.

The artist François Biard too saw to be sure something different in Læstadius than his partner Léonie d'Aunet, and in Karesuando he used the opportunity to make studies for a large painting: *Pastor Læstadius preaches to the Sámi* that was exhibited at the Paris Salon two years later.

On September 16th, the ten other members of the expedition arrived in Karesuando. Only two of these were along on the journey through Lappland, namely Xavier Marmier and Paul Gaimard. The latter got to take along both Læstadius' meteorological observations for all of the 1830s and a number of other natural science materials for printing in the official publications.

One of the members of this year's expedition was the young painter Charles Giraud, who in Karesuando sketched the well-known portrait of Læstadius, later lithographed by Émile Lassalle. In an updated brochure, published by Gaimard about 1843, which among other things discusses the expedition's picture atlases, it says:

Among the portraits there is one that cannot be passed in silence, the one of Pastor Læstadius. This exceptional man has devoted his entire life to a mission wherein salvation is superior to all salvation in this world. He spreads civilization among his fellow rural citizens, he enlightens them and aids them in their suffering. M. Giraud knew how he in the portrait was going to preserve the expression of kindness and of mild sympathy that animates this spokesman of the Gospel.

About the expedition's visit this fall Læstadius writes in a letter to the zoologist Sven Nilsson in Lund, the 18th of November:

Our Frenchmen took the same route this fall, as last year, namely from Alta to Karesuando, and were mostly concerned with painting Lapps, for which they had with them a couple skillful artists, so that I presume this portion of their studies will be most successful.

The work on Sámi mythology must have gone forward now. In a letter to J. M. Vahl of November 2nd, Læstadius gives thanks for the *Lappska Grammatikk* that was sent, and he also hopes to get in touch with the author:

I really wished to know whether Rask was still alive, and whether I might not give him my Lappska Mythologi for his examination and correction, before it is delivered to the Frenchmen for translation.

Rasmus Rask, though, had been dead for several years. But the point here is that it might seem as if Læstadius already at this point in time, at the beginning of November 1839, was finished with in any case parts of the manuscript for his Sámi mythology.

Now Læstadius had found out that the Finnish pastor Jacob Fellman was working on a monograph about the Finnish Sámis' mythology, and in a letter to Fellmann from December 15, 1839 he writes:

The so-called French scientific Expedition's members have now two years in a row wanted to prevail upon me to write a monograph on Lapp mythology, for which I, as born and raised in the purest part of the Lappmark, suppose I have good materials. This, their wish I have probably not at all been able to refuse.

As in the letter to C. A. Gottlund, Læstadius presents the matter as him having to be compelled to accept the task. Then comes his real errand:

/.../ but as the Lappmarks are far-flung and the mythological objects, just as the language, the dress and manner of living, turn out to be very different in different Lappmarks, so I have dared to have recourse to Mr. Rector's experience in that part of Lapp mythology that concerns the Finnish Lappmarks.

Læstadius then asks Jacob Fellman whether his monograph will soon go to press. If that is not the case, he wants to borrow the manuscript *to make excerpts from it*.

During the spring Læstadius works diligently on his manuscript, and in a letter of July 3, 1840 to J. J. Berzelius in Stockholm he writes:

I have on Messieurs Gaimard's and Marmier's entreaty written a monograph on Lapp Mythology, of which a portion is ready in manuscript, but since it sounds so poor with their monetary concerns, that I don't know whether I can get anything for my hard work, as was promised.

Here Læstadius mentions for the first time that he is finished with the first part of the mythology. But he is accordingly concerned about the economy of the project. The allusion to the Frenchmen's poor economy points to the fact that P. Gaimard actally has not settled up for himself in several places in Norway and Sweden and owed a large amount of money. Læstadius, who was not well off, was then reasonably anxious he would not get the agreed amount for his work. He therefore asks Berzelius for help in notifying Gaimard that he wants 100 riksdaler for this first part of the mythology, which treats the Sámi doctrine of the gods.

A week later, the 10th of July, the Hungarian linguist Antal Reguly travels from Muonioniska to Karesuando where he gets in touch with Læstadius. In his notes from the trip, Reguly writes in the 23rd chapter, dated July 11:

I have never before discussed so much with anyone as with this pastor, but I am learning much too; his speech is for me like desired, long sought treasure, – he dismisses every doubt in me – sometimes with a single word.

July 15th to 18th Reguly worked with Læstadius' manuscript and got permission to make the excerpts he desired. Læstadius at the same time wanted to assure himself that his material would not be published by others before he himself got it out. Reguly therefore had to write a statement, dated July 22nd, where he promised not to misuse the confidence he had been shown:

The undersigned has with Pastor L. L. Læstadius been able to use all the books, manuscripts and oral information that could be granted concerning the Lapps' an-

Portrait of Lars Levi Læstadius, drawn by Charles Giraud during the stopover in Karesuando in September of 1839. On February 26, 1841 Læstadius, together with several other of the Scandinavian participants in the Recherche expedition, were named knights of the French Legion of Honor. When Émile Lassalle later drew the lithograph, he included the medal in the portrait as a gesture to Læstadius. Plate nr. 165 in the Recherche expedition's *Atlas historique et pittoresque*.
Lithograph, Norsk Polarinstitutt, Tromsø. Photo: Mari Hildung, Tromsø.

cient and present conditions, especially what this people's mythology concerns; but as the aforesaid Pastor concluded a special contract with Messrs. Gaimard and Marmier (leaders of the so-called French Scientific Expedition) to write on their account a Lapp Mythology, of which a portion is already in manuscript, and such a work can only be sold by Europe's antiquarian dealers, so Pastor L. L. Læstadius only under those conditions has allowed the undersigned to make use of his materials, that the forthcoming Lapp Mythology's readers will not in any way be compromised with reports and excerpts; on these grounds I pledge not to publish in any language my annotations here made on Lapp Mythology, until it is printed at full length, either in France, Germany or Sweden, and I will consider myself to have misused the hospitality, and be obliged to compensate the prospective publisher for the damage that such an early publication can yield.

The 30th of July Læstadius received from J. Fellman a manuscript draft, almost a rough draft, discussing Sámi mythology. However, Fellman wanted the manuscript back quickly. He was namely himself in a phase where he was trying to get it published through the Finnish Literature Society. Læstadius had at that point in time a visit from a student, Friedrich Leonhard Heller from the old university town of Dorpat, now Tartu, in Estonia. He was going to travel on soon, and Læstadius worked hard to finish going through the manuscript, so that Heller could take it along back to Fellman. And when the Dorpat student left Karesuando at six in the morning the 1st of August, he had the manuscript in his bag.

In an enclosed letter to J. Fellman, Læstadius wrote that he had read through the manuscript a couple of times and made a few remarks in the margin. He had actually thought about copying parts of the manuscript to weave into his own. But both because of the lack of time and because Fellman's manuscript was actually a rough draft, *which because of the many interpolations and deletions occurring there, was difficult to keep track of*, so this was not done.

Jacob Fellman had earlier suggested to Læstadius that they should together publish a book on Sámi mythology. This however Læstadius did not want. He said that in Fellman's manuscript he had found a good deal of interesting information, but he was critical of Fellman's selection and use of sources, and he called attention to certain flaws in the manuscript, something he went into in detail. Læstadius' refusal of Fellman's offer of cooperation may also have had an economic aspect and be connected to his already having both a publisher and financing in order. Læstadius needed money for his steadily growing family, and as sole author he would be spared sharing the honorarium.

Læstadius is absorbed however that Fellman is going to get his monograph published, and in a statement that went back with the manuscript, dated August 1st, he explained that there was not a competative relationship between the two monographs:

Of the undersigned's fragments in Lappish mythology the 1st part or doctrine of the gods is ready in manuscript, which according to a special agreement with the French

Expedition will be handed over to Prof. Marmier; and although the manuscript will be returned to me, after it is used, it is probably yet uncertain whether it will ever be printed in Swedish, at least not until all parts are finished and translated into French. Thus, my work and that of the author of the enclosed manuscript, which is hereby gratefully returned, do not collide, but it would be my wish that the Author therefore rather sooner allows said manuscript to be published.

But it wouldn't turn out that way. Jacob Fellman's manuscript was not published until 1906, more than 30 years after the author's death.

Læstadius' introduction to *Fragmenter i Lappska Mythologien* is dated May 8th 1840, and in the course of the summer and fall he wrote in several letters that the first part, *Gudalära*, was ready in manuscript. But he was clearly not entirely satisfied yet and among other things tried to find a natural scientific explanation for a number of mythological phenomena; in addition, he did not make contact with P. Gaimard about finances. In a long letter to the zoologist Sven Nilsson in Lund, dated December 6th 1840, Læstadius writes:

The first part of "Fragmenter i Lappska Mythologien" I now have ready in manuscript; but since nothing is heard from the Frenchmen, for whose reckoning I in fact took the pains, so the manuscript will probably remain with me for a while. Among which are some mythological objects, about whose natural basis I would gladly like to learn an experienced zoologist's opinion. Among them can first of all be mentioned the Norrland and Lapp common folk's belief in the miraculous power of the worm stone; from an old book, called Francisci Redi Experimenta, I find that belief in the worm stone's miraculous power is supposedly still found in India. As a child I saw with a settler in Luleå Lappmark a couple so-called worm stones. I thus dare ask whether it is possible that there are some worm stones, i.e. whether in certain individuals of the serpent family there can be some stone formations, which might give rise to the common folk belief? And I wonder whether this folk belief is also found in Southern Sweden? – Another mythological object is the so-called Gan fly (mentioned by Norwegian authors), from which the old Ganviken likely got its name. Now it is a common belief in the northern portions of Finnland that in certain marshes there is a very poisonous insect that causes plague among the livestock, and a human is even in mortal danger if bitten by this insect. But it is supposed to be very small and hard to get out. The farmers in Råvaniemi swear they have seen how it shoots as they say, or goes like an arrow toward the beast, and immediately afterwards the beast begins to shake and be tormented dreadfully, and die within a day. I wonder thus whether the information Linné got in the district of Kemi about the so-called Furia infernalis, can have any basis? Is there such a poisonous insect, which I, considering much supporting information, am inclined to believe, then it is even likely that the old noaidis knew the art of capturing this insect in their gan boxes, and that they thereby actually harmed people.

Another mythological object is the Marmæler as they are called in Norwegian who are thought to be the young of the marine animal Trichæcus manatus L. but these live only in the sea? When Anonymous in Leem tells according to the Lapps' stories that a kind of childlike creature resides in cold cellars, and is captured and eaten because it is tasty, one asks whether there is such an animal similar to a child who lives on land

Lars Levi Læstadius was an especially diligent botanist. He was on a number of botanical excursions and trips, and his herbarium was very extensive, above all with plants from Lappland. He sold about 6,600 plants to the expedition leader Paul Gaimard in Paris.
The illustration shows Northern Gentian (*Gentianella aurea*, earlier gentianella involucrata), found by Læstadius in Kåfjord in Alta the summer of 1838. Naturhistoriska Riksmuseet, Stockholm.

or in cold cellars? A settler here in Karesuando says he has seen such an animal in the river. One might otherwise guess the young of beavers or otters, but these animals are too well known by the people to be mixed up with mythological creatures. I should be very interested to hear my Dear Professor's judgment concerning the objects now mentioned; if possible, before I send off my manuscript.

Whether Sven Nilsson answered these rather special questions, and what he eventually replied, is not known. Læstadius in any case considered himself finished with his manuscript, but would still not release it until P. Gaimard has discharged his economic pledges. In a letter to J. M Vahl in January of 1841 he writes:

The 1st part of my Mythologia Lapponica has been finished for a long time, and the manuscript is only waiting for the Frenchman to pay something for the trouble. Otherwise, I will make use of the manuscript myself, nor do I dare relinquish it either until I have heard something from the Frenchmen.

A month later, the 26th of February, both J. M. Vahl and L. L. Læstadius, together with among others the Danish zoologist Henrik Krøyer and the Norwegian physiologist and zoologist Christian Boeck, all of whom had participated in the Recherche Expedition, had been nominated as knights of the French legion of honor. In a short autobiography, dated June 12th 1841, which Læstadius sent to the legion of honor's chancery, he listed his publications, and also mentioned the monograph on Sámi mythology, which would be transmitted to M. Gaimard.

The spring passes though without there being any economic clarification; nothing is heard from France. And now Læstadius faced an especially difficult time, something that set him way back in his work. First his only brother died, Petrus Læstadius, in August, and then he himself became seriously ill, so ill he was absolutely certain he would die. In a letter to the botanist Göran Wahlenberg from October 1841 he writes:

While I still have strength, it is my duty to write a few words. I have long felt death in my chest, and already between 20 and 30 years of age I had severe pains in my chest. Nevertheless, I have tried to be careful; but last summer I rowed rather intensely in a loaded boat down some rapids, and then got cold, which caused a bad and persistent head cold that continued with expectoration throughout the summer.

Læstadius is concerned about his family's situation after he himself has died, and he continues the letter by asking G. Wahlenberg to take care of some practical and economic matters. He wishes among other things that Wahlenberg might be able to sell his large herbarium to England or Sweden for 1000 riksdaler. The letter clearly remained unsent from October, and in a postscript, dated the 6th of December, it becomes apparent that Læstadius has gotten somewhat better and looks a little more optimistically toward the future. But he is no better than that in a letter to Sundevall, dated December 2nd, he repeats a wish he also had for Wahlenberg:

If you dear Professor after my death will support the request, which I have asked Prof. Wahlenberg to do something about, viz. an annual stipend from Vetenskaps Academien for my surviving children, that would be good.

At the same time Læstadius gets good news from C. J. Sundevall, who at that point in time was in Paris. He had spoken with P. Gaimard who still wanted to publish the Sámi mythology in the expedition's official publications and who also would pay what Læstadius was asking. In an answer to Sundevall from January 10th 1842 Læstadius wrote that he would send the manuscript with some Norwegians passing through. He writes further that it has been a lot of work with the manuscript, also because he had to make an extra copy:

/…/ *which was necessary for the continuation of the work (if my life should last so long) since, you see, I cannot expect to see the book published for a long time. M. Gaimard has gotten, I hope, two conditions to choose from, either some copies of the entire Commision's forthcoming works, or cash. As a poor man, I would rather accept the latter, and will be satisfied if I get 100 riksdaler in the bank for this manuscript.*

The Norwegian passersby, who were parliament representatives from Finnmark County, however took another route, and Læstadius had to find alternative ways of forwarding. He eventually had the manuscript brought to Haparanda to the apothecary Claes Fredrik Östman, who was going to Stockholm in April.

In a letter to Læstadius from June 15th Sundevall confirms that the manuscript for "Lappska Mythologien" has arrived in Stockholm, and on September 2nd he writes to Gaimard that he has received the manuscript from Læstadius and thereupon entrusted it to the French Ambassador in Stockholm for forwarding to Paris. He adds that Læstadius is now working on the other parts of the mythology.

In a letter to Læstadius from January 20th 1843, C. J. Sundevall offers to advance the amount P. Gaimard owes for the manuscript. March 7th Læstadius writes back to Sundevall that since he:

/…/ *believes he can be advanced 100 riksdaler from P. Gaimard, he will accept the offer – better something than nothing. In me Thomas still sits, how he can fulfill his promises. /…/ The continuation of the Lappska Mythologien though cannot come in a hurry; I have to go to Härnösand this summer for the pastoral exam, which in addition to a presumed move to Kengis or Pajala will interrupt my usual occupations.*

Læstadius had on November 1st 1842 sought transfer to Pajala. But to be able to get a parish that lay outside the Lappmarks one had to take the so-called pastoral exam at that time. In the course of the spring of 1843, Læstadius was thus busily occupied with the preparations for his stay in Härnösand.

In Paris however sits an impatient P. Gaimard, and he writes to C. J. Sundevall on April 9th and wonders what has become of the second part of the *Mythologie Lappone*. He also asks Sundevall to evaluate, either alone or in consultation with Læstadius, whether sketches should be made of objects that could be relevant illustrations to this text, such as for example a magic drum.

In July of 1843 Læstadius set to work on his further clerical education in Härnösand, and in the course of the summer he received several letters from C. J. Sundevall; for one thing, he got the 100 riksdaler for the first part of the Sámi mythology. In a letter from Härnösand, written in August/September, Læstadius thanked Sundevall for the money and repeated that the continuation of the monograph must be delayed a bit because he first *had to fulfill what belongs to the pastoral [exam]*.

Caricature of Lars Levi Læstadius from the summer of 1860. Water color by Gustaf Albert Hüttling. Wadströmska Collection/Museiverket, Helsinki. Læstadius would die early the following year. – Reduced.

In a letter to G. Wahlenberg, dated November 20th, he wrote that he was using free time to:

/.../ *to write a few things on the Frenchman's behalf, e.g. Fragmenter i Lappska Mythologien, of which the first part now at this location is probably being translated into French, and being printed in Paris, which I can find from the parts of their large opus that came into my hands this summer.*

The parts of the large opus Læstadius refers to here must be an undated prospectus: *Voyages de la Commission Scientifique du nord pendant les années 1835, 1836, 1838, 1839 et 1840, publié par ordre du Roi, sous la direction de M. Paul Gaimard, président de la commission*, apparently printed in the spring of 1843. It is stated here that the eighth part of the official publications will consist of four works, namely, "Historie de la Scandinavie," "Littérature scandinavie" and "Relation du voyage," all three by Xavier Marmier, plus "Histoire et Mythologie des Lapons" by L. L. Læstadius. It is also stated that these four works will be illustrated with 240 lithographs in large folio format, and finally it says strangely enough that they are being printed – *sous presse*. It is in all likelihood this Læstadius refers to in the letter to G. Wahlenberg, when he says that the manuscript *is being printed in Paris.*

In a letter to P. Gaimard of December 16th, C. J. Sundevall advised that Læstadius had been busy with his pastoral exam and that it would take some time before the next part of the manuscript came.

The same day C. J. Sundevall sends his letter to Paris, Læstadius concludes his stay in Härnösand and goes on a visitation trip around Sweden's Lappmarks. On this trip at the beginning of January 1844, Læstadius meets the young Sámi girl Maria in Åsele Lappmark, a meeting that has decisive importance for his faith and further activity as a pastor.

In March Læstadius was back in Karesuando and then found a letter from "the Recherche participant" P. A. Siljeström, dated December 23, 1843. Here Læstadius learned that Siljeström had received 213 francs from P. Gaimard that would be paid to Læstadius as remuneration for the next parts of the mythology. And gradually Læstadius also began fully on this work. The introduction to the 2nd part of the monograph is dated May of 1844, and in a letter to C. J. Sundevall of June 10th the same year Læstadius wrote: *I am just now in the thick of working on the 2nd part of Lappska Mythologien.* Læstadius must have worked effectively that summer and fall, for already on October 9th he sent a new letter to Sundevall where he wrote:

The second, third and 4th parts of my Lappska Mythologi are now so nearly finished, that I only await a manuscript from Rector Fellman in Finnland, from which I will make a few excerpts on the same subject, to make my work so much more complete.

Læstadius further asks Sundevall to inform Gaimard about this and in addition that he has received the 100 riksdaler through P. A. Siljeström, a payment he is pleased with. This Sundevall does in a letter to Gaimard of November 1st.

The fourth part of Læstadius' manuscript was concluded with the following note:
The author has gotten this far by November of 1844, and unless Rector Fellman's manuscript is not to be expected, I will have concluded the work here and sent it off.

Some time or other in the winter however Jacob Fellman sent his manuscript to Læstadius, and it seems here as if he had come back to his earlier suggestion of cooperating on publication. Læstadius though had the same view of this as earlier; he wanted to publish his Sámi mythology alone.

In a supplement to *Fragmenter i Lappska Mythologien*, dated May of 1845, Læstadius wrote by way of introduction that he had finally been able to borrow J. Fellman's manuscript and he continues:

It is the author's unselfish liberality I have to thank for this loan. The manuscript contains much important information, which I, with the author's good consent, have taken the liberty to use, in the following supplement.

Læstadius also reported this good news to C. J. Sundevall in a letter of May 12th, and continues:

I am now in the thick of making excerpts from it on behalf of the French, and the manuscript will probably be sent to you [Sundevall] next autumn; for though it is now mostly ready, I have to make excerpts from it so as to have something left, in case the manuscript should not arrive. Since the original manuscript arrived properly and, as desired, was properly used by the French, I have decided to turn over the excerpting to Pastor Stockfleth who requested the same, so as to publish them through the Vet. Societeten in Trondhjem in Norwegian, NB: since they first appeared in French there will be no detriment to the French thereby.

Missionary Nils Vibe Stockfleth had visited Læstadius in the first days of December 1844, and about this he wrote:

For the French scientific expedition, the pastor had prepared Fragments of Finnish-Lapp mythology; from the first part, the doctrine of the gods with appurtenant mythological objects, then printed among the Society's publications the pastor entrusted me with the manuscript.

It is evident from this that Læstadius in all likelihood thought that *Gudalära* at this point in time was already in print.

At the same time as Læstadius was in the final phase of his work on mythology, P. Gaimard wrote a letter to J. J. Berzelius, dated May 9th 1845, where he said he wanted to start printing *Mythologie des Lapons* as soon as the last parts were at hand. Gaimard had in several earlier letters mentioned that the pictorial artist Auguste Mayer would travel to Stockholm, and now he repeated this to Berzelius: *M. Mayer during his stay in Stockholm wants to sketch some Sámi objects such that he can make a number of plates to illustrate Læstadius' work.*

Later in the summer of 1845 Læstadius finished copying and adapting J. Fellman's material to his own, and at the end of July he finally managed to send these last parts of the mythology with a passerby, Baron Fabian Wrede, who was on his way to Stockholm. Læstadius informed Sundevall about this in a letter of July 16th and asked that the manuscript be sent on to P. Gaimard. At the same time, Læstadius received a letter from Sundevall, dated July 17th, where he found out that he finnarnes Vuoro, eller Silmen vuoro, en gångbar ögonsjukdom, hvarmed äfven Vuornies Lådde torde stå i någon förbindelse. möjligt är, att Lapparne under sitt Vuolekeo, tänkte sig en infernalisk ande, såsom orsak till en gångbar sjukdom, hvartill ingen naturlig orsak kunde tänkas; och att denna Dæmon uppenbarade sig under skepnad af en fogel, var så mycket lättare att föreställa sig, som Nåidarne, enligt hvad vi ofvanföre visat, hade flere underjordiska Trollfoglar i sin tjenst. (§. 76.)

§. 142.

Hvad föröfrigt de så kallade Ganflugor beträffar, som Nåiden skolat uppbrännt af den infernaliska fogelns fjädrar, och sedan förvara i en aska, får jag anmärka, att det utan tvifvel finns ett giftigt insect, som de gamla Lapparne haft sig bekant, ehuru ofvan åberopade författare icke fått reda på denna insectens Lappska namn. Den Anonyme hos Leem anför väl ett Lappskt namn: Zhiokkush, men jag kan icke rikteligen begripa, om detta skall vara namnet på Normännens Ganfluga, eller

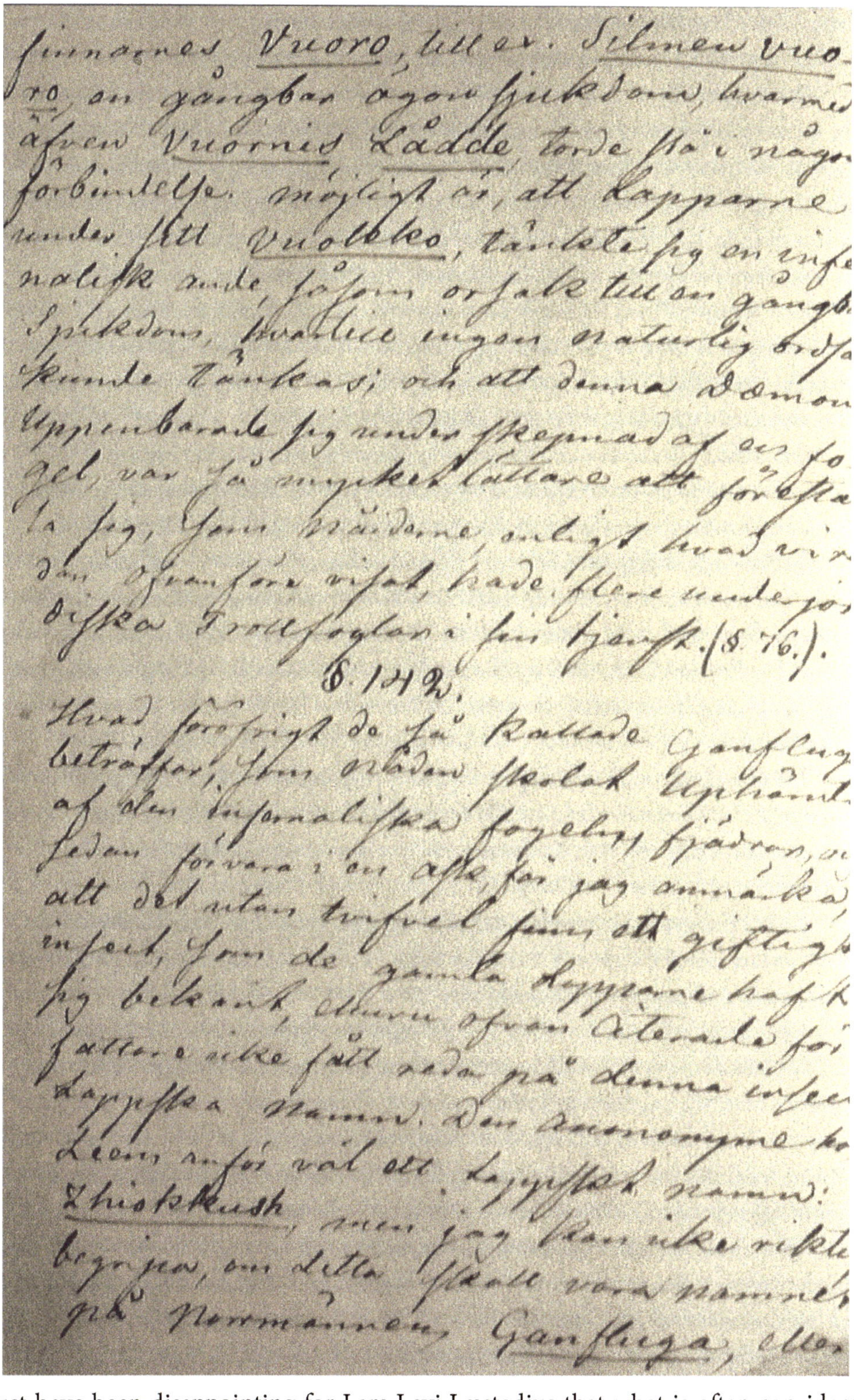

It must have been disappointing for Lars Levi Læstadius that what is often considered to be his magnum opus, *Fragmenter i Lappska Mythologien*, was not published during his lifetime. A whole 160 years would pass before all parts of the monograph were rediscovered. The illustration shows one of the pages of the original manuscript that was found in 2001. Musée de Pontarlier, France.

would be sent some of the expedition's plates. In a reply to Sundevall from October 12th Læstadius wrote:

Of course, I can't use the Frenchman's plates myself, but I request that you, Sir [Sundevall] in the best manner try to convert said plates into money – get whatever you can. If I can get 200 in cash for each specimen, then I will certainly be contented, and it would be, with the scant income I have, a great help. I have no more than a boy in Pite School, but he already consumes half of the parsonage's income – and besides I have 8 children at home to feed and clothe.

In the fall of 1845 C. J. Sundevall received Læstadius' manuscript from Baron F. Wrede, and he took time to read it before he sent it to Paris. Sundevall was very surprised at the free tone of Læstadius, and in a letter to P. Gaimard, dated October 1st, with signature in great haste, Sundevall says: *the author is a little too temperamental in defense of his Sámi, and discusses a highly esteemed pastor from here (Gravallius) in a not very suitable manner*. The cause was remarks Gravallius had made, especially in relation to the magic drum's existence in Lappland, in a lecture to the Stockholm Pastors' Society October 31, 1843. And Læstadius was really crass and on the border of slander in his comments, both in the introduction and in several later paragraphs in the mythology's second part, *Offerlära* [Doctrine of Sacrifice]. Sundevall didn't think that belonged here and was also apprehensive about Gravallius' reputation. In the letter to Gaimard, he therefore comes out with suggestions for a number of changes in the text, something he thinks will have no significance for the content, but rather will strengthen the work. The 10th of December Sundevall again writes to Gaimard and hopes both the manuscript and his own suggestions for changes have long since arrived in Paris.

In December Læstadius returned J. Fellman's manuscript with expressions of great thanks, but asserted that:

/…/ I cannot concern myself any longer with this deserving manuscript, because my attention – turned in another direction – is required by other subjects belonging to religion, which seem to me to possess incomparably greater weight than the mythological. Approximately one fifth of the manuscript I have borrowed, and included in my work.

This time Læstadius had more time than the previous time he went through Fellman's mythology, and the manuscript was also in better condition; he therefore made considerably more comments and additions in the margin.

As earlier mentioned, Læstadius had sought in November of 1842 to be transferred to Pajala without success. However, he wrote on several occasions that Karesuando was Sweden's poorest parish and he could imagine a somewhat better mission. In a letter to J. M. Vahl from February 7th 1845 he writes: *My family has over time increased, so that I now have 9 living children, and 3 dead. My intention is to move away from the Lappmark, and seek a somewhat better pastoral calling*. On July 12th, 1847, he again sought to become parish pastor in Pajala pastorate. This time he succeeded, and in October the following year he was appointed.

This year, 1848, Læstadius mentions the Sámi mythology to C. J. Sundevall for the first time since the manuscript's completion. In a letter from June 28th he says:

Have you [Sundevall] heard whether Gaimard is still alive, or has he been massacred in the February battle? [I wonder] whether the revolution caused any delay in the work's publication.

The next time Læstadius mentions the monograph is in a letter to Sundevall from December 2nd 1851: *From Gaimard probably nothing further of note. You [Sundevall] probably don't know whether my Lapp Mythology is being used in any way.*

In March of 1852 the final synopsis of the lithographs in the Recherche expedition's *Atlas Historique* was at hand, also called *Atlas Pittoresque*. This *Table explicative des Planches des Voyages en Scandinavie, en Laponie, au Spitzberg et aux Feröe* contained 310 titles, one picture appeared later, so that the atlas came to comprise 311 images. Among these were supposed to be the illustrations for Læstadius' monograph, but unfortunately there are no images here that refer to Sámi mythology. Auguste Mayer had a finger in nearly every pie on his Sweden trip. He produced all of 49 lithographs from southern Sweden of which about half were from the Stockholm area.

Læstadius mentions his Sámi mythology a last time to C. J. Sundevall, before he in all likelihood gives up hope of ever seeing the monograph in book form. In a letter of June 26th 1853 he says:

Nothing at all from Gaimard any more, all those works he was going to publish in addition to the others. That would be a shame if my Lapp Mythology should thus be entirely consigned to oblivion, when so much effort went into it.

The reason P. Gaimard was not heard from any longer, was that on March 8th 1853 Victor Lottin had taken over the responsibility for the completion of the Recherche expedition's publications. Ten days later, March 18th, he thus sent a letter to all the collaborators, where he says he has been *appointed by the Navy Department to supervise the publication of the collected material from La commission scientifique du Nord, something the French government wished to conclude as quickly as possible.* But when Lottin did not receive more manuscripts in spite of a reminder in May of 1853, the French government decided early in 1854 that the publication would be concluded in the course of 1855 with the sections that had already been commenced.

At this point in time, Læstadius' Sámi mythology, to all appearances, had been shelved long ago. The reason seems to have been an unfortunate combination of several circumstances, but some of the fault must be put on Læstadius himself. From when he told his Stallo stories on the mountain above Kåfjord in Alta in the autumn of 1838, there passed, as we have seen, all of seven years before the entire monograph was delivered to Paris. Nor was the manuscript especially easy to translate into French with its technical terms and etymological observations, where in addition to Sámi and Swedish, Finnish was brought in, and, in some cases, Norwegian and Latin.

The translator, Xavier Marmier, did not have all the time in the world to set aside for this project either, especially considering the uneven and somewhat unpredictable manuscript deliveries from Karesuando. From 1840 Marmier was permanently employed as librarian in Paris. He was also an inveterate traveler, and he was work-

Title page from the original edition of Johannes Schefferus: *Lapponia* (Frankfurt, 1673). Læstadius was lacking this important source when he was working on *Gudalära*. When he finally got hold of the book, probably the summer/fall of 1842, he prepared Further supplement to Lapp Mythology, which he sent on to Paris.
Universitetsbiblioteket i Tromsø.

ing steadily on his own literary projects. During this period, the first half of the 1840's, he was busy completing the Recherche expedition's official travel accounts, *Relation du voyage*, a two-volume work of over 800 pages.

And it did not get any easier after the February revolution in France in 1848. An important supporter of the entire Recherche project, King Louis-Philippe, had been toppled, and the new rulers were not as enthusiastic about completing this prestigious project.

It must have been very disappointing for Læstadius that *Fragmenter i Lappska Mythologien* was not published during his lifetime. But in the middle of the 1850's, when it was entirely obvious that the mythology was not included in the Recherche expedition's official publications, Læstadius had, to be sure, lost some of his interest in the whole project. First of all, it had been all of ten years since he had sent the last parts of the manuscript to Paris, and his great religious engagement now took up most of his time. His correspondance with C. J. Sundevall had in all likelihood also ceased; in any case, no letters are known from this period. Thereby the contact with Paris was also gone. In addition, both P. Gaimard and V. Lottin died in 1858, and with them "disappeared" too Læstadius' original manuscripts for the Sámi mythology. Læstadius himself probably had no complete copies of the entire manuscript, so an edition in Swedish was not of current interest either. Nils Vibe Stockfleth had, as previously mentioned, taken over some of the manuscript for publication in Norway, but nothing came of that either.

A last factor in Læstadius not setting everything under the sun in motion to get the mythology published in Scandinavia, was his age and gradually failing health. At the end of the 1850's his eyesight gradually became poorer, and late in the autumn of 1860 he became seriously ill. He died on February 21st of 1861 in his home in Pajala.

*

Throughout his entire adult life Læstadius was an assiduous author and letter writer. There are more than 200 letters preserved after him in public libraries and archives, mostly in Sweden. His authorship comprises most essentially botanical and religious writings, written in Swedish, Finnish, Sámi or Latin. Much of this material was printed during his lifetime, a few were published after his death, while a few manuscripts remained unpublished.

Only once later in Læstadius' own century in an official connection would one find traces of his manuscript on Sámi mythology. That was in 1871 when the Norwegian author and philologist Jens Andreas Friis published: *Lappisk Mythologi, Eventyr og Folkesagn* [*Lapp Mythology, Folktales and Legends*]. In the introduction he lists his most important sources, and under Lars Levi Læstadius stands the following:

Defective manuscript, containing some "Fragmenter i lapska Mythologien," written 1840 and at one time turned over by the author to Pastor Stockfleth to make use of.

As mentioned earlier, N. V. Stockfleth got a manuscript from Læstadius during a visit to Karesuando at the beginning of December 1844. He himself wrote in his *Dagbog over mine Missionsreiser i Finmarken* [*Diary of my Missionary Travels in Finnmark*] from 1860 that this treats the first part of the mythology, *Gudalära*. Læstadius also wrote this in a letter of February 7th 1845 to J. M. Vahl where it says:

The Pastor and Fellow of the Order Stockfleth intends through Videnskaps Sällskapet in Trondhjem to publish my Lappska Mythologie in Norwegian after it is first published in French; and I have therefore entrusted to Stockfleth's translation my draft of the first part.

J. A. Friis has in his book on Sámi mythology 26 references to Læstadius' manuscript. Eight refer to *Gudalära*, five to *Offerlära*, one to the supplement Læstadius wrote on the basis of J. Fellman's manuscript, while 12 of the 48 folktales Friis includes in his book, have the addendum: *Fra sv. Lapmark. Efter L. Læstadius*. This means that the Læstadius manuscript Friis refers to in his foreword, and which he had gotten from his old teacher and friend N. V. Stockfleth, must have encompassed the entire *Fragmenter i Lappska Mythologien*, not just the first part, *Gudalära*.

J. A. Friis died in 1896. Some years later Universitetsbiblioteket (University Library) i Oslo got access to a number of his archives. In this material, there is a little manuscript of 28 pages, written by Lars Levi Læstadius. This then must necessarily be a remnant from the manuscript Friis used for his book on Sámi mythology. The manuscript is sort of a rough draft, written on old letters Læstadius had received. Several of these letters are from the 1830's, one from 1842, while the latest registered date is on a letter from September 12th 1843. Purely theoretically, Stockfleth could then have taken along this manuscript when he left Karesuando in December of 1844. But as long as one of the aforementioned references in Friis' Sámi mythology is from the supplement of J. Fellman, written down by Læstadius in the spring of 1845, this is not possible. The content of this very battered manuscript, which quite appropriately referred to by Friis as *defective*, is precisely also from this supplement of Fellman. It goes from the middle of *No 30* up to and including the last paragraph, *No 40*; only a little is missing at the end.

How then has N. V. Stockfleth gotten hold of Læstadius' complete manuscript? This is unknown, but most probably Læstadius has sent him his "kladde-manuscript (rough copy)" for the last parts of the mythology sometime after the summer of 1845. The idea was, as earlier mentioned, translation and publication in Norwegian, something which was never implemented.

In 1875 Jacob Fellman died, and he did not have the pleasure of seeing his Sámi mythology in book form either. Only in 1906 did his four-volume work: *Anteckningar under min vistelse i Lappmarken* appear, published by his son, Isak Fellman. In *Andra delen* [*Second part*] that has the title *Ur Lappsk Mytologi och Lappländsk Sägen* [*From Lapp Mythology and Lapplandic Legend*] there is text from the manuscript Læstadius borrowed.

In the ten-page introduction to this volume, Isak Fellman discusses the exchange of letters between Læstadius and Jacob Fellman. He quotes among other things excerpts from five letters, written by Læstadius in the period December 1839 to December 1845, and he fabulizes a little about the fate of the two manuscripts. He also cites portions of a statement to Jacob Fellman from the Finnish Literary Society from 1839, penned by the poet Johan Ludvig Runeberg where among other things it says that Fellman's *Lapp Mythological Lexicon probably contains not insignificant contributions to knowledge about the Lapps' doctrine of the gods*. Runeberg explains why the Finnish Literary Society cannot publish the manuscript, but says that they all the same wish to keep it for their own possible use. This Fellman did not accept, and in the middle of the 1840's he instead turned it over to Gabriel Rein for adaptation and publication, something that for unknown reasons did not come about.

About Læstadius' manuscript Isak Fellman says at the end if his introduction:

But what fate has befallen Læstadius' above-mentioned manuscript? Is it maybe located somewhere in Paris or in Stockholm? Or has it, after already having been presented to Gaimard's agent in the latter-mentioned place, been withdrawn by the author and possibly destroyed; or has it in some other way gone lost?

Fellman's mythology begins with a general overview of 61 pages, and it seems as if this was written later than the rest and thereby did not belong to the material loaned to Læstadius. Here there was no commentary in the margin in Læstadius' hand either. The next 116 pages consist of what J. L. Runeberg refers to as the *Lapp Mythological Lexicon*. It was this manuscript Læstadius borrowed, and it was indeed here he made his roughly 60 annotations and additions in the margin. These are included in Fellman's book as signed footnotes.

In addition to this "lexicon" Læstadius had also been able to borrow Fellman's manuscript with the title: *Lapska Sånger og Sagor* [*Lapp Songs and Folktales*]. This is evident from Læstadius' own supplement of Fellman, No 40, where it says:

Among the many Lapp and Finnish troll songs, which appear in Rector Fellman's manuscript, most are of the nature that they would not be of interest to other than native researchers, who are at home in the language. Through translations of such pieces, most of the language's particular beauty would also be lost, for which reason I did not risk including them in this work, for I would hope that the author according to his intention in the future will get the opportunity to have them published.

But Læstadius let himself be fascinated by the text of one of these songs, which existed both in Sámi linguistic form and in Fellman's Swedish translation, and included portions of it right at the end of his mythology. The reference he found in "the lexicon section" under the word S*ame ædnam, – Land found*, and as a curiosity is here reproduced with Fellman's explanation:

The Lapps give their land this appelation, since it was found by them and, after expelling another migrating people, by them occupied. That people who lived here before the Lapps, are supposed to have lived most recently by the Porsse stream that falls into the Tana river. In a prolix national song, the Lapps describe their fate before and after the land's taking them in; which can be seen in the song "*Same ædnam alggo-olbmui pirra [The first inhabitants of Samiland]*."

In Fellman's translation the song has the title *Om Lapplands första inbyggare* [*About Lappland's first inhabitants*].

Visiting some Norwegian Sámi in Kautokeino.

More than a quarter century would pass before anything was again heard about Læstadius' lost manuscript. It was in 1932 when the Finnish politician Kaarlo Castrén, who devoted his old age to Læstadius research, published a Læstadius biography in Finnish. While working on the book, he made contact with Eero K. Neuvonen, librarian at the Nordic section of Bibliothèque Sainte-Geneviève in Paris. On Castrén's initiative Neuvonen made thorough investigations of archives and libraries in France, to find, if possible, material that might throw new light on the fate of Læstadius' manuscript on Sámi mythology. At Bibliothèque Nationale in Paris Neuvonen then found correspondence between C. J. Sundevall and P. Gaimard, and he found the previously mentioned statement from the Hungarian Antal Reguly. In this way, one was able to understand who Reguly actually was; you see, his name had been misinterpreted earlier and his material incorrectly archived in Budapest. Now this was cleared up, and his notes from the stay in Norden were loaned to the Finnish Literary Society in Helsinki for copying.

In Reguly's notes, chapters 25 and 26 constitute excerpts from Læstadius' *Gudalära*. Reguly made a sort of résumé of the manuscript: he picked a little here and there, and, versed in languages as he was, he wrote the whole thing in Swedish, with a few elements in German and Latin. The copy, made by the Finnish Literary Society, fills 30 typewritten pages in A-4 format. When Kaarlo Castrén came out with his Læstadius book in 1932, he thought he had now "rescued" the first part of Læstadius' mythology. On closer inspection though it turns out that Reguly's material only makes up about ⅙ of Læstadius' manuscript.

In Paris Eero K. Neuvonen continued his hunt for the original manuscript. In the Gaimard correspondance in Bibliothèque Nationale he in this manner found information that Xavier Marmier had received the first part of the manuscript for translation, but that this was too little for a separate volume, and that Marmier would keep the manuscript awaiting the rest. Therefore, letters were written to a number of Marmier's relatives to find traces of the manuscript if possible. One of the letters ended up with Lektor Aymonier in Bordeaux who was a good friend of the archivist in Pontarlier, the birthplace of Marmier. Marmier had bequeathed his large collection of books to this town, and the archivist was now written by Aymonier with an inquiry about Læstadius' manuscript. And especially good news came in return; Læstadius' manuscript was there and had always been among the books in Marmier's copious library. This was in 1933.

The manuscript now found, has the title: *Fragmenter i Lappska Mythologien by Lars Levi Læstadius, Pastor in Karesuando, from Torneå Lappmark, Member of the Royal Scientific Society in Up[p]sala, Corresponding Member of the Royal Hunters' Society in Stockholm, as well as the Botanical society in Edinburg. Member of the Royal French Legion of Honor.* The last sentence was added later with a different pen, for as mentioned, the appointment to the Legion of Honor happened in February of 1841, i.e. after the title page was written. The manuscript begins with *Erinran til Läsaren* {Reminder to the Reader], dated May 8th 1840, and continues with *Första delen* [first part]. *Gudalära with appurtenant mythological objects*, from §1 to §111.

Læstadius' monograph is written in a thick notebook, width 5 ⅔ inches and length 8.62 inches and comprises 291 pages. The book was later bound in a brown marbled cardboard binding with brown leather spine. At the top of the spine are three words engraved in gold: *Scandinavie, Laponie* og *Spitzberg*, while at the bottom stand *Zoologie* and *Læstadius*. The end papers are a brownish marble, and on the next opening page's left side stands the title. In the upper left corner of the same page a company label from Paris is pasted in: *Papeterie Brot 17, Rue de l'Ecole de Médecine, Faub St Germain.*

13 years later, in 1946, a new sensational discovery was made within Læstadius research. The Swedish librarian Olof von Feilitzen was then going through the collection of older Swedish manuscripts and prints at the Yale University library in the USA. In the printed catalogue of the book collection of older Swedish literature, which had belonged to the French count Paul Riant, he found a reference to the 2nd, 3rd and 4th parts of Læstadius' manuscript on Sámi mythology.

The manuscript's path from Paul Gaimard to Yale's library likely cannot be reconstructed in all details. But at one time or other in any case, Count Paul Edouard Riant, who was a history scholar and passionate book collector with a particular interest in older Scandinavian literature, acquired the manuscript for these last parts of Læstadius' mythology. It is possible he bought it from a second-hand bookstore in 1872 for 30 francs. In any case, written in pencil at the upper left of the cover's inside is: *30 fr. 1872.* Paul Riant died in 1888, and the Swedish part of his library eventually landed at Yale University.

This part of Læstadius' monograph has the title: *Fortsättning af Fragmenter i Lappska Mythologien, af Laurentius Levi Læstadius, Pastor och Provost i Karesuando Församling af Torneå Lappmark: Riddare af Kongl. Franska Heders Legions Orden; Ledamot af Kongl. Vetenskaps Societeten i Upsala; af Kongl. Jägarförbundet i Stockholm samt Corresponderande Ledamot af Botaniska Föreningen i Edinburg.* It begins with *Erinran til Läsaren*, dated May of 1844, and continues *2nd Part of Lapp Mythology, containing the doctrine of sacrifice* – 71 §§, *The third part, containing the doctrine of prophecy, or brief information on the Lapps' notorious witchcraft* – 32 §§, *Fourth and Last part of Fragmenter i Lappska Mythologien, containing various scraps of the Lapps' legendary practices* – 40 §§. The supplement which Læstadius wrote on the basis of J. Fellman's manuscript, is dated May of 1845 and is of 40 items.

The whole work was written in a thick notebook with cardboard covers and a leather spine, width 5 ⅔ inches and length just over 8 inches and comes to 355 pages, including title page. On the front of the cover stands: *2. 3. 4. Part of Læstadii Fragmenter i Lappska Mythologien i Manuscript, Partes secunda, tertia et quarta Mythologiæ Lapponicæ a Laestadio manu scriptæ, ad celeber. Dominum P. Gaimard 1845.* On the inside of the cover in the upper left corner is a company label with the text: *Maisonneuve & Cie, 15 Quai Voltaire, Paris.* In the middle of the page, a sort of ex libris is pasted with text: *Bibliothèque de Ms le comte Riant.* At the bottom stands Yale University's stamp with a printed marking: *Gift of Mrs. Henry Farnam 1896 (Library of Count Riant.)* What this marking refers to, is unknown.

Paul Gaimard
Leader of the Recherche expedition. Sailed around the world as a navy doctor 1817-20 and again 1826-29. He led a research journey to Iceland in 1836 and led the expedition to Scandinavia and Spitzbergen 1838-40. Urged Læstadius to write about Lapp mythology.

Xavier Marmier
Man of letters, Scandinavianist and translator. From Pontarlier. Wrote a book on Goethe and became interested in Danish literature. Joined Gaimard's expedition to Iceland in 1836. Published the official report of the Recherche espedition in 1841.

Thus, there were now the manuscript's beginning, found in Pontarlier in 1933, and the three last parts, found in the USA in 1946. However, another 13 years would pass before Læstadius' manuscript was finally printed. That occurred in 1959 when Landsmål- och Folkminnesarkivet in Uppsala issued the mythology in its publication series, under the editorship of theologian and scholar Harald Grundström. In the introduction Grundström accounts for the manuscript's path from Læstadius' hand to the last parts being found in the USA. However, he does not wish to use space on quotations in this first printed version of Læstadius' mythology, and says in the introduction:

Since all the cited source writings are accessible in print and Læstadius' own reflections are not of especially great significance in this case, the undersigned editor has not found it necessary to cite all the quotations in extenso.

In *Erinran til Läsaren [Reminder to the Reader]*, *Gudalära* og *Offerläran* he has thus to a large degree omitted the quotations and instead written brief summaries of the content with references to the paragraphs in question.

Grundström has also omitted the entire supplement which Læstadius wrote on the basis of J. Fellman's manuscript. His argumentation is that Fellman's material was already in print, as soon as the publication of *Anteckningar under min vistelse i Lappmarken* in 1906 with Læstadius' marginal notes as footnotes. And even if Grundström writes that the supplement of Fellman *is provided with various supplementary information by Læstadius*, then he does not see the necessity of printing it.

In spite of Grundström's edition of *Fragmenter i Lappska Mythologien* being somewhat amputated relative to the original manuscript, a long time would pass before this was corrected. Not until 1994 was the mannuscript printed in its entirety, edited and translated into Finnish by theologian and scholar Niila Outakoski. And finally, in 1997, the whole manuscript was printed in the original language, Swedish, and published in Åbo in Finland in NIF Publications 37. Historian of religion Juha Pentikäinen wrote here a lengthy article entitled: *Lars Levi Læstadius som samisk mytolog och mytograf* [L. L. L. as Sámi mythologist and mythographer], and the folklorist Reimund Kvideland wrote a three-page article with the title: *Læstadius' Lapp mythology – the manuscript and its fate*, where it says:

Niila Outakoski's Finnish translation is the first complete version of the manuscript. The present work however is the first complete version in the original language.

Kvideland is of course in good faith when he writes "första **fullständiga** utgåvan," for since 1946 Finnish, Swedish and Norwegian Læstadius scholars believed that all parts of the original manuscript had actually been found. This though would prove to be wrong, for 68 years after the first discovery in Pontarlier, a new discovery was made in the same place. During work on the previously mentioned book about the Recherche expedition: *La Recherche – En ekspedisjonen mot nord* [*La Recherche – en expedition to the north*] (Angelica Forlag 2002), the authors traveled to Pontarlier in the autumn of 2001 to study Xavier Marmier's copious collection of books, and to take a closer look at Læstadius' manuscript that had been found in 1933. After elegant scrutiny of the library's handwritten catalogues, a manuscript of Læstadius, unknown until now, was discovered. It turned out to be a continuation of part 1,

Gudalära, from the middle of §111 up to and including §146, with supplements to a number of paragraphs, and concluding with "a further supplement."

The manuscript was written in a thin notebook, width just over 5 ½ inches, length 8 ⅝ inches and comprising 108 pages. The book was bound in a green cardboard binding where it stands on the front cover with gold characters: L. L. LESTADIUS. MYTHOLOGIE LAPONNE. Otherwise, there is no title, and at the top of page 1 there is only: (to §111). The whole thing begins in other words in the middle of §111, a paragraph which in the original manuscript seemed a little short and stopped rather abruptly. The last paragraph is §146 which ends on the 70th page with the words: *Slut på Gudaläran [End of Gudaläran]*. Thereafter follows a ten-page *supplement*, with commentary on some of the paragraphs, also some for §111. The supplement concludes with a remark from Læstadius:

After the book's printing, an index has to be appended of all the mythological objects occurring in the work, whether in Swedish, Finnish or Lapp, together with a brief résumé of their functions, which in particular will be useful for detailed researcch in the general mythology of nations.

This note was actually on the last page of the notebook. But Læstadius was not entirely finished yet, and the manuscript concludes with *Ytterligare tillägg till Lappska Mythologien*, written on 14 sheets, which are bound between the last page and the back cover. This last section consists of 28 pages, width 4 ⅓ inches and length 7 ½ inches. Læstadius begins by saying /.../ *while preparing the work at hand, I did not have access to Schefferus' Lapponia, which only later came into my hands. It is probably necessary to make some excerpts from it, to the extent they concern the present subject.* This appendix contains, as mentioned here, additional commentary to a number of the paragraphs with support in the Uppsala professor Johannes Schefferus' standard work on the Sámi, *Lapponia*, written in Latin and published in Frankfurt in 1673.

On the last page of this manuscript stands an especially interesting greeting of transmission from Læstadius:

To M. Gaimard, president of the so-called French North Pole expedition, is presented this manuscript written by the undersigned in his own handwriting, containing **Fragmenter i Lappska Mythologien.** *Part 1 Gudalära, plus enclosed supplement, in return for 100 riksdaler Banco, plus 10 copies of the printed book. Karesuando the 4th of December 1842. Lars Levi Læstadius. Past. I Karesuando.*

Striking here is the dating, for Læstadius had already sent his manuscript with apothecary C. F. Östman to Stockholm in the spring of 1842. C. J. Sundevall confirms receiving it in a letter of June 15th, and on September 2nd he writes to Gaimard that the manuscript has been taken care of and sent to Paris. How then could Læstadius on the last page of the newly discovered fragments date the letter of transmission as late as December 4th 1842?

One possibility is that Læstadius held back the notebook that starts with §111, in expectation of Schefferus' book, *Lapponia*. This must have come in the summer/fall of 1842, and when *Ytterligare tillägg till Lappska Mythologien* had been finished,

Anders Person, Norwegian Sámi from
Kautokeino in Finnmark.

he formulated the letter of transmission which then would be valid for the entire first part of the manuscript.

Another possibility is that the rough draft book that begins with §111 was sent from Karesuando in the spring of 1842 together with the main part. And when Læstadius got access to Schefferus' *Lapponia*, he formulated *Ytterligare tillägg …* which he sent along with the mentioned letter of transmission. This was later bound into the back of the rough draft book. The strange thing though is that the transmission of this last bit is not mentioned in any letter from Læstadius to Sundevall nor in the correspondance between Sundevall and Gaimard.

But this is just speculation. The essential is that the whole manuscript had now turned up, in that this last part of *Gudalära* was found in Marmier's library in Pontarlier in 2001.

It is a little surprising though that it has not been pointed out before that the manuscript of *Gudalära* ended so abruptly, and that thereby the possibilities that there could be a continuation of this first part of the manuscript had not been discussed. A good indication that something had to be missing, is found in Læstadius' own references in the manuscript's parts 2, 3 and 4 as well as the supplement. Here there are namely references to part 1, §134; in part 3, §12 to part 1, §§138 and 141 and in part 4, §15 to §111, above all the newly discovered part. In the supplement of Fellman No 24, Læstadius refers to part 1, without specification of paragraph. The theme dealt with however is not mentioned in the paragraphs befire §111, but is dealt with though in §120.

It is interesting to note that Harald Grundström probably noticed these references to the paragraphs after §111. He skirted the problem however either by omitting Læstadius' references or changing paragraph numbers in reference to numbers before §111, where the same theme is discussed.

Juha Pentikäinen says in his article on the mythologist and mythographer Læstadius:

His idea was that the Lapps not only believed in the soul's immortality, but also in the resurrection of the dead or a renewal of the body after death. Here Læstadius is satisfied however with only a few quotes from Norwegian sources, without trying to draw any conclusions about Lapp belief in e.g. reincarnation.

But that is exactly what Læstadius does in the following paragraphs after §111, where the main theme was precisely the Sámi's conceptions about mankind's state after death.

Here there is in other words a lot of new material to understand, both for historians of religion, mythologists, folklorists and Læstadius scholars in general. It is therefore to be hoped that these newly discovered fragments will be thoroughly studied, and that they will perhaps contribute to new knowledge, both about Sámi mythology and popular belief and about the mythologist and human being Lars Levi Læstadius.

Norwegian Sámi in Kåfjord in Finnmark.

Sources

1. Printed works

d'Aunet, Léonie — *Voyage d'une Femme au Spitzberg.* 7. utgave. Paris 1881.

Castrén, Kaarlo — *Kiveliön suuri herättäjä Lars Levi Laestadius: elämäkerta* Helsinki 1932.

Castrén, Mathias A. — "Några Dagar i Lappland," i Joukahainen XIV Helsingfors 1913.

Fellman, Jacob — *Anteckningar under min vistelse i Lappmarken* I-IV. Helsingfors 1906.

Friis, Jens Andreas — *Lappisk Mythologi, Eventyr og Folkesagn.* Christiania 1871.

Gaimard, Paul (ed.) — *Voyages de la commission scientifique du nord, en Scandinavie, en Laponie, au Spitzberg et aux Feröe, pendant les années 1838, 1839 et 1840...Prospectus mars 1842.* Paris 1842.

Gaimard, Paul (ed.) — *Voyages de la commission scientifique du nord Pendant les années 1835, 1836, 1838, 1839 et 1840...* Paris u. å. (ca. 1843).

Kvideland, Reimund — "Læstadius' lapska mytologi – manuskriptet och dess öden." Etterord i: *Fragmenter i Lappska' Mythologien*, NIF Publications 37. Åbo 1997.

Læstadius, Lars Levi — *Ens Ropandes Röst i Öknen*, 1852-54. Genomsedd och ordnad af J. F. Hellman. Uleåborg 1909.

Læstadius, Lars Levi   *Fragmenter i Lappska Mythologien*. Svenska Landsmål och svenskt Folkliv. B. 61. Innledning og kommentarer av Harald Grundström. Stockholm 1959.

Læstadius, Lars Levi   *Fragmenter i Lappska Mythologien*. NIF Publications 37. Åbo 1997.

Læstadius, Petrus   *Journal för Första året av hans tjänstgöring såsom Missionär i Lappmarken*. Stockholm 1928.

Marmier, Xavier   *Lettres sur le Nord. Danemark, Suède, Norvège, Laponie et Spitzberg*. Paris 1845.

Marmier, Xavier   *Voyage en Scandinavie, en Laponie, au Spitzberg et aux Feröe, pendant les années 1838, 1839 et 1840, sur la Corvette la Recherche. Relation du Voyage*. Paris u.å (ca. 1845)

Pentikäinen, Juha   "Lars Levi Læstadius som samisk mytolog och mytograf." Etterord i *Fragmenter i Lappska Mythologien*, NIF Publications 37, Åbo 1997.

Stockfleth, Nils Vibe   *Dagbog over mine Missionsreiser i Finmarken*. Christiania 1860.

Willers, Uno   *Xavier Marmier och Sverige*. Stockholm 1949.

2. Newspapers and journals

Castrén, Kaarlo   "Lars Levi Læstadiuksen lappalaismytologian jäljilä" i *Suomen kirkkohistoriallisen seuran vuosikirja*, volum 23, 1933.

Collinder, Björn   "Lars Levi Læstadius, förkunnaren och forskaren – I anledning av ett sensationellt handskriftsfynd" i *Upsala nya tidning*, 23. Mai 1933.

Lavirer-Anders   "En Spadseregang fra Øvretorneå til Talvig" i *Tromsø Tidende* nr. 87, 31. Oktober 1847.

Neuvonen, Eero K.   "Kåsikirjoitus Lapista – ranskalaisen pikkukaupunkiin" i *Suomen Kuvalehti*. 1933.

Nissen, Kristian	"Lars Levi Læstadius' portrett, en ordensdekorajon og et Karikaturbilde" i *Morgenbladet*, 26 februar 1941.	
Læstadius, Lars Levi	"Franska wetenskapliga expeditionen till Spitsbergen" i NORE (Norrlandsposten) nr 9 (68), 12 (71), 13 (72), 14 (73) 1838.	

3. Manuscripts, letters

Fra Lars Levi Læstadius til:

Berzelius, Jøns Jacob	3. juli 1840	KVA
Fries, Bengt Fredrik	28. april 1834	GUB
Gottlund, Carl Axel	5. and 6. 1839	HU
Hartman, Carl Johan	11. mai 1839	UU
Marklin, Gabriel	30. mars 1830	UU
Nilsson, Sven	18. november 1839	LU
	6. desember 1840	LU
Sundevall, Carl Jacob	2. desember 1841	KVA
	10 januar 1842	KVA
	7. mars 1843	KVA
	august/september 1843	KVA
	10. juni 1844	KVA
	9. oktober 1844	KVA
	12. mai 1845	KVA
	16. juli 1845	KVA
	12. oktober 1845	KVA
	28. juni 1848	KVA
	2. desember 1851	KVA
	24. juni 1853	KVA
Vahl, Jens Moestue	12. january 1839	BCK
	2. november 1839	BCK
	januar 1841	BCK
	7. februar 1845	BCK

Wahlberg, Peter F.	11. april 1838	KVA
Wahlenberg, Göran	oktober 1841	UU
	20. november 1843	UU

Fra Paul Gaimard til:

Berzelius, Jøns Jacob	9. mai 1845	KVA
Sundevall, Carl Jacob	9. april 1843	KVA

Fra Victor Lottin til:

Christian Boeck	18. mars 1853	NBO

Fra Carl Jacob Sundevall til:

Paul Gaimard	2. september 1842	BN
	16. desember 1843	BN
	1. november 1844	BN
	1. oktober 1845	BN
	10. desember 1845	BN

4. Manuscripts

– F. L. Hellers erklæring til L. L. Læstadius (1840)	BN
– Kirkebok for Alta/Talvik 1838	ST
– Sven Lovéns dagbok 1837	KVA

– Fragmeneter i Lappska Mythologien av L. L. Læstadius
Del 1 – Gudalära → §111   MP/SOFI
Del 1 – Gudalära §111 →   MP
Del 2, 3, 4, Supplement   SOFI

– Opptegnelsr om lappenes mytologi av L. L. Læstadius
Defekt manuskript i J. A. Friis' papirer.   NBO

– Kristian Nissens udaterte manuskript:
Lars Levi Læstadius som lappisk mytolog og folklorist   TMU

– Antal Regulys avskrifter etter *Gudalära* (1840)   FLH

– Carl Jacob Sundevalls dagbok 1838   KVA

Abbreviations:

BCK   Botanisk Cemtralbibliotek. København
BN   Bibliotèque Nordique, Paris
FLH   Finska Litteratursällskapet, Helsinki
GUB   Göteborgs Universitetsbibliotek
HU   Helsingfors Universitetsbibliotek
KVA   Kongl. Vetenskapsakademien, Stockholm
LU   Lund Universitetsbibliotek
MP   Musée de Pontarlier
NBO   Nasjonalbiblioteket, Oslo
SOFI Språk- och Folkminnesinstitutet, Uppsala
ST   Statsarkivet i Tromsø
TMU   Tromsø Museum, Universitetsmuseet i Tromsø
UU   Uppsala Universitetsbibliotek

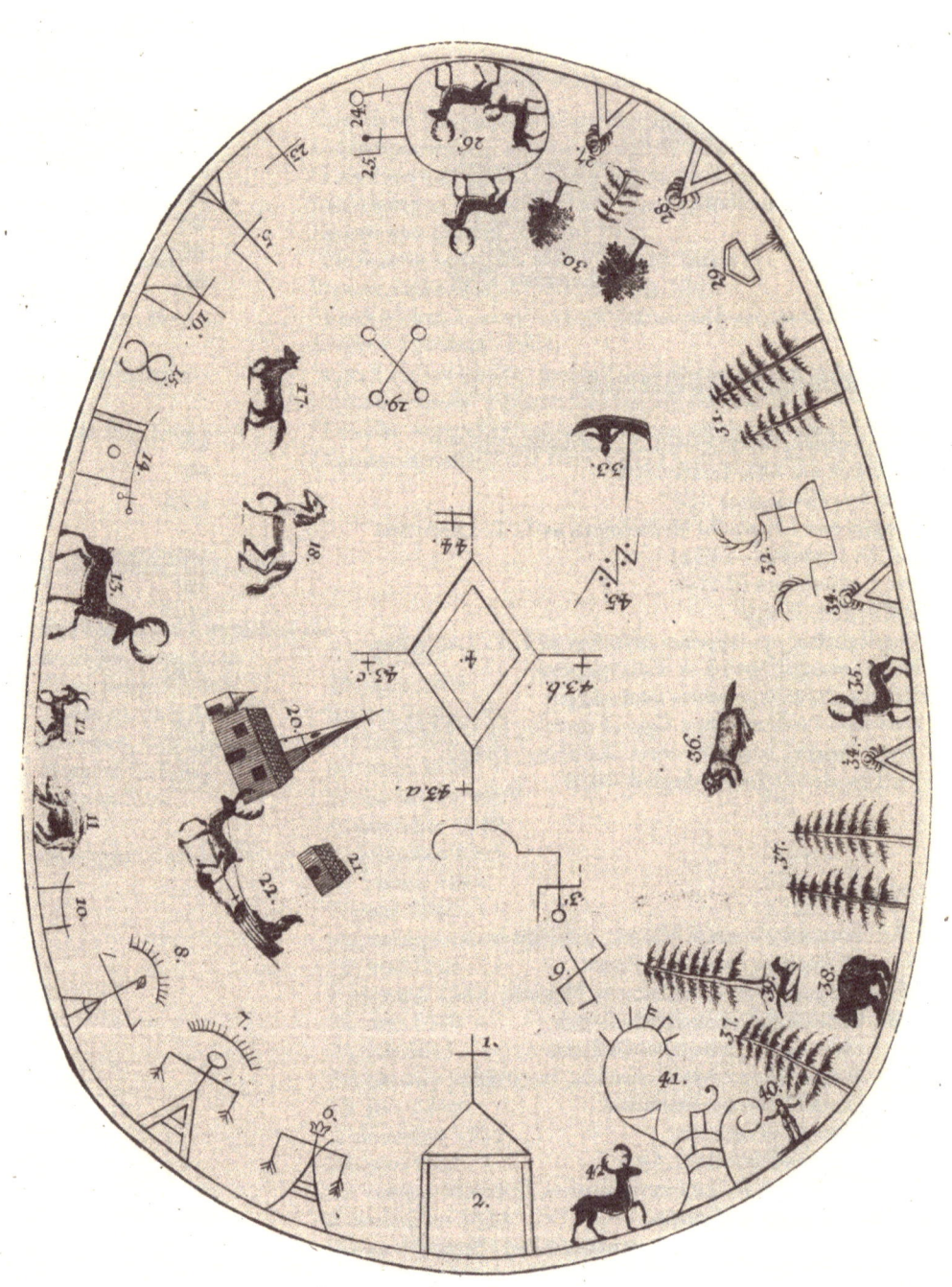

In *Fragmenter i Lappska Mythologien* Læstadius often refers to figures on this magic drum. The drawing is from Erich Johan Jessen: *Afhandling om de Norske Finners og Lappers hedenske Religion*, included at the end of Knud Leem: *Beskrivelse over Finmarkens Lapper* (København, 1767). Universitetsbiblioteket i Tromsø.

Fragments
of
Lapp Mythology
by
Lars Levi Læstadius

Pastor in Karesuando, from Torneå Lapland
Fellow of the Royal Science Society in Uppsala,
Corresponding Member of the Royal Hunters Association in Stockholm,
along with the Botanical Society in Edinburgh.
Member of the Royal French Legion of Honor.

Part 1
Doctrine of the gods, with associated mythological objects.

Reminder to the Reader

The notes on Lapp[1] Mythology contained in this work could rightly be called fragments, since most of the Lapps' ancient mythology has presumably been lost since the introduction of Christianity. Nowadays the Lapps know their ancient gods only by name, and even the names have been forgotten in many places. Yet much disbelief and superstition still reign among them as an obscure feeling from a forgotten past. It is also no wonder, since one finds among the Swedish peasantry itself in certain remote backwoods almost as much superstition as among the Lapps. It has not been much more than 200 years since the Lapps more generally began to accept Christianity, and even 100 years ago there were genuine pagans in Luleå Lapland. On the other hand, the Swedish peasantry has had Christianity for nearly 1000 years, and yet among them are found numerous superstitious ideas which undoubtedly derive from paganism, such as *vittra* [sirens], *underboninga* [underground forest spirits], *trollkäringa* [witches], *bjäran* [supernatural creatures] and others of which examples will be cited in this work.

For the information we still have left about the Lapps' ancient mythology, we have to thank some assiduous pastors in Lapland and Finnmark, who at the request of the Antique Collegium in Stockholm, as well as the Collegium of Missions in Copenhagen, collected and recorded everything they could lay their hands on of the Lapps' pagan religion; but unfortunately, it was not possible for these clergymen to get hold of everything belonging to this topic. For above all, they were not really fluent in the language; and secondly, they were in a way obligated to persecute precisely those persons who were conversant in all the Lapps' secrets, and from whom the pastors could get the most important information, if they had been approached more accommodatingly. One need not imagine that the multitude of Lapps were learnèd in all the magic arts; it was reserved for the *noaidis* (shamans) alone to more intimately know these magic secrets, for which the Lapps had become far and wide so notorious. These *noaidis* (magus, shamans, wizards) were highly respected among the Lapps, and were as a matter of fact the people's sages or priests.

But because through their alleged or real art of divination they placed the greatest obstacles in the way of the new faith's more rapid spreading among the masses, it was natural that they were detested and persecuted by the pastors who considered the *noaidis* as instruments of the very Devil. Therefore, it was less likely for the cler-

---

[1] In the North Sámi language, the name of the people today is Sámi and the area where many live is Sápmi.

gy to be taken into the *noaidis*' secrets, and even today the Lapps are very guarded with information concerning their superstitions. The pastors in particular should not acquire knowledge about that sort of thing; it was only through children and settlers' reports that one might get to hear one thing or other of that kind.

Once the first pastors in Swedish Lapland persecuted the *noaidis*, we haven't gotten much information from that side about the Lapps' original mythology. But on the Norwegian side, the pastors seem to have proceeded more amenably with the *noaidis*, and it is from that side we have the most important information on this topic.

However, not all the information merits equal credibility. A more detailed familiarity with the Lapps' past and present circumstances is required, so as to be able to distinguish the true from the false in the authors' information. The one writing this was born and raised in Lapland. He has perhaps more than anyone else wandered through Lapland in all directions; yet, he admits candidly that there is still a lot in the Lapps' inner affairs he does not feel himself able to judge infallibly. How much less credibility then do those authors deserve who only as outsiders, with preconceived ideas and prejudices, visited the land? Their reports had to be based on information from people who are just as unfamiliar with the Lapps' inner affairs as the traveler himself. One should not imagine that those Swedes and Norwegians who live in the vicinity of Lapland and Finnmark are familiar with the Lapps' inner affairs even if they annually see Lapps and are together with them. Even pastors in Lapland and Finnmark are not very well acquainted with the Lapps' situations and circumstances unless they are born and raised, or also resided for a longer period in Lapland, and visited the Lapps in their turf huts. On such unreliable persons' information, mentioned above, a number of more recent authors seem to have based their reports on the Lapp areas, and therefore too their works abound with mistakes and unfounded accounts; such as for example Zetterstedt, Blom, Rosenvinge, Brooke and others. The most credible authors on this topic which will be discussed here are the following:

Johannes Schefferus [1621-79] was the first author to write about Swedish Lapland with any criticism and judgment. His work *Lapponia* appeared first in Frankfurt in 1673 in quarto; followed by a second edition in 1674, and a third in 1677, also published in Frankfurt. These editions were in Latin; but according to Loenbom's[2] estimable foreword to *Johannis Tornei Lapponia*, Schefferus' work was translated into English, and published in Oxford in 1674; and the same year, the entire book was also translated into German; a revised edition also in German appeared in 1675. In French, Schefferus' work was translated by one P. Lubin, and printed in Paris in 1678, all this according to Loenbom.

Schefferus had good manuscripts to work with, and can therefore be considered a fairly good author for his era, and for those portions of Lapland he described. It follows from Loenbom's foreword that all of Lapland's pastors were instructed by the Royal Collegium of Antiquities to collect and record everything worth remem-

---

[2] Sam[uel] S. Loenbom (1725-76) wrote an introduction to Johannis J. Tornæus' *Beskrifning öfwer Torneå och Kemi Lappmark*. (1772).

bering, regarding the Lapps' customs and way of life. The pastors then sent these reports to the aforementioned Collegium, each one for his particular Lapp area. It is a shame that some of these manuscripts have gone missing. One would perhaps have been able to decide which of these pastors were most skilled in the Lapps' languages and ways of life. Judging from the quotations Schefferus provides, Samuel Rhe[e]n [1614-1680] seems to have been the most reliable and detailed of them.

Tornæus (1605-1681), whose manuscript Loenbom published in 1772, also became quite familiar with the Lapps' conditions in Torneå-Kemi Lapland; yet mistakes are also found in his work, e.g. p. 55 where he mistakenly gives the names of reindeer according to age. Tornæus' manuscript was used by Schefferus, and was thus written before 1670.

Gabriel Tuderus' (1754-1805) report on Sodankylä, Kuolajärvi, Kitka and Maanselkä Lappars, in Kemi Lapland, idol worship, superstition etc. was written around 1670, but not published in print until 1773 under the direction of the aforementioned Loenbom. This work which Schefferus did not get to use, contains important contributions to this topic, which will be treated in this work.

Pehr Fjellström's (1697-1764) report on the Lapps' bear hunt, and their superstitions related to it, was printed in Stockholm in 1755. This author reveals a great deal of knowledge about the Lapps' customs and way of life. His report on the bear hunt is the only complete one we have on this subject and sheds much light on Lapp mythology.

Pehr Högström's (1714-1784) *Account of Lapland under the jurisdiction of the Crown of Sweden* etc. [was] printed in Stockholm in 1847. "Of all real so-called accounts of these places, this one is presumably the most complete," says Loenbom in his foreword to the work of Tornæus mentioned above. Anyone who knows Lapland would have to concur with Loenbom's testimonial that Högström's account is not only the most complete, but also the most reliable of all earlier and more recent works dealing with Lapland. Högström does not feed his readers idle chat. He is not seeking a Don Quixote adventure in Lapland. He examines things before he expresses judgment. Such a man should have been in Lapland a century earlier, while paganism was still flourishing. Then one would not be groping in the dark concerning the significance of the figures on the magic drum, as well as the meaning of the figures on the Lapp Calendar which were touched on briefly by the older authors, but not entirely explained.

In the eleventh chapter of his account, the author goes into everything belonging to the Lapps' idolatry and superstitions; but the era when Högström was living and working in Lapland was not such that the author could be completely let in on the *noaidis'* mysteries. For above all, Christianity had already gotten the upper hand so that most of their ancient mythology had fallen into neglect; secondly, the Lapps had been so frightened by the earlier pastors that they didn't dare reveal the little that remained of their old superstitions. The author discusses this distinctly in §§28 and 34 of the chapter mentioned. Accordingly, it was only byways through settlers and such persons the author could get information on the Lapps' superstitions. And that is the situation even today. Thus, the one who wants to treat all the Lapps' mysteries completely should have gone to the *noaidis'* school.

Among the more recent authors could be mentioned Petrus Læstadius' *Journal*, printed in Stockholm 1831-33 and [Andreas Johan] Sjögren's notes[3] on Kemi Lappmark, printed in Helsingfors 1828. All other authors who only as travelers visited the Lappmarks, and who in their works included one thing or other touching on the Lapps' superstitions, do not merit any credibility to the extent I have studied them. – Holmström's *Attempt at an account of Lappmark's oldest inhabitants, the Lapps* etc. inserted in *Westerbottens Lähns Kongl. Hushålls sällskaps Handlingar* for the year 1829, I have not had the opportunity to use.[4] Judging from Zetterstedt's *Resa genom Umeå Lappmarker* (printed in Örebro in 1833)[5] and the statistical information inserted in Engström's *Resa genom Södra Lappmarken* (printed in Calmar in 1835),[6] Mr. Holmström does not seem to have much to report on the Lapps' mythology. In Lindahl and Öhrlings' *Lexicon Lapponicum*, printed in Stockholm in 1780, there are a number of interesting items in regard to Lapp mythology.

Among the Norwegian authors who have dealt with the Lapps, Lapp mythology is much more thoroughly taken up than with the Swedes and Finns. It is well-known historically that Norwegians had contact with the Lapps long before the Swedes. The Lapps' witchcraft or art of divination was known by Norwegians long before the introduction of Christianity into Norway, and is found among Icelandic authors under the names *Seid, Gan[d], Finnekonst*, etc. But except for the few Norwegians who put their children in schools to learn the art with renowned *noaidis*, not many have gotten to know what the art actually consisted of, until the Danish government at the end of the 17th and beginning of the 18th centuries began to send missionaries to Finnmark. The so-called missions Collegium in Köpenhamn had called upon the missionaries to hand in reports about the Lapps' pagan religion, and from that time there has been more precise information about the so renowned *Finnekonsten*.

Nor can it be denied that Lapp mythology is much richer with the Norwegian authors who managed to penetrate the Lapps' inner household through a more complete knowledge of the language. Yet one can make the same observation about them as about the Swedish authors, that they are not all equally credible. For some of them have never been able to penetrate the wall of prejudices, which the way of life and the language for ever raised between Norwegian and Lapp. Others have tried to make Lapp mythology more dazzling and systematic than it could possibly have been in the mind of the *noaidi* himself.

Here we will enumerate some of the Norwegian authors who according to the criteria whereby authors of this work base their judgment, could be considered to merit credibility.

---

[3] *Anteckningar om församlingarne i Kemi-Lappmark* (1828).

[4] *Holmström, Eric, [1777 – 1847]: Kort berättelse öfver Lappmarkens äldsta inbyggare... 1700 – 1827.*

[5] Johan Wilhelm Zetterstedt [1785-1874].

[6] Jon Engström [1794-1870]: *Resa genom södra Lappland, Jemtland, Trondhem o. Dalarna år 1834.*

In Erich Johan Jessen's treatise on the Norwegian Finns'[7] and Lapps' pagan religion (introduced at the end of [Knud] Leem's [1697-1774] *Description of Finnmark*) the author mentions that the information he gives in this work was gotten from the reports to the Mission Collegium in Köpenhamn that had come in occasionally from the missionaries in Finnmark. Since Jessen's treatise is accordingly a summary of the missionaries' reports, it is thus necessary to investigate at what times, in

---

[7] Most Norwegian, Danish and Icelandic authors call the Lapps Finns, and the Finns Kvens, Bjarmians, etc. The Lapp name does not often appear officially in Swedish history until after the first invasion of Finland, proof that the Swedes borrowed this name from the Finns, for which Lappalainen was known from time immemorial. According to Finnish myths (runes) the Finns' oldest divinity Väinämöinen was shot by an arrow from Lappalainen. Thus Lappalainen (Lapp) was contemporary with Väinämöinen. Presumably the Swedes didn't know so exactly the difference between Finn and Lapp before the Finnish war under Erik the Holy (Erik IX ruled 1156-60). They considered them as one and the same nation, and thus called the Lapps 'Skridfinnar (skiing Finns)' in connection with their skiing. Maybe it's just on the occasion of this mixing up by the Swedes of the nations 'Finn' and 'Skridfinn' that the Finns ever since that time kept the Finn name which originally belonged to the Lapps, during which the actual Finns were called 'Kvens,' which is nothing other than a Geatish shortened pronunciation of the Finnish word '*Kainulainen*,' which again designated a certain Finnish group of which remnants or descendants are still found in the present *Kainun maa*. Österbotten or actually *Kajana Län*, also as 'Alakainio' and 'Ylikainio' in Norrbotten. The Lapps also have their 'Kainolats' which according to the Lapp etymology should mean: one who handles rope. That Tacitus' description of the Finns rather more fits the Lapps, than today's Finns, is my complete conviction, although [Carl Axel] Gottlund in his "Attempt to explain Tacitus' opinion of the Finns" (printed in Stockholm in 1834) [*Försök att förklara Caj. Corn. Taciti omdömen öfver finnarne*], tries to show the opposite, e.g. Tacitus' words *Victui herba*, don't fit the old Finns who according to Mr. Gottlund's own testimonial were familiar with burn-beating [slash and burn], and thus did not have to eat grass, as the Lapps, about whom one knows that they still to this very day eat grass, viz. *Angelicha, Rumex acetosa, Rhoeum digynum, Sonchus alpinus*, likewise the leaves of *Epilobium angustifolium*, and *Ribes Sonchus*, which plants the Lapps on the one hand eat raw, as the stems of Angelicha and Sonchus, on the other, boiled and mixed with reindeer milk. The Lapps along the Norwegian seacoast also eat *Cochlearia*, either by itself, or mixed with fish liver. And these are the words of Tacitus: *Sola in sagittis spes, quas inopia Ferri ossibus asperant* [Their only dependence is on their arrows, which, for want of iron, are headed with bone]; this cannot fit the Finns who had iron and other metals. But the Lapps can report clearly that their ancestors used loon beaks (Rostrum Columbi Septemtrionalis) as arrow points. These are also Tacitus' words: *in aliquo ramorum nexu contegantur* [a covering of branches twisted together].

Mr. Gottlund himself has admitted (ibid.) that the Finns had houses or huts. Tacitus could not say about them that they had a *nexum ramorum* [branches twisted together] for protection against bad weather. But about the Lapps' *Laudnje kååtte*, one can probably say that it is a *nexus ramorum*, consisting of a few raised poles, with birch branches or spruce branches protecting against the wind. The use of tents belongs to later times. According to the Lapps' own accounts, *Ädnam kåte*, or turf huts didn't come into use until during the Chudes' and Karelians' raids. Everything Gottlund has cited from Danish, Norwegian and Icelandic authors about Finns and witchcraft, etc. only concerns Lapps, from whom Finnmark too has gotten its name. Anyone who reads history impartially will probably discover that these authors did not understand or mean Finns, but Lapps, when they speak about the people in Finnmark. Besides these Danish-Norwegian-Icelandic authors even in their own places spoke about Kvens, and that the Norwegian's Kvens are the same people the Swedes call Finns, is besides now a definite fact. That the Norwegian called the Finns Kvens even in ancient times can best be demonstrated by the name *Quænangern*, a fjord in Finnmark that got its name from Kvens at the time when *Anger* (bay or fjord) was still usual in the language.

which parts of Finnmark, as well as how long each of these missionaries stayed in these districts so as to be able to assess their authority on Lapp mythology.

Blom mentions on his trip, p. 186, that the first person who got serious about the conversion effort in Nordland and Finnmark was Magister Erik Bredal [1607-72] who during the time of Fredrik III was banished from Trondhjem as a consequence of the Swedes' conquest. This Bredal is supposed to have lived in Trondenes in Senjen which at that time was part of the Trondhjem bishopric. Bredal is supposed to have visited the Lapps' place of residence.[8]

Since Jessen does not mention the missionaries' names from whom the reports about the Lapps' superstitions came in, then one cannot know whether this Bredal has handed in any such, nor can it be known whether he had command of the language.

Thomas v[on] Vesten has indeed been one of the most fervent missionaries on the Norwegian side, which can be seen from his letter to the Swedish clergy from the year 1723. In this letter, which Loenbom had published in 1773, the author enumerates a multitude of Lapp divinities; but considering the publisher's ignorance of the language, the Lapp names have been spelled in a strange manner, which makes the document itself less useful. From this letter as well as *Budsticken's* (the Messenger's) 7th annual volume one finds that von Vesten visited the Norwegian coast from Trondhjem to the districts of Kola: that he made these journeys several times in particular, during which he offered to convert the pagan Lapps to Christianity. It is likely that this thesis, which Leem included in his description, of the Lapps' ancient doctrine of the gods, is in von Vesten's hand, although Leem assumes the treatise's authors as anonymous.

Högström too cites von Vesten as the author of a mythological work, but does not mention whether and where it was published. The treatises of von Vesten that are included in *Budsticken's* 7th annual volume do not concern mythological objects.

Almost contemporary with von Vesten or a little later was Morten Lund, missionary in Alta and Hammerfest; from him there is a Lapp translation of Luther's lesser catechism, printed in Köpenhamn in 1728. As this Mr. Lund was an authority

---

[8] Here is presumably meant Lapps along the seacoast, or the so-called *Sjöfinnar* [Sea Sámi]. If one excludes Koutokeino [Kautokeino], Karasjoki [Karasjok] and the district of Porsanger Fjord, then in the rest of Nordland and Finnmark there are rather few places suitable for reindeer Lapps to spend the winter, from which it follows that most reindeer Lapps (Lapps with reindeer herds) already from ancient time wintered on the Swedish side. These in turn have always been considered as Swedish subjects (likewise Koutokeino and Karasjoki up to 1751).

From this it follows that the Lapps the Norwegian missionaries had to deal with were for the most part *Sjöfinnar* (Sea Sámi), who through their dealings with Norwegians and German merchants from a long time ago managed to get a step ahead of their brothers the Mountain Lapps in culture, which also had an evident effect on their mythology, so that one finds Lapp, Catholic and Old Geatish concepts mixed together in their doctrine of the gods. Distinguishing true from false in the authors' information, that in the Norwegian Lapps' mythology, separating purely Lapp mythological objects from foreign, is no easy matter.

on the language, one must assume he was together with the Lapps for a longer time. How he handed in a report to the Missions Collegium is not known.

Lennart Sidenius (1702-63), according to (Christfried) Ganander's [1741-90] testimonial, wrote a report on the Lapps' doctrine of gods, and sent a copy of it in manuscript to the Vicar Johan Tornberg in Juckasjärwi [Jukkasjärvi] the 17th of October 1726, who in turn gave it to the Dean, Magister Henrik Forbus (1674-1737), the 1st of January 1728. From this manuscript *Ganander* has on his own testimonial taken his information on Lapp Mythology, which he entered into his *Finnish Mythology*, printed in Åbo in 1789. This Sidenius report has much similarity with the anonymous author who is cited by Leem. Ganander also says that Sidenius' manuscript corresponds to another Danish missionary's, Jöns Kijhldal's [Jens Kildal] report. (This author is not known to me).

The anonymous author whom Leem published in his classical work betrays a lot of knowledge of the Lapps' doctrine of gods. Yet Leem observes that the anonymous author's information chiefly concerns Trondhjem's and Helgeland's Lapps, since the Lapps in Finnmark could not be acknowledged all the mythological objects enumerated by the anonymous author. Most likely it seems that the anonymous author is von Vesten.

After these older missionaries who more or less have contributed to the information on Lapp mythology, Knud Leem appears with a thoroughness in inquiry, and a clarity in presentation that distinguishes him above all others, and puts him abreast Högström on the Swedish side. Leem was a scholar who not only verified what others before him wrote about the Lapps' superstitions; he himself also sought during his ten-year duties in Finnmark to penetrate the Lapps' mysteries, and can therefore be viewed as a classic author in his way. In what concerns Finnmark's Lapps Leem is beyond all doubt the most reliable, and it is therefore incomprehensible why a number of younger researchers, ignoring these classical authors, are so bent upon treating the public with empty talk, but authors who want to pass as reliable in their information, such as Zetterstedt, Blom, Brooke, Rosenvinge, et al. The crazy Acerbi and his like it is not worth talking about.

Yet the same remark has to be made about Leem that we have already made about Högström, that he lived and worked at a time when Christianity had already gotten the upper hand. The Lapps in Leem's time had already forgotten a large portion of their superstitions, and what was still left of their ancient doctrine of gods, naturally had to be viewed as shameful to reveal. Yet Leem has found out the most that he could possibly lay his hands on at that time. His lengthy work was printed in Copenhagen in 1767 in large quarto format with Danish and Latin text.

These are the most distinguished authors in Lapp mythology. I sincerely regret that I did not have the opportunity to consult [Hans] Hammond's *Nordiska Missions-historie* (Copenhagen 1787), nor have I been informed of Pastor [Jacob] Fellman's *Lapp Mythology*, which is said to have been written by the well regarded pastor, and according to a letter from Mr. Gottlund, submitted to the judgment of the Finnish Literature Society, but still not, as far as is known, sent to be printed.[9] I

---

[9] After the above was written, and the entire manuscript ready, the vicar Mr. Fellman kindly sent me

presume that Mr. Fellman's *Lapp Mythology* will contain roughly the same as found in this work, to the degree he perhaps had a better opportunity than I to study the relevant authors. What remains of the Lapps' ancient superstitions among the present Lapps, I believe I know as well and maybe somewhat better than Fellman.

For comparison with Lapp mythology, and to ascertain whether the Lapps could have borrowed certain mythological objects from neighboring nations, I have also used: *Norske Sagn* by Andreas Faye, printed in Arendal in 1833; *Ordbok öfver Nordiska Mythologien*, printed in Nyköping in 1815, (author anonymous); as well as *Handlexicon i Gamla Classika Mythologien*, by J[ohann] G[ottfried] Gruber, Stockholm, 1834. One must regret, that although several learnèd native Finns are ardently studying Finnish mythology, yet none of them to my knowledge has published his views regarding their ancestors' religion and doctrine of gods; they haven't even given a summary draft of a Finnish mythology, for which they nevertheless have good materials in the store of Finnish songs (runes), which in more recent times have been collected and in part printed. (Among great experts of Finnish mythology who deserve mention are Carl Axel Gottlund, Doctor [Elias] Lönnroth and Magister [Matthias] Castrén). I have accordingly not had any other author at my disposal than Ganander's *Mythologia Fennica* which was published in Åbo in 1789. But this author has a rather modest testimonial of today's greatest experts in matters Finnish, which can be confirmed by the following: excerpts of a letter from Carl Ax. Gottlund (1796-1875) dated Kuopio August 4th, 1839.

"In summary you mention that among other things you have also undertaken to write a Lapp mythology on behalf of the French, in connection with which you turn to me with a request for information on various questions, in any case you presume Lapp and Finnish mythology ought to be in closer contact with each other. I must admit that in this case you have turned to the wrong person, not because in this I consider my judgment inferior to that of others: on the contrary I cite all the knowledge and experience I possess."

"But if one is to understand by the word mythology what it denotes for the Romans and Greeks, namely not just a list of the gods, but a science of the gods, or faith as a subject of human worship, etc. then I must say what I already said 22 years ago, and what you probably read in *Svensk Litteratur Tidning* [Swedish literature journal] from 1818 where in a review of [Friedrich] Rühs: *Finnland och dess invånare*[10] discusses the Finns' mythology (which consists in that they do not have or possess one); and since that time my views have not at all changed."

"Everything Ganander, Petterson, Rühs et al. have written about this is sheer nonsense. Anyhow: the Finns do not have once in their language any words that mean: church, temple, worship, sacrifice, altar, priests, etc. The very word *Jumala* (God) is not an appellative noun, but a *proprium* (a proper noun), and cannot as

---

a portion of his manuscript; but as he intends to publish it, and requests it back at the earliest opportunity, I didn't have a chance to take excerpts from it; in that part of the manuscript I borrowed there wasn't much that could belong to the Lapp doctrine of gods; and what belongs to the later portions of my work I hope to be able to read in print.

[10] *Finland und seine Bewohner.*

such be construed with, or together with other proper nouns. One rather says Jumala-Isä, Jumala-poika instead of Isä Jumala, Poika Jumala, etc.; but it is not Finnish, and against the nature of the language, introduced with Christianity. This alone ought to convince you to some extent what Finnish mythology is at its foundation."

"The old myth about the Jumala temple and the image in Bjarmaland is already what the language itself and the tale reveal, only a political warrior poem, a legend without the least historical precedent. But if on the other hand one wants to understand mythology not as nature-worship (worship of nature) but as nature poetry, an idolatrous, incarnate and mystifying nature, yet without any sort of worship; well then the Finns have a rich mythology, actually fantasy, poetry; of which to be sure if greater individual poets, artists, painters, sculptors, et al. have made from it an object of art on the one hand and of superstition in the people on the other – over time a mythology could have arisen, like the Greek and Roman, but interrupted in this process of development, or delayed art of the people's moral and religious thoughts, through the introduction of Christian faith, Finnish poetic art did not attain this point of culmination."

"With a Finnish mythology of that nature consisting only of nature poetry, you are not content. Therefore, you must study Ganander and his kind of people, and learn what you can from them; between you and me, all of his explanations, interpretations and learned commentary are just empty talk. Only the Finnish rune (song) can be referred to as basic, deserves to be read, but not as psalm, hymn, article of faith."

"Whether the Finns under paganism were convinced of the soul's immortality, of punishment and reward in another world, etc., about that nothing more can be said for certain. Only what one can indirectly conclude from their speculations, proverbs and old sayings, that you can learn in the essay on the old Finns' philosophy, introduced in the first part of *Otava*, of which a translation into German from Brockhaus in Leipzig, taken care of by Sederholm in Moscow, after an excerpt had previously appeared in *Morgenblatt* published by Cotta in Augsburg in 1835."

So much for Mr. Gottlund.

I suppose not all Finnish mythologists share Gottlund's views on this subject; but since I cannot be taken into Finnish mythology's, or as Gottlund calls it, nature poetry's mysteries, so I don't dare embark upon lengthy discussions about this question, but will be satisfied by citing the following for the elucidation of Lapp mythology:

By mythology I mean a common popular belief in supernatural beings and effects. All ideas about supernatural beings and effects not part of the common popular belief, but only belonging to single individuals' fantasies, could not according to my simple-minded opinion belong to mythology; but if a poetic painting, a frightened imagination or ghost story becomes part of common popular belief, then it also enters into the realm of mythology.

If we now look at Roman/Greek mythology according to this distinction, then we soon find that the countless number of extant mythological objects – whose number according to some mythologists' calculations reached 7000 – consisted mostly of deified and metamorphosed human beings who only belong to mythology because their divine or supernatural power and metamorphosis was generally believed in a particular town or rural area. But, that not all could be objects of a general folk belief only proves their countless number which no one but a professional studying the poets' writings could know about. If we separate these deified humans from the genuine mythological objects, then Greco-Roman mythology's extent becomes significantly less, though its content, in relation to the poets' free play is rich in bold creations. Probably the poets themselves did not believe in the reality of their creations; and so much less then could all, perhaps not even ¼ of their fantasies become objects of a general folk belief. Only such objects that had a temple, or in one way or other were worshiped, that were called upon or believed by the people, could be viewed as genuinely mythological.

If according to these distinctions we compare Finnish mythology – called by Gottlund nature poetry – with other nations' mythology, then we soon find that its content cannot be poetry alone. There must also be actual mythological objects. For example, *mahinen*, a kind of human creature that lives under the earth; *manalaiset*, deceased people's souls; *äpärä*, murdered child's ghost. All of these still constitute, at least in northern Finland, objects of common folk belief.

Besides, Mr. Gottlund himself, in his treatise on Tacitus' opinion of the Finns, has acknowledged that among them there are veritable sorcerers (*noaidis*), who have come so far in their art that they even conjure one another to death. I wonder whether this also happened via nature poetry? Or via mystification or personification? To be sure, he mentions in another place in the same treatise that the sorcerers made appalling grimaces toward each other when they met. But didn't they conjure each other to death simply with grimaces? If it didn't happen via natural magic, then at least an exalted imagination must have played a role. But just the force of this exalted imagination, which can have a detrimental effect on the organism itself, I consider to be the real myth's fosterer. It differs thereby from any sort of poetry in that it believes in the reality of its own creation.

One meets the force of this exalted imagination in children and neurotic persons, in particular among women. One encounters it more often with coarse, uneducated persons than with educated. Therefore, myth too actually belongs to the people. Yet, most of all, it is encountered among uneducated persons who live alone in the forests, which seems to have its natural basis in the loneliness and desolate emptiness that surrounds the recluse's cabin. The soul is always active; but with the uneducated, the mental power is not directed inward as with the thinker and poet; it is directed outward toward external objects. What images could not arise in the lonesome wanderer's soul when he finally goes to bed by a log fire in the desolate forest? Must not the dark shape that appears before his eyes through the bewildering morning mist be a troll that nevertheless upon closer inspection is just a gray rock? Must not the howl of a wolf, the hoot of an owl, or the weasel's rustling in the dry leaves come from marvelous creatures on and beneath the earth? The one who merely tried to lie alone in the forest on a gloomy autumn night will soon experience the strange magic power the forest possesses together with loneliness to awaken fantasies, and it will no longer seem strange to him, why mythology is so especially full and varied in the most remote forest tracts where one finds so many gnomes, elves and trolls with all their odd epithets and shapes. In a larger town one doesn't have time to listen for spooks and trolls. If something peculiar is heard from a distant garret or wine cellar, then one immediately suspects thieves. The din of people who wander back and forth on the streets soon puts an end to ghost stories.

But entirely different are the circumstances in a remote forest village where one seldom gets to see people, where no exchanges take place, and where nature alone with its surroundings occupies the lonely hunter's or herder's attention. The least sound from a bird, a hare, a stone rolling off a cliff immediately arouses the lonely wanderer's attention. If he cannot immediately explain the cause of the strange sound or confusing sight, then he suspects something mysterious or supernatural in the chance incident. His frightened imagination paints nothing but horrors and frightening pictures. He thinks he sees the spook, troll and evil creatures that surround him. This seems entirely natural, and I think it would happen to any person whatsoever if he were put in the same circumstance as the lonely forest peasant.

This magic power whereby a wild nature together with loneliness engenders man's power of imagination, is according to my simple opinion the real basis of myth. The solitary wanderer relates what he sees with a solemn mien; it becomes a legend among the people, and the tale is believed by the foolish multitude. Then the myth is completed. Such a myth is, according to my conception, not poetry, but it can become a splendid subject for poetry, if the poet attires it in poetic dress, and gives it a more noble color, i.e. turns it into a real poem. Mythology has always provided the poets with magnificent material for the poem; but the poet does not confine himself to the myth in its original form. He reshapes and embellishes it with his own additions, and it is difficult and maybe impossible to discern in the poets' writings the original myth from the poetic ornaments. Even the Finnish rune has a good portion of poetic ornamentation which does not belong to the myth but the poem. When Ganander placed the rune as the basis of his mythology, then Mr. Gottlund may indeed be correct that Ganander was not always right when he wanted to explain the rune as myth. But that myth is also the basis of the rune, I think no impartial researcher can deny.

On the other hand, Lapp mythology is rather free of all poetic ornamentation. The Lapps have nothing that can be compared with other nations' poetry. Their song "moves," as Blom observes, "within a fourth or fifth, and is extremely repulsive to a musical ear." This is so nevertheless only for the unaccustomed; for when one becomes inured to the Lapps' song, one finds it not entirely unpleasant. Maybe neither Blom nor Zetterstedt (who also condemns their song) has heard anyone other than inebriated Lapps yoiking (singing). The late conductor Hæffner in Uppsala has said that the Lapps' song is in certain cases sublime. NB: As a sound of nature, or as the purest expression of the intrinsic feeling, it can in certain cases be called sublime when it is performed by a pure female voice in the resounding forest.

But otherwise, and although in a musical sense it can be said "to move within a fourth or fifth," one should not imagine that it is without variations. There are special songs for sorrow, and others for joy, particular modulations for courage and cowardice. Each animal has in Lapp its song with attached words, expressing the animal's natural temperament. To each more remarkable person, a song is dedicated that is supposed to express the person's particular manner, or special way of being. These songs in their modulations are just as unchangeable as they are innumerable in number. But although the improvised words to the song do not lack all poetic inspiration, one cannot however discover any trace of rhythm in them. Besides, I have seen Lapps so captivated or inspired by their songs, in spite of any of the Phosphorists' school, which proves they are not so unemotional as a few later authors would promise. (Zetterstedt's *Journey* 2, p. 56).

The Lapps' poetry has as said no real connection with their mythology. The latter is always related in prose. Naturally, the prosaic tale can also be dressed up with additions, but the additions are not of poetic nature. They are incidental. Accordingly, one often hears one and the same story told in different ways in different parts of Lapland. Yet the basic idea is always the same.

But entirely different is the situation with the Finnish rune. There it is the poet or rune master who gives the myth color. There nothing can be removed or added without spoiling the entire context. No single verse or strophe can be omitted without regret. In such a case the rune or song represents correctly the original myth such as it was perceived in the rune master's brain. But the original myth such as it was in the common folk belief, the poet cannot reproduce because of the rhythm. The entire difference between prosaic and poetic mythology consists in that the additions in the former are by many, in the latter by one alone, namely the poet.

That is roughly how I conceive of mythology's origin. – Besides what Mr. Gottlund remarks about the word 'Jumala,' namely, that it is a proper noun; that I think was the case with 'Jehovah' itself. God can never be the subject of a concept, accordingly, not its name either. Jumala thus represents a certain separate object (individual) in the same way as *Väinämöinen, Ilmarinen*, et al. each designate its own mythological object. That in Finnish there is no word for church, temple, worship et al. proves nothing of what is supposed to be proved. In the Lapps' language there are not any words either to represent these concepts. Yet one knows that the Lapps had their *Passe* sanctuary; that they crept on four feet before the idol *Seite*; that they sacrificed large piles of reindeer antlers to their idols, etc.

I wonder whether the Finnish word *Pyhä* doesn't refer to a place or object purified for divinities? Why otherwise should *Pyhä ouda,* a sacred forest, exist as far up as Finnmark? Inasmuch as this is not just a translation of the Lapps' sacred places. I wonder whether the Finnish word *kumarta* refers to a sort of bending down before the gods?

Mr. Gottlund in general wants to elevate his pagan ancestors beyond other pagans; he wants to acquit them of all idolatry and superstition; he wants to make them real natural philosophers and nature poets; but I am afraid that Old Adam or more correctly Old Erik was playing with them, as well as with other nations. Already the circumstance that they had their *Noidat* (*noaidis*) sorcerers; *Luvut* readings or incantation formulas; *loitimiset* secret cures, etc. already shows that the people believed in supernatural effects. Mr. Gottlund even mentions in the above-mentioned work, about Tacitus' opinion of the Finns etc., that the *noaidis* were believed to be in contact with "the slippery one" [the Devil], and that they (the *noaidis*) nevertheless were feared and honored by the people; so much the worse. That shows that the old Finns believed that an evil, powerful being existed that could do both good and evil through the *noaidis*.

Mr. Gottlund asserts of course in *Otava* 1, p. 31 and following, that the essence of prophecy belongs to a later period; but when he wants to adapt Tacitus' observation "*incantantionibus dediti* (addicted to incantations) etc." to the Finns, then their art of divination must already have been flourishing in Tacitus' era. Then he cannot blame Catholicism for having been the cause of sorcery. But where then have the Finns learned to practice witchcraft? And how would they have been able to become so popular for their witchcraft, if the people didn't believe in their conjuring tricks? If the *noaidis* themselves didn't believe in the power of their witchcraft (i.e. that it happened only through natural means, which they assiduously kept secret), the people all the same believed it happened through supernatural effects. Just this belief of the people in supernatural forces and effects is already sufficient to prove the existence of a Finnish mythology.

Mr. Gottlund will likewise explain away the whole Thorir Hund story about the Bjarmians' god, who is called *Jumala*, which story is found in Snorri Sturlason. Since this belongs to history and not mythology, I can't decide whether the story is true or false. That it should be a 'political warrior poem' I cannot detect; for the whole story about Thorir Hund's journey to Bjarmaland is so lengthy and detailed that it does not seem it could have been fabricated. Scholars are still said not quite to agree about Bjarmaland's geographical location. Some claim it would have been in the district of Archangel. But it could be possible that Bjarmaland lay in the district of Kola, in which case *Jumala* would more likely be a Lapp divinity.

von Vesten mentions in a treatise from 1717 included in *Budstikken's* 7th annual volume, p. 13, that a Lapp village at the end of Nordfjellet (in Lapp: *Nuorta Tunturi*) on the Archangel side is called *Bjarmiri*.[11] Magister Emanuel Kohlström, missionary in Enontekiö in the Lapp area, has told me, that his father, the late parish pastor Math. Kohlström, is supposed to have seen a large idol of hewn stone (?) in the district of *Aviovaara*, now Karasjok. If this is true, then one is easily led to the thought that the Lapps had brought in idols from foreign nations, for there is no example of the Lapps having cut in stone. Germany is called in Finnish: *Saxan maa*, and the Lapps in Torneå in the Lapp area as well as farther north, call Germany *Saxa ädnam*,

---

[11] *Budstikken* is a Norwegian journal published in more recent times (1820-26). There were several interesting treatises about Nordland and Finnmark including the above mentioned by v. Vesten who himself has traveled widely in these northeastern districts all the way to Kola together with a Russian clergyman.

from which it seems to follow that the Saxons were the first Germans who visited and came in contact with these northern countries. It is possible that either they themselves or through Norwegian adventurers, provided the Lapps in Finnmark with one or other *Jumala* image of hewn stone. But the *Jumala* image in Bjarmaland seems to have been of wood, because the neck came off and the whole *Jumala* tumbled over when Thorir Hund's companion went to cut off the chain around *Jumala's* neck.

When now Mr. Gottlund claims that the old Finns did not have any idols (of which at least reports should exist if there really were such images), then it is likely that it was a Lapp god that Thorir Hund and his foster brother wrecked. That the word *Jumala* sounds more Finnish than Lapp makes little difference, seeing that the Lapp dialect in the Kola district is closer to Finnish than to Lapp.

I hereby conclude my remarks regarding Finnish mythology, which I am not capable of assessing, as long as the opinions are divided among the native researchers. For purposes of comparison I have to use it as it appears in Ganander, along with the runes or songs I had a chance to consult.

With so few sources of help I have not been able to make many comparisons with foreign nations' mythology, but present the Lapp as it appears in the previously published sources, together with the little I could add from my own experience. I have never made mythology a primary object of study. As a child, I heard quite a lot belonging to Lapp [mythology], and as a student I did excerpts from Leem. I would probably not so soon have undertaken to write these 'fragments,' if some members of the so-called French scientific expedition hadn't encouraged me to do so. If I can thereby serve those interested parties and researchers in the human family's cultural history, it will be a pleasure for me.

If the work finds a publisher and outlets, it will continue with the following sections: viz. doctrine of sacrifice, doctrine of divination and doctrine of fables. The last mentioned will contain a selection of the Lapps' tales.

Karesuando in Torneå Lapland May 8, 1840

L. L. Læstadius

Study of Sámi. Painting by F. Biard. Nordnorsk Kunstmuseum, Tromsø.

Fragments of Lapp Mythology
Part One. Doctrine of Gods.

§. 1.

The Lapps, not having either educational institutions or the art of writing, could never become such great philosophers that through thinking they might come to an acknowledgment of a single god. For the same reason, they could not become naturalists, rationalists or deists. Needed of course is a certain power of thought to be able to arrive at such a result in religion. But the feeling for religion, or belief in the supernatural, was just as alive in the Lapps as in other nations. Nor can one claim that their doctrine of gods was more unreasonable than that of other pagans. To be sure, they had idols, but these were only to represent the divine. At its height, perhaps, the very densest believed some of the god's power was communicated to the hallowed idol. Sacrifices were usual; but that they also supposedly used human sacrifices is probably less believable. In their worship they have been very zealous, and the least fault against accepted practices would be reconciled with sacrifice.

Belief in a life after this one seems to have been common among the entire nation. Bound up with that too was the idea of punishment and reward in another world. In their belief in the resurrection of the dead the Lapps have gone much further than Greeks and Romans. For the Lapps believed that both humans and animals would get new bodies in another world. If the Greeks' heroes journeyed to the realm of the dead, then the Lapps too were not unfamiliar with that journey; every renowned *noaidi* or soothsayer had, in important cases, to undertake a trip to the realm of the dead, though not in the body but in spirit. If the Greeks had their oracle, then the Lapps too were not without. Their magic drum was that oracle which was diligently consulted for advice. This is in brief the content of the Lapps' mythology.

§. 2.

Since man thinks in terms of time and space, and since one idea always gives rise to another, I have presented Lapp mythology as a sort of system. With alphabetic order too much continuity is lost, and an index at the end serves the same purpose as alphabetical order. It is therefore not the idea that the mythological objects should have come about in the order the system indicates. You see, it is likely that evil beings or creatures harmful to humans first appeared in the imagination, and that the fear of them provided the occasion to imagine good ones, – as opposed to the former, superior divine forces. The whole essence of mythology seems to be nothing but a battle between good and evil forces, just like the battle between good and evil in man's inner being is the axis around which one's entire life and essence revolves.

As the Lapps' mythology is found much more complete in the Norwegian-Danish than in the Swedish authors, and Jessen's aforementioned treatise is based on several missionaries' reports; I have thought it best to take it as the basis, and for each individual object, append the others' information together with my own remarks.

§. 3.

The ranking of the Lapp Gods, and their division into classes. The *noaidis* presumably did not classify their gods. Yet there occurs in the missionaries' reports a sort of precedence, which though based on the *noaidis*' information, can serve as a basis for the classification, so as to better understand the connection.

"The Lapps' divinities," Jessen says, "are divided into three classes; namely, superhuman, heavenly and terrestrial," to which could probably be added subterranean, as well as mythological objects which without having been seen or worshiped as divine, nevertheless were kept for supernatural essence, and played an important role in their mythology.

Sidenius in Ganander has divided the Lapps' gods into four classes, viz. upper celestial, lower celestial, terrestrial and subterranean. The same basis of classification is also followed by Anonymous in Leem.

The Swedish authors who generally recognize a smaller number, do not mention the upper celestial. With them however there are a few terrestrial gods not clearly perceived by the Norwegians. That happens naturally in that the Lapps' gods were different in particular Lappmarks.[12]

§. 4.

Radien or the upper God. Among the upper celestial Gods *Radien atzhie* who was the Very highest and greatest God is counted first. He was denoted by a single cross standing above *Radien kiedde* (N° 2 on the drum diagram). NB: Here is meant the magic drum [*govadas*] that Jessen had drawn up, and engraved on sticks, about which drum the same author remarks that it had been given by Thomas von Vesten in Trondhjem; because all the specimens of magic drums given to the missions Collegium in Köpenhamn, and continued to their archive at Kongl. Waysenhuus, had perished in the Köpenhamn fire of 1728. The figure on this drum also appears in Leem, and seems to be taken from a copy belonging to the Lapps of Helgeland.

"*Radien atzhie* was believed to reign with absolute power over heaven and earth, over all other Gods, as well as over the Lapps themselves. Therefore, they had given him the name *Radien* which means power and domination, and besides they attached the word *Atzhie* which means: source and origin." Jessen, ibid.

---

[12] Lappmark is used for Swedish *Lappmark* and refers to individual Lapp areas such as Kemi, etc. rather than to the entire Lapp area.

§. 5.

In the idea of a supreme god ruling over everything there is nothing unreasonable. It occurs in all nations' mythologies, and is a necessary consequence of the evolution of human ideas. It shows that the actual thought appeals in the end to a supreme power which is the main source of everything.

But whether the name *Radien* is originally Lapp can no longer be determined with certainty. That it was taken from the Helgeland Lapps seems likely, because the shaman drum on which *Radien* is marked by a cross, is thought to be from the Helgeland Lapps.

Sidenius, v. Vesten, and the anonymous author in Leem all write *Radien*; they affirm that among the Gods who dwell highest up in the firmament, *Radien* is the most distinguished.

Except for Lindahl and Öhrling, none of the Swedish authors were familiar with *Radien*. Lindahl (*Lexicon Lapponium*) has cited the name *Radien*, and it is possible he heard it mentioned in Lycksele Lappmark. In Jockmock and Arjeplog I have not heard it mentioned, nor does the name appear in Högström.

§. 6.

Jessen thinks that *Radien* means "power and control," but that depends on how the Lapp informant pronounced the word. If that was so, as Jessen thinks, then the word could be derived from the verb *raddit*, which means prevail, possess, rule, but *raddit* is not originally Lapp, but borrowed from the Swedish word *råda*, in the same way as Finnish got its *raadi* from Swedish *råd* 'senate, magistrate,' and *raadia* from the same *råda*. According to this derivation, *Radien* would not be a real Lapp divinity, but a loan. Rather the word and the divinity should be Lapp, if one derived Radien from the Lapp word *radje*, or *raje*, which means border, *terminus*; then *Radien Attje* would mean: the border father. NB: According to Leem's orthography *Atzhie* is the same as *Attje* according to Lindahl and Öhrling, and means father.

§. 7.

Anonymous in Leem says that "some Lapps distinguished between *Radien* and *Zhioaarve Radien*, who is supposed to be subordinate to the former. This *Zhioaarve Radien's* task is to send the soul down at a person's conception into the womb, which soul the female *Madder Akko* receives from *Radien*, but delivers immediately to her daughter *Zarakka* who makes a body grow on the soul."

This distinction no other author knows. In Jessen the above mentioned act is ascribed to *Madder-Attje*, and it is possible that *Zhioaarve Radien* is the same entity. NB: *Zhioaarve*, according to Lindahl and Öhrling *tjårwe*, actually means antler, *cornu*, a metonym. Might, the most distinguished of its kind. Usually the richest Lapp in the parish is called: *Tjårwe*.

§. 8.
"*Radien kiedde*, indicated under N⁰ 2 on the drum diagram, was said to be a son of *Radien Attje*. One thought of him as a building whose two colonnades on each side were supposed to represent both of his hands with which he made, managed and controlled everything. *Radian attje* was so sacred among the Lapps that they didn't dare call him by any other name. Even his only son *Radien kiedde* had to respect and honor him like a temple. *Radien Attje* actually creates nothing himself; however, through his son he exerts so great a force that his son creates everything. These two control everything, all other gods, whether celestial, terrestrial or subterranean. It was even thought that *Radien Attje* controlled *Radien Kiedde*, and through him influenced everything. However, *Radien Kiedde* did not do anything by himself, but his power to effect depended on *Radien Attje*." Jessen, ibid. p. 11.

Nevertheless, one can call into question to what extent this idea is originally Lapp. I think that the story about *Radien Kiedde* betrays too much acquaintance with the first chapter of the gospel of John. *Radien Kiedde* is not mentioned by anyone else other than v. Vesten and Jessen. It is thus difficult to know from which district of Helgeland or the Trondhjem district the story emanated. '*Kiedde*' means a moor or a grass-grown open space where the Lapps usually put up their tents, and milk their reindeer. So much stranger then seems the sense Jessen gives *Radien Kiedde*. The fact that *Radien Kiedde* was depicted on the drum in the form of a building would seem to indicate that *Radien Kiedde* was regarded as a dwelling place for *Radien Attje*, which according to the Lapps' concept could not be put on a better spot than a grass-grown plain. But that this *Kiedde* afterwards was transformed into a son of *Radien Attje*, seems to originate from the narrator's familiarity with Christianity.

§. 9.
In Sidenius there are two other divinities with similar names, viz. *Radier* and *Rariet*, but these only seem to be either synonyms of *Radien*, or derived from different pronunciations, or a spelling error. "*Radier*, though highest up in the firmament is somewhat smaller than *Rariet*, which is supposed to send down the soul to the human fetus in the womb." Sidenius in Ganander. One sees that the same function is devoted to *Madder Attje, Tjårwe Radien* and *Radier*, from which one can conclude that they all indicate the same thing. When one finally unites all the information on *Radien, Radier, Rariet, Radien Attje* and *Radien Kiedde*, plus Tjårwe Radien, then one can draw the following conclusions: 1) All these names were taken from Lapps of Helgeland; 2) They represent originally one and the same thing; 3) They seem to be false, or not originally Lapp, as far as one can conclude from the names, which are derived from Swedish or Danish. Without the signs which are on the drum previously mentioned, it does not state that the Lapps imagined any of these divinities as idols or images. The aforementioned *Madder Attje* will appear later on.

Comment: *Radien Gudde* mentioned by v. Vesten in his letter is clearly a misprint, and should be read: *Radien Kiedde. Alskin* in v. Vesten's B. is also surely a misprint, and ought to be read with the preceding *Radien*. Probably it should be *Attje*, since *Alskin* is a name that doesn't appear at all with any of the other authors. *Veralden Olmai* in the same place should, according to v. Vesten, be a synonym of *Radien Kiedde*. *Veralden Olmai* means man of the world, and is proof that this name is from Helgeland, because *Verald* is from Swedish *Verld* [world], and does not appear in the Finnmark dialect.

§. 10.
"Next to *Radien* in rank" Anonymous says in Leem, "is *Ruonaneid*. She dwells highest up in the firmament not far down from *Radien*. *Ruonaneid* is the deity of the mountains which do not turn green until spring. She causes new grass to grow for the reindeer's nourishment, and that the first green may be good for the reindeer, the Lapps sacrifice in the spring to this god." Sidenius in Ganander has the very same description of this deity, but he writes *Rananeid*, which without a doubt is the correct spelling. Jessen also writes *Rananeid*, but he does not cite it as among the inhabitants of the firmament; though he mentions on p. 63 that *Rananeid* was the Lapps' *Flora* who brought forth grass and herbs to the earth. Neither v. Vesten nor the Swedish authors know anything about this deity.

That this *Rananeid* was a real Lapp deity is probably not to be doubted, but from where the Lapps got the word *Rana* is not so easy to fathom, since to my knowledge it has no meaning in the language. Lindahl and Öhrling have accepted *ranot* and *ranom* from a dialect of South Lapp, but these words clearly come from Swedish *råna* and *rån*. In Ganander's *Mythologia fennica* occur *Rauni* as *Ukko's* (*Thunder's*) wife and goddess of spring sowing; *Rauna* is also a fairly common woman's name in the northernmost Lappmarks, although it is considered to be a contraction of *Ragnhild*. In Scandinavian mythology, it is said that *Ran* was Ægir's wife and a goddess of the ocean. Since *Rana* has no meaning in Lapp, then it is likely that the word was borrowed either from Finnish *Rauni* or Geatish *Ran*; it is likely the latter alternative because *Rana neid* seems rather to belong to the Helgeland Lapps than those of Finnmark. *Neid* means maiden, and indicates that *Rananeid* was a female deity.

§. 11.
"To the second class of gods or the celestial ones belong *Beiwe* and *Ailekis olmak*. *Beiwe* – or the sun – is denoted by a rhombus, N° 4 on the drum diagram. From each angle of the indicated rhombus goes a separate path (line) which in Lapp is called *Beiwe labtje* (the sun's reins, i.e. rays). These reins were four in number, and indicate the sun's power to act in the four cardinal directions." Jessen, ibid.

"Those gods who have their refuge farther down in the air are: *Solen Peiwe*. To her one sacrificed white creatures so that she might shine well, and on Midsummer Eve one ate in her honor a porridge called sun porridge." Anonymous in Leem.

"The Lapps count the sun among their gods which are farther down in the air. They sacrificed to the sun white creatures so that she might shine well and promote the growth of grass, and also ate porridge on Midsummer Eve in honor of the Sun. They also sacrificed to the sun for various illnesses, curiously for lack of intelligence." Sidenius, ibid.

NB: due to a misunderstanding, Ganander has written "The sun shall foster white creatures." Sidenius' intention seems to be that one sacrifices the white creatures.

"Among the sacrifices delivered according to the drum's instructions, the sun should annually have a *Jubtse*, porridge (really, gruel), which both men and women ate in her honor on Midsummer Eve, when before the meal they always fell to their knees, and summoned the sun that she would spread a merciful light on their reindeer and other animals. In the same way, they summoned her after the meal with very deep reverence that the Sun not begrudge them a good summer of milk, and their reindeer serenity." Jessen, ibid. p. 18.

The same author also speaks of a *Sola Neid* (the Sun's daughter), who was also honored with sacrifices; she seems to have been added at a later time.

§. 12.
How things are bound up with the Sun's worship cannot now be decided with any certainty. All the Norwegian authors are in agreement that the Sun really was the object of the Lapps' worship. v. Vesten too affirms the same.

NB: *Pare* which is in his letter, is a misprint, and ought to read: *Peiwe*.

Schefferus too has reported that the Sun was one of the Lapps' deities, and Högström states it was probably not known in his time; yet the Lapps had told him it had been customary in earlier times.

This affirmation of Högström is according to my thinking decisive. Thus, one has to believe that the Lapps really worshiped the sun, though I have not discovered any kind of superstitious use that might relate to ancient worship of the sun. Yet, much consideration is still made as to what is or happens against the sun [counterclockwise, in Swedish *motsols*] and with the sun [clockwise, in Swedish *medsols*].

Since much more civilized nations have elevated the sun to a deity, one should not be surprised that the Lapps, who really need light and heat from this heavenly body, honored her with some form of worship.

§. 13.
"On three of the Sun's above-mentioned *Labtjeh* (reins or rays) stand the Lapps' *Ailekis Olmak*, i.e. holy day's men, or such deities who for their holiness were honored with a cross; namely, on the first *labtje* or rein (indicated by N° 43a on the drum diagram) stands *Burres* or *Sodna-peiwe-ailek*, i.e. the deity for Sunday, which day they consider the most powerful and most distinguished to hold *noaidi* services on." (NB: By *noaidi* services is meant casting spells, or the act itself consisting of

hammering on the drum with all the ancillary ceremonies which will be discussed later on.) "On the second *Peiwe labtje* or sun rein (indicated by N° 43b on the drum illustration) is seen *Lawa-Ailek*, or the deity for Saturday, which should be the most powerful next to the previous one. On the third *Peiwe labtje* (indicated by N° 43c on the drum diagram) is found *Frid-Ailek*, or the deity for Friday which was also held to be sacred as an excellent day for casting runes; but this day was thought to be less sacred than the two others." Jessen, ibid.

"On Friday and Saturday everything was forbidden: cutting wood for fuel, for it was alleged that *Ailekes olmak* became angered at this, and the first blow one gave to a tree on these days, blood came from the cut." Jessen, ibid. p. 80.

"In honor of the three *Ailekis olmas,* one celebrated Friday, Saturday and Sunday, though other Lapps say they held Friday sacred in honor of *Zarakka*, Saturday in honor of *Radien*, and Sunday in honor of the 3 *Ailekis olmak*; what is more, if a Lapp happened to provide himself with work on these three days, the offense ought to be made up with sacrifices to the three deities mentioned." Anonymous in Leem.

"*Aklikes olmai*, three Lapp deities lower down in the air, in whose honor Saturday and Sunday were sacred. Most Lapps have hallowed Friday for *Zarakka*, Saturday for *Rariet*, and Sunday for the three *Aklikes olmai*. Therefore, when the Lapps have arranged to work on Friday, Saturday and Sunday, they have made sacrifices in conciliation." Sidenius in Ganander.

NB: Due to mistake and unfamiliarity with the language, Ganander has written *Aklikes* instead of *Ailikes olmat*.

§. 14.
This entire story about the three *Ailekis olmak*, seems to have quite the flavor of the papacy. None of the Swedish authors knows anything about them. There are to be sure a few words in the language, *ailes*, *aileg* and *ailestattet* et al. that relate to something sacred, delimited for the gods that could not be broken or cut up, but which had to be complete and flawless (Lindahl and Öhrling *Lexicon* under *Ailes*). *Aileg* also means in the middle Lapplandic dialect a holy day, holiday or Sunday; but otherwise there are no examples in ancient times of Lapps celebrating any holy day at a particular time, if one excludes certain sacrificial holidays, and the days that were consecrated for engaging in casting runes and drumming. They do not even have a special word in their language for month, week. (*Manno* and *Vakko* are clearly loanwords). Only two weekdays have Lapp names: *Kaskavakko*, mid-week, i.e. Wednesday, and *Perjetag*, Friday. Whether these day names must have been borrowed from Finnish (*Keskiviiko* and *Perjantai*) or the reverse, I cannot decide, since not once did Gottlund himself embark on an investigation into *Perje*, which cannot readily be derived from Frey.

Arka, workday (I wonder whether this word doesn't come from *örk* 'workday'? – consider *yrka* 'profession') is probably the opposite of *Passe*; but with *Passe peiwe* the ancient Lapps probably meant the day on which one sacrificed to *Passe*, a deity about whom more later on. But such a *Passe-Peiwe* couldn't take place so often as every Sunday for us. So much less believable is it that the Lapps should hold an entire three days in the week as holy.

But the idea of the three *Ailekis olmak* is presumably taken from Catholicism, the adoration of the saints, All Saints' Day, etc. The three *Ailekis olmak* are consequently, according to my simple way of thinking, an obscure representation of some Catholic Saints' images, confused with an equally obscure representation of the trinity. One can see from the entire Norwegian-Lapp mythology that the Lapps in that area absorbed much of Catholicism, which could not be avoided in Helgeland and close to Trondhjem.

§. 15.
The deities, which we so far have described, according to the Norwegian missionaries' information, could be considered as less legitimate, or not originally Lapp. Jessen too is of the opinion that many of these deities were borrowed from Christianity, like *Radien Attje* and *Radien pardne,* and some had *Jubmel Attje* (God the father), *Jubmel pardne* (God's son) and *Jubmel ailes vuoigenis* (God the holy spirit) on their drums, but these were not held in as great reverence as their ancient idols. Jessen, ibid. p. 17. We come now to a class of gods that have a more Lapp character.

§. 16.
"To the third class of gods belong those lower in the sky who stay in the air, of which *Madder Attje* is the highest beneath the heaven, or right under the Sun. Others stay in the middlemost air section such as *Madder-Akka* and *Hora Galles*. Others resided farthest down in the air, or closest to the earth. These include the many *Akkerna* such as *Zar-akka Uks-akka* and *Juks-akka*." Jessen ibid.

"The sign on the drum for *Madder-Attje* is denoted sometimes by a little circle, sometimes by a triangle, now and then by a hexagon. On this specimen (of which the figure in Leem is cited several times) *Madder-Attje* is denoted by a man lying flat on his face. Sometimes he is found by *Radien Kiedde*, aslant of the sun, so that from *Madder Attje's* opening a path goes to the Sun's uppermost *Labtje* (rein). Others place him, as here, always by the Sun's rein. This *Madder-Attje* according to the Lapp *noaidi's* thinking contributes to the union of the sun with all kinds of creatures' lives, whose power is sent to him by *Radien-Kiedde*." Jessen, ibid.

§. 17.
No one but Jessen mentions *Madder-Attje*, from which we can conclude that he had more manuscripts available than those we now have in print. Anonymous in Leem, as mentioned above, ascribes the same function to *Tjärwe-Radien* as Jessen does to *Madder-Attje*. This is probably due to the mythological objects having different names in particular districts. *Madder-Attje* means a progenitor, and the idea seems

quite natural. Of course, one has to imagine a progenitor of the human race, whom one cannot put on any lower place than it occupies here. And since one has imagined a progenitor, then it would also be quite in order to imagine a first ancestress, *Madder-Akka*, who as a woman would have to occupy a lower place in the heavens, since the woman was (among the Lapps) by far subordinate to the man. Curiously, this *Madder-Akka* did not have any sons but only three daughters, namely: *Zarakka*, *Uksakka* and *Juksakka*. Since the functions of these four individuals hang together very closely, one cannot separate their personages into specific §§, but their story has to be presented as a whole.

§. 18.
"From the Sun's fourth and lowest rein (see drum diagram) goes a horizontal line to *Madder-Akka*, *Madder-Attje's* consort. This *Madder-Akka* has her dwelling in the middle of the air. *Madder-Attje's* ability to give life to all creatures under the Sun, took place in this way. *Radien-Kiedde* got the power from *Radien-Attje* to create souls and spirits. As soon as this *Radien-Kiedde* brought forth a soul, he sent it to *Madder-Attje* who on *Radien-Kiedde's* order brought it to his consort *Madder-Akka*, which happened thus: *Madder-Attje* opened his stomach, then took the soul with him, and then traveled around the Sun by way of its *labtjeh* (reins), continued his journey thereafter from the lowest *labtje* by way of a horizontal line, (on the drum diagram) to his *Madder-akka*, who received the soul and created a body around it."

"If this body was to become a male, *Madder-Akka* sent it further to *Uks* or *Juks Akka* (N° 24 on the drum diagram) who is also called *Stauk-Edne* or *Stilko-Edne*, i.e. a mother (housewife?). However, if it was to become a female, then *Madder-Akka* gave the child to *Zarakka* (N° 23 on the drum diagram) that she might endow it with a female nature. But whether the child came to *Juksakka* or *Zarakka*, the one to whom it was first sent took it, the child (the spirit) into its body and brought it then to the woman who was going to give birth to the fetus into the world. This matter was so well performed that the evil gods, *Fudno*, *Rutu*, *Paha Engel* or *Mubben Olmai*, were not able to put obstacles in the way." Jessen, ibid. pp. 14-15.

§. 19.
One has to admit it was a very intricate process that preceded a human being's birth into the world. Yet the idea seems to be well carried out, provided it arches around the circumstance that evil forces were pursuing the human's life, even before it was ready to be born into the world. The *noaidis* seem to have imagined that the evil gods had a keen scent, since the newly created soul had to take so many roundabout ways, and pass through so many creatures' lives before it came to the human mother. The *noaidis* presumably were thinking about the many roundabout ways the Lapps had to take to mislead their enemies, *Pädnak-Njunne* (man with dog-like face), *Tjuder* (Chudes) and *Kareler* (Karelians), from the track. That is the way I

roughly visualize how the idea of the strange soul wandering came about. The idea is quite peculiar, yet one cannot assume it to be other than genuine, since with other closely bordering nations to my knowledge no such theory of human beings' origin has occurred. Jessen is on this point, as also in much else, the most complete, and therefore we have cited his words first. For better comparison, the other authors' attestations follow, about the so-called *Akkerna* and their functions.

§. 20.
"Other *noaidis* said that *Radien Attje* and *Radien kiedde* were one and the same, namely Jubmel; but *Radien Attje* had a spouse by the name of *Sergve-Edne* (more correctly *Sierg-Edne*), and *Radien* had given her the power to create souls, which she thereupon conveyed to *Madder-Akka*; she was supposed to create bodies around the soul. Besides, they ascribed conception of all animals to *Maddar-Zar-Uks-* and *Juks akka*." Jessen, ibid. p. 15.

One gathers from these remarks that the *noaidis* were not in complete agreement in their views about the functions of the divine figures. This *Sergve-* or *Sierg-Edne* is not met with in anyone but Jessen, and I think it superfluous to enter into an investigation of this name's mythological meaning. *Sierg*, *Siedga* or *Sädga* actually means *Vide* (Salix – willow). *Edne* 'mother'.

§. 21.
"Among the gods who reside on the earth belong also *Madder-Akka*, who with her three daughters is help for women. She receives sacrifices so that she might let her daughters be of help to women. Some claim that she gives a hand in the matter."

"*Madder-Akka's* first daughter *Zarakka* gives a body to the child in the womb, when *Radien* has provided a soul, and this *Zarakka* will suffer pain herself together with the mother who gives birth to the child. As a result of this (says the author [Anonymous in Leem]) some Lapps during his time ate and drank this *Zarakka's* body and blood together with the holy sacrament. Women, especially those who were pregnant, worshiped this *Zarakka* diligently. For good childbirth one ate a porridge in her honor."

"*Madder-Akka's* second daughter was named *Juks-Akka* who changed daughter to son in the womb. To her was sacrificed a lot, because the Lapps seemed better served with a boy than a girl; for the latter could neither hunt nor shoot."

"*Madder-Akka's* third daughter was named *Uks-Akka*; she was seen as an old woman of the earth who receives the child at its birth, and protects it from an instance of misfortune. She also helps the women maintain their monthly purification; therefore, one sacrifices to her too." Anonymous in Leem.

§. 22.
In this report, the idea about the *Akkers'* function is somewhat different than in Jessen, from which one can conclude that the information is from another source.

Sidenius' report on *Madder- Zar- Juks- and Uks-akka* is very much in agreement with Anonymous in Leem, with the sole difference that *Juks-Akka's* function is appropriated by *Uks-Akka*. This mix-up probably arose through a misprint, or else Ganander has not taken a close look at the manuscript. He says namely: "That Uksakka Madder-Akka's second daughter was worshiped by the Lapps; that she was supposed to change a daughter to a son in the womb; that the Lapps sacrificed to her, since they thought they were better served with boys than girls who weren't good at shooting." Etc.

In case Sidenius is someone other than Anonymous in Leem, then I must observe that I consider Anonymous' information to be the correct reading, because the name *Juks-* itself or perhaps more correctly *Juoks-Akka* just implies that she was concerned with bows and hunting equipment. It was presumably this goddess of the hunt who "changed a daughter to a son in the womb."

§. 23.

Uks-Akka means: door wife, door woman, in the Västerbotten dialect: *Döråkäringa*, a sort of female Janus who was thought to reside in the doorway. The peasantry in Norrland still say: "*Döråkäringen* is blowing out the candle." As the women's place in the Lapp's hut [turf hut] is by the door, where they even have to give birth to their children, then it was natural that *Uks-Akka* had to act as midwife. Strange that Jessen regards *Uks-* and *Juks-Akka* as one and the same person. He says namely ibid. p. 21 that "*Uks-* or *Juks-Akka* got its name from the bows (*Juks*) that were placed by the door.[13] This deity guarded the exit and entrance. Therefore, a little food and drink was sacrificed to her at every meal, without hallowed feast sacrifices especially for her.

It looks like Jessen had not taken advantage of Anonymous' manuscript, or also he was led astray by the conflicting information in the missionaries' reports to mix up *Uks-* and *Juks-Akka*. In my view, they were separate entities.

§. 24.

On *Juks-Akka,* Lindahl and Öhrling have the following: "*Juks-Akka,* one of the daughters of the deity *Madder-Akka,* who the Lapps believe cares for children [*Juks akka,* una ex filiabus Deæ *Madder-akka,* cui curæ esse infantes, prisei Lappones sibi persvaserant]." It almost looks as if Lindahl has had one of the Norwegian authors before himself, when he wrote this, without further reflection on the origin of the name. If the Norwegian authors got this explanation from the Lapps themselves, that the name is derived from their bows, then it should not be written: '*Juks*' but

---

[13] This information does not seem to be in agreement with the correct state of things. The bows, just as shotguns, were sacred objects, which were not to be touched by women. Placing them by the profane door through which the women necessarily had to pass, doesn't seem to be in agreement with the Lapps' views. Even today belief in their places is prevalent, that a shotgun is spoiled if a woman chances to step over it.

'*Juoks*,' the latter which according to Lindahl's own orthography means bow. '*Juks*' on the contrary means the thongs whereby the Lapps strap their skis onto their feet. If that is so, that the goddess got her name from '*Juks*' which also belonged to hunting, then the name should be written *Juks-akka*, but if the name comes from bow, as Jessen thinks, then it should be written '*Juoks akka*.'

§. 25.

Where *Sarakka* got her name is not so easy to explain. Some write this name with S, others with Z. v. Vesten writes *Sader-Akka*, but his orthography isn't much to be guided by, because the publisher of his letters butchered the Lapp names. Lindahl and Öhrling say that '*Saret*' means create, and Högström observes on p. 179 that in some Lappmarks the word *Saragads* was used as an appellative noun for Creator. In view of this, one should be able to conclude that *Sarakka* got her name from *Saret*; according to which *Sarakka* should mean 'the creating woman, or the [female] creator.' This explanation gains even more credibility when Lindahl and Öhrling cite the following example under the word *Saret*: *Naute le mo Sarakka Sarem. Ita me formavit Sarakka,* [This is how *Sarakka* created me.] from which it is likely that *Sarakka* was seen as the actual creator, or that it was she who created the body on the previously provided soul (which Anonymous and Sidenius state), although Jessen ascribes this act to *Madder-Akka*. Lindahl and Öhrling also state: "*Sarakka: Dea partus, olim a Lapponibus culta, cui adscribebant partus formositatem et felicitatem parturæ; hodie de partu felici et facili dicitur:* "*Sarakkan edne nuolei*," i.e. *Mater Sarakkæ ligamina solvit* etc. [Sarakka: goddess of birth whom the Lapps worshiped and from whom they hoped for a happy and beautiful birth. Even today a happy and beautiful birth is called: "*Sarakkan edne nuolei*," i.e. *Mater Sarakkæ ligamina solvit etc.* or Mother Sarakka delivers from shrouds etc.][14] With this translation it should be noted that the word *nuolei* likely does not mean: *ligamina solvit*, but rather: *lingebat*, et metaph. *Adoptavit* 'licked' and metaphorically *adoptavit* 'take into one's care.' '*Nuolei*' is actually an imperfect of the obsolete Finnish *nuolis* or the same as *njållot* in Lapp.

§. 26.

About *Madder-Akka* Lindahl and Öhrling say *Mudder-Akka olim Dea gravidis inserviens*, etc. [*Mudder-akka* long serving goddess of pregnant women], etc. In all of three places they have written *Mudder-Akka*, so it cannot be a misprint; but *Mudder-Akka* can never be the correct spelling, for *Mudder* sounds more German than Lapp. Lindahl has either heard badly or too, read wrong, when he wrote *Mudder-Akka*.

If we should presume that the Lapps borrowed their *Madder-* (more correctly written *Maadder*, v. Vesten writes *Mader*) *akka* from some other Finnish tribe, then Tacitus' remark about the Estonians, *matrem deum venerantur* [they venerate the

---

[14] To be sure, there is also a verb *nuollet* or *njuollat* 'release;' but I have never heard this word used in the sense that Lindahl mentions.

mother god] could lend itself to the often mentioned *Madder akka*, who without a doubt is a very old deity among the Lapps. This is of course a guess; for since I am not familiar with the Estonians' mythology, I cannot adduce other than a guess in this case.

§. 27.
Högström only mentions *Sarakka* in passing and cites thereby v. Vesten. However, he speaks about *Viros-Akka*, which Torneus calls *Viran akka*, which is supposed to mean 'de Lifflanders kärring' (the Livonians' old woman). Certainly, *virolainen* in Finnish means Livonian, but what reason the Lapps may have had to deify an old woman from Livonia, I am unable to find out. Ganander knows nothing about *Viran akka*. He mentions very briefly *Viran-kannos* who fostered the growth of oats.

Torneus says about *Viran akka* that "a renowned *Seita* [ritual site] has in days of old stood in the middle of Torneå Lappmark; it is called *Viran-akka*, i.e. the Livonians' old woman. All surrounding Lapps have sacrificed to her. Birkarls[15] threw her once far away from her place, since she was nothing other than a tree stump; nevertheless, she got back to her place again. But now she has rotted away." Torneus, p. 16.

This *Viran-Akka* I have placed here among the other *Akker*, since it is likely that in the eastern Lappmarks that border on Finland she was worshiped instead of, or along with the others. What this *Viran-Akka's* function was Torneus has not informed us about.

§. 28.
It is not for want of a reason that these *Akker* still live in the Lapps' memory. *Sarakka* is a very familiar name among them. In Kautokeino there is still a Lapp family with the surname *Sarak*, Otherwise, one calls a younger reindeer bull, who has been driven away from the reindeer herd by the strongest bull, *Sarak*. I've heard a very vague tale in southern Lappmark about a rock on which a sort of runic inscription is supposed to have been carved, which according to an old Lapp's explanation is supposed to have contained the following verse: *Sarakkam. Sarakkam mijab vaivaisit teki powti kålmå tjuote japeh mangel tulwe*, i.e. My *Sarakka*, my *Sarakka* has made us wretched here three hundred years after the flood. I heard this story from my father who got it from his ancestors who for a long time were pastors in Piteå Lappmark. Whether this story emanated from the Lapps seems uncertain. It only merits mention as proof that *Sarakka* was known among the Lapps.

§. 29.
Since the *Akkers* played such an important role in Lapp mythology, then one probably ought to offer some proof of the sacrifices that were dedicated to them.

---

[15] The *birkarls* were merchants who traded with the Sámi in Northern Sweden from the 13th to 17th centuries.

"While eating, the *Akkers* were honored with water and brandy, but especially with a sort of porridge. Among these *Akkers* though *Sarakka* was foremost." Jessen, ibid. p. 16.

"*Sarakka*, who was also called *Sarag-Akka*, had her place by the hearth. As sacrifices she was offered drinks. They invoked her often in all their activities. They sacrificed to her without consulting the drum. She had a temple too that is represented under N° 28 on the drum diagram." Jessen, ibid. p. 21.

NB: The author did not state whether these temples were found in nature or only on the drum. I find it most likely that the idea of temples was borrowed from the Christians, and that those temples mentioned here consisted either of a pile of antlers, or some other enclosure of wood with a tree stump or rock in the middle. The Norwegian authors seldom mention whether the enumerated deities were represented with images.

§. 30.
"Women giving birth drank *Sarakka's* wine before delivery, and also, with other women present, ate porridge after they had given birth. Some prepared a feast in *Sarakka's* honor."

"In the porridge mentioned they put two sticks, the one split, on which were hanging three rings; the other stick was black, and the third white. These sticks were put under the bow for two or three days; if one then found that the black stick was missing, then it meant that either the mother or the child would die. If on the other hand the white stick was invisible, both would live. The porridge was not eaten then until the drum gave a response."

"Roosters, hens, reindeer calves and bitches *were* sacrificed to *Sarakka*, but of the latter offering only women got to eat."

"To *Madder-Attje* and *Madder-Akka* one made sacrifices according to the magic drum's directions. *Madder-Akka* as the protector of womankind, was held in greater esteem than *Madder-Attje*. The latter was honored with a temple too." Jessen, ibid. p. 16.

§. 31.
"Except for roosters no male animal could be sacrificed to *Sarakka*." Jessen, p. 48.
"What was sacrificed to *Sarakka* was only eaten by women." Jessen, p. 49.
"They believed that *Sarakka* would strengthen their wives and children." Jessen, p. 68.
"Pregnant women drank to *Sarakka's* health, and ate her porridge." Jessen, p. 44.
"Children were baptized anew in *Sarakka's* name; the Lapps ate *Sarakka's* body and blood." Jessen.
"They begged forgiveness at the same moment, for having to go to *Jubmel kare* 'God's table' [take communion]." v. Vesten, ibid.

NB: the idea of baptism, and the eating of *Sarakka's* body and blood are without a doubt borrowed concepts.

§. 32.
"When one sacrificed to Sarakka and other deities, a tree stump was erected, which was called *värro-muor* 'the offer tree'. This stump was placed so the root, which was supposed to represent the head, was at the top, but the trunk, which was supposed to represent the body, was at the bottom." Jessen, ibid.

If things were as Jessen seemed to have thought, that such a tree stump was also set up for other deities on the actual sacrificial occasion, then it should follow that the Lapps did not attribute to these tree stumps any divine power, but to the extent it was granted by the presumed deity, to whom one on the occasion sacrificed. This is an important explanation in the Lapp doctrine of the gods; for there is a great difference in worshiping a tree stump, and under the image of a tree stump worshiping a supposed spiritual being, which the imagination has called forth and superstition ascribed divine or supernatural capacity. In the former case, it is the tree stump, whereas in the latter case it is a spiritual being visualized beneath a tree stump that is worshiped.

We probably cannot support Jessen's view in the case where the tree stump is made for each particular sacrificial case; for from Swedish authors it is a well-known fact that the tree stump once fabricated, represented the supposed deity as long as it could resist decay; yet the image was renewed often enough when it took on visible damage, also as it often had to be smeared with blood or fat, and in other ways cleaned and groomed with a lower bed of birch or spruce twigs, etc. What is stated about the offering etc. really belongs to the doctrine of sacrifice, about which more later on.

§. 33.
"One of the Lapps' oldest and most honored gods was *Horagalles*, who on the drum (drum diagram N° 9) is represented by a double hammer. He was also called *Horan-galles*, *Horan-orias*, *Hores gudsk* and *Attje-gadze*, which names mean simply a servant of the father of might. He actually corresponded to *Thor*, which is why some Lapps called him *Turaturos-podnje*. This powerful man lived, as did *Madder-Akka*, in the middlemost air. When some animal was bewitched, one was supposed to persuade him [*Horagalles*] through *Juoigning* (as Lapp song is called) and hammering on the drum, as well as through sacrifice, to free the misfortunate one. He could also harm other humans at the request of the *noaidis*, plus avenge wrongs they suffered; but if he didn't run across the person intended, or if he in some manner was prophesied against, then he turned his ruinous force against the *noaidi* himself, who thereby had to make many sacrifices to him, whereby many became impoverished, and were reduced to begging. *Horagalles* could also foster the growth of grass, and

the reindeer's subsistence. He is visualized as being bound, and has to be freed to be able to effect anything." Jessen, ibid. pp. 19-20.

§. 34.
That so majestic a phenomenon as thunder should become an object of the simple multitude's reverence and admiration was not surprising at all. Most pagan nations have had thunder among their most powerful deities. Thunder has left many traces in the Lappmarks too. No wonder then that the Lapps considered it as a large and powerful divine force.

Jessen's explanation of the meaning of the names cited seems to be a decent free translation when he says they should mean "a servant of the father of might."

Galles, which more correctly is written *Kaalles* (Lindahl and Öhrling write *Kalles*) means a hero, a very strong and venerable man. *Hora* seems to be onomatopoetic or an imitation of the sound of thunder; similarly, *Hurri* (*Tetrao bonasias*) [hazel hen] for its noisy flight. In Finnish there is a verb *huran*, [Lat. *murmuro* 'rumble, ripple']; a Lapp family in Karesuando is named *Hurri*, and a man in Jukkasjärvi who is very loud-voiced and noisy in his speech is called *Huru* Jussa.

Horagalles thus means the noisy hero, or as one says in Swedish a *dunderkuse* 'noisy kid' or *bullerbas* 'ill-behaved young man'. *Horan* is genitive of *hora*; *orias* is not so easy to derive, since there are so many similar sounding words both in Lapp and Finnish; but whether, as is likely, *o* in this place ought to be pronounced as Greek *w*, or Finnish *u*, then *orias* has its nearest root in Finnish *uros* which also means a venerable man, a hero (cf. Renvalls *Lexicon*[16]), whereby even the Lapp word *ores* 'male' et al. is most closely related.

Gudsk, more correctly written *kutsch*, is a kind of adjective ending, which added to a noun gives the meaning of something old – before this, which has been; for example, *kaalleskutsch*, formerly, the hero, but for the present either weakened by age, or deceased; *jamikutsch*, the deceased. *Horekutsch* thus denotes formerly *dunderkusen* considering the thunder god's supposed age, the long intervals when he doesn't let himself be heard, etc. The explanation of the name *Attje Gadse* we will save until further on, where *Gadse* often occurs.

Toratoros- or *Turaturos-podnje*, is likewise onomatopoetic, or mimicking the sound of thunder. The word seems to be a compound of *Turat*, (NB: *u*, should be read as Greek *w*) presumably borrowed from Swedish *Thor*; *Uros* [Finnish for male], hero; *Podnje*, old man. *Turat-uros-podnje* thus becomes *Thordöns Gubben* 'old man thunder' which was probably one of his honorifics.

§. 35.
Sidenius in Ganander calls the god of thunder *Torden*, which is roughly the same as Swedish *Thordön*. He says that "the Lapps feared it as a god who often becomes angry, and knocks off large chunks of the mountains, topples trees, kills cattle and hu-

---
[16] Gustavo Renvall: *Lexicon Linguæ Finnicæ*, 1826.

mans. For the thunder often rumbles in the Lappmarks because of the high mountains. When in her wrath she lets herself be heard in the air, they have promised her sacrifices which they also kept." Sidenius in Ganander.

Anonymous in Leem mentions "*Horan Galles* who often gets angry, who not only knocks chunks of the mountains loose and fells trees, but also kills people and animals, which is why the Lapps appease *Horan Galles* when he lets himself be heard in the clouds, and bring him sacrifices."

Another name of the god of thunder is *Tiermes* which occurs in Schefferus and Sidenius. The latter adds that "*Tiermes* was a Lapp high god who ruled over thunder, *Thordön*, rainbow, as well as humans' health and lives; then over weather and wind, over the sea and the water, has received sacrifices that he might shut down the storm at sea." Sidenius in Ganander.

That *Torden* is borrowed from Swedish, and taken from Helgeland's Lapps or the district of Trondhjem cannot be doubted, but where *Tiermes* came from is more difficult to explain. Presumably, Schefferus has picked up *Tiermes* from southern Lapland or Jämtland. That, like Ganander, going all the way back to Hermes, I suppose, is the last resort that can be taken in etymology. One can sooner derive the word from *terme*, or *tierme*, Finnish *Törmä* 'riverbank' *ripa altior prærupta* [rugged edge higher]; from thunder's characteristic of striking down on hills, the Lapps could have come to this idea of calling the thunder god *Tiermes*, i.e. the backer [from *backe* 'to give a proper slope to'] or the hill digger.

§. 36.
The most common name for *Tordöns Guden* [the thunder god] in Central Lapland is *Aija*, 'grandfather' [father's father]; *Aijek* 'little grandfather;' *Atjekatsch* 'little father.' These names occur mostly in the Swedish Lappmarks, and show the reverence one holds for *Thordön* 'thunder.' *Attje* and *Aija* are the greatest honorary titles Lapps can bestow on a very venerable person. Out of reverence for the bear, they have given him the name *Puold-Aija* 'backfarfar' [hill grandfather]. The pastor is usually called *Attje* 'father.' *Attje* and *Aija* are thus such names one dedicates to *Thordöns Guden* out of the importance of respect.

In Torneå Lappmark thunder is called *Pajan*, i.e. the smith, from Finnish *Paja* 'smith.' Maybe in these Lappmarks one has called thunder *Pajan* in reference to *Ilmarinen* who also was a smith, and is not so very unknown in the Lappmarks bordering on Finland. The name *Ilmaris* even occurs in Leem, but it is no doubt an adopted name.

§. 37.
On the above mentioned *Aija, Aijek* or *Atjekatsch* Högström has the following curious story: "With my Lapps I have noticed that they hold it (thunder) as a separate being from God, and likewise one that is both good and evil, because this nature,

according to their story, was created by *Perkel* [devil] 'the stealer' inside a rock cliff without *Jubmel* being able to find out about it. But then *Jubmel* or God found out about this and fetched him out and fed him. And because this *Thor Gubbe* is consequently the child of the devil, but God's foster child (according to their own literal way), then he is both good and evil; his most distinguished and real work being killing and destroying all trolls and ghosts, as well as their *Säite* 'ritual sites' – to be discussed later on – are more often affected by thunder, which he in their opinion does with his bow, which they call *Ajan joksa* 'the rainbow' or the *Storfadrens* [big father's or grandfather's] bow. And while he thusly does good for the people, in that he roots out these forms of witchcraft, which fact they find themselves obliged to recognize, especially since he can do them harm in other ways, particularly when he touches their sanctuaries, he ought likewise to be counted among their ancient idols." Högström pp. 177-78.[17]

§. 38.
This report about the origin of the god Thor is certainly interesting, but does not seem to be so old, nor as genuinely Lapp as one might guess from the nature of the matter. *Perkel* is namely a being that does not appear in the Lapps' oldest legends. The god Thor's persecution of trolls and such rather belongs to Scandinavian folklore. The Lapps' trolls were moreover such creatures that neither they nor their *Aijek* had any reason to persecute, and therefore it seems probable, or more than likely that this story was borrowed from Norway.

§. 39.
Högström relates further: "But otherwise I have once again learned about the following incident from other Lapps that when a girl had sat down by a tree in the forest, the evil one came and asked her to put dry, tarry wood in her reindeer fur coat, which she was wearing. But when she set fire to this wood, and she noticed that the man had horns, she became frightened, and wanted to flee, but she didn't escape his violence, from which she became pregnant and gave birth to a son who cried non-stop and became fidgety. God came and took the child with him up into the sky, and asked which one he wanted to be of help to, either his father or mother. The child answered that he wanted to help his mother, and pursue his father and all his kin, which he now does, dashes through the air and cleaves mountains, and sets fire to trees when they (the trolls) hide under them." Högström, p. 178.

This tale does not seem to be Lapp originally. It has too much the taste of the papacy and the many stories about the devil which since that time have been circulating among the Swedish and Norwegian country folk. An evil spirit with horns I hardly think the Lapps would have been able to imagine. However, in and through the papacy the evil one has acquired both horns and claws.

---

[17] Page numbers provided in *Fragments of Lappish Mythology*, 1997.

§. 40.
One can also add the following to the renown of the rumbling god: "To *Horagalles* no female nor castrated reindeer could be sacrificed. Of the sacrifice offered to him no woman could eat." Jessen, ibid. p. 48.

Linnæus cites the following anecdote, which could belong to this topic. "When thunder rumbles, our timid Lapp usually takes refuge under a birch tree, as did emperor Tiberius under the crown of the laurel as if this might protect him from the wrath of the rumbling Jupiter. I have attempted to find an explanation as to why he does this, but have not found one."

The reason why the Lapps usually get under a birch tree when thunder rumbles loud is presumably that one has found it strikes more often in pine and spruce trees than in birches, which can have its natural cause.

Whether any Lapp today considers thunder to be a special being cannot be ascertained so precisely. Certainly, some have great respect for thunder. In Luleå Lappmark one dedicates a thunderbolt to thunder, which is called *tjuolonis*; with this thunderbolt she is believed to split trees and other objects.

§. 41.
Since *jubma* in Lapp means 'roar, rumble,' and it is used in particular for the roar of thunder, *Atjekatsch jubma*, i.e. the thunder roars, then one inevitably is led to the thought that *Jubmel* (God) is derived from this *jubma* just as *Jumala* in Finnish can most naturally be derived from *jumisen* '*susurrans tono*' [whisper tone] (Renvall's *Lexicon*, p. 131).

I think, that since nothing in nature has more power than thunder to awaken a reverent perception of a mighty, supernatural being, then this majestic natural phenomenon must also have given most nations reason to imagine a deity that so powerfully and majestically reveals itself in that very phenomenon.

This thought is so much more insistent, as if the cause of the phenomenon were entirely incomprehensible, both for learned and unlettered, right down to more recent times. Therefore, I think it is absolutely unnecessary to trace its derivations back to Hebrew, Greek, et al. as long as one can find the stem closer to hand, even still alive in the language.

§. 42.
What is more natural than for example *Jubma lä almen* (the rumble is in the sky) being transformed through a more rapid pronunciation, and through the second vowel's contraction to *Jubma l'almen*. This is not just a guess, but something that may even be said today. *Jubmal' almen*: the rumble is the sky. But this *Jubma*, could it possibly be something other than a large, powerful supernatural creature that lets itself be heard up there, and that sometimes in a moment shattered mountains and split the strongest trees into splinters? And must not this force according to the

thought process that takes place in an uneducated mind quickly flow together to a unit in the consciousness with the rumble itself, so that the cause of the rumble gets the same name as the rumble, thus: *Jubmal almen* 'God is in the sky.'

§. 43.

We must above all not forget our own childish ideas with this and similar words' derivations. A child who hears thunder for the first time involuntarily must connect it to the idea of a large glorious, supernatural and powerful being who causes such a rumble. I have seen the same thing happen to many an adult human among the country folk. Thus, *Thor*, who is nothing other than an imitation (onomatopoeia) of the sound of thunder, must be a great and powerful being, namely, the strong Ása Thor who struck with his hammer. One still says in many places in Västerbotten: *Thorn* (i.e. the thunder) *går, höres, dånar,* etc. [walks, is heard, rumbles], i.e. *Thorn* who is supposed to denote the cause of the rumble, has here come to denote the rumble itself, and so too it has gone with *Jubma* in Lapp. What originally denoted the rumble finally came to denote the cause of the rumble; but the cause of that which produced the rumble could be nothing other than God himself.

§. 44.

That *Jubma* provided the Lapps with the first occasion for the idea of a powerful supernatural being seems to be in accord with the development of human ideas; for involuntarily, the raw, uneducated human must visualize a real living being as a reason for the urgent rumble of reverence, from which it also follows that *Jubmel* can most naturally be derived from the same *Jubma*; That *Jubmel* was the first deity the Lapps could imagine seems more than likely. Its intellectual fellowship with the Finns' *Jumala* seems to affirm this; for that *Ibmel, Immel, Jubmel, Jummel* and *Jumala* originally represent one and the same object can I suppose hardly be doubted. Now if one accepts that Lapps and Finns were originally one and the same people, then *Jubmel* or *Jumala* must have arisen at a time where there was an insignificant difference between these two peoples. If on the other hand one assumes that Lapps and Finns do not belong to one and the same human race, then one must either have borrowed *Jubmel* or *Jumala* from the other. In whichever case *Jubmel* must be very old, since he is one among few deities these nations have in common.

§. 45.

It follows from the nature of the matter that *Jubmel* originally signified a single entity, whose name thus had to be a proper noun; but logically it is clear that a proper noun can become a common noun as soon as the idea of a single object can be adapted to several, i.e. the idea then becomes a concept, and that word which designates the concept also becomes a common noun. This is not just supposition but a theorem which can be proved. For that reason, it follows that *Jubmel* which originally designated a single object, e.g. the Thunder God, over time came to be a common noun, as soon as one together with the original Thunder God embraced other gods, to whose representation and name *Jubmel* could be adapted. The word which first designated a single object, ultimately designated a concept, and thus became a common noun.

§. 46.

In this way, *Jumala* could also become a common noun; for though *Isä Jumala*, *Poika Jumala*, etc. are, as Gottlund correctly observes, unFinnish, all the same, *Isä on Jumala*, *Poika on Jumala* (the Father is God, the Son is God), etc. can be said. In these sentences the predicate *Jumala* is already a common noun, as it can refer to several subjects like a predicate. The proper nouns *Jubmel* and *Jumala* have thus become common nouns, in the same way as the word Caesar, from being a proper noun, over time became a common noun. That this word now designates a concept is a clear logical truth.

But as soon as *Jumala* and *Jubmel* became common nouns, then likewise the original Thunder God had to get a specific name, for *Jubmel* which came to designate several objects, could not since that time designate a single object, just as Caesar, who after the era of Julius, came to mean emperor, could no longer designate a particular person. In the same way, the word *Jumala* can again become a proper noun, when after the advent of the Christian religion it designates a single object. Subsequently, it also seems the Lapps' story about a single supreme god has this in view, about which Högström states "that the Lapps in his time recognized a single supreme master over everything, whom they call *Jubmel,* and this *Jubmel* they considered as the head of the good natural forces." Ibid. Ch. 11, §§3. 4.

§. 47.

If it is the case that some of Schefferus' informants got the story about *Jumi* or *Jumo* from the Lapps, then this story also has reference to the original Thunder God; for whether one reads *Jumi* or *Jumo*, then the word must still be most closely related to *Jubma*, or Finnish *Juminä*, *Jumiä*, et al., all of which mean a roar, thunder, rumbling; also, why too the insect larva, which in Swedish is called "wall smith" (Callidium violaceum), is called in Finnish *jumi* for its clicking sound in the wall.

Thus we do not need to derive *Jumo* from the fabulous *Yme*, nor do we need to bolt off all the way to Greek for the derivation of *Jubmel*, when, as said, the stem word for these names still exists in the language. In short, on etymological grounds *Jubmel* is an original Lapp deity, and on logical grounds he must have been their oldest god. For the idea of an object whose name several objects have, must be older than the idea of the objects denoted with an already given name belonging to the first named object. So the idea of the object *Jubmel* must be older than the objects that bear *Jubmel's* name, just as the idea of the individual Caesar has to be older than the individuals who have gotten Caesar's name. This can be sufficient for *Jubmel*. We now turn to other deities.

§. 48.

Among those gods, who are lower in the air, Sidenius also counts *Bjegs-Olmai* and *Gissen-Olmai*; but *Bjegsolmai* is put by Jessen in *Fudnos-aimo*, i.e. the Devil's world or Hell. Ganander has only taken the name of this *Bjegs Olmai* from Sidenius; but Anonymous in Leem says that "Bieg-olmai is a god of weather and wind, water and sea. He was offered sacrifices so that he might calm the sea's storms."

Jessen adds "that storms and rainclouds had their place in *Funos aimo* (Hell), where *Biegs Galles* (the weather hero) with his shovel (*kåiwo*) threw hail and tempest, plus wind and storm." Jessen, p. 66.

If this deity is a real mythological object, and not just a symbol of wind, then it has very likely belonged to the seacoast's Lapps. None of the Swedish authors knows anything about him. v. Vesten in *Letters*, ibid. writes *Bier-Salmai*, which is a misprint, and ought to read *Biegs olmai*. *Gissen olmai* which is most correctly written *Kiesse-olmai*, means *Sommar mannen* [the summer man], an object that only appears with a name in Anonymous and Sidenius. NB: *Biegs-* or *Bjegs-olmai* is most correctly written *Pjegg-olmai*, from the word *Pjegg* (weather, wind) and *Olmai* (man).

§. 49.

Now we come to the class of gods who are supposed to have their refuge on earth. Among them Sidenius places the so-called *Junkars* first, but the other Norwegian authors know nothing about them. It is possible Sidenius got the name *Junkars* in Salten, or it may be he has taken them from Schefferus. According to Swedish authors both *Stor-* and *Lill-Junker* [Big and Little Junker] belonged to Luleå Lappmark. Both Torneus and Högström speak about them, and the name *Junkar* is not entirely unknown in this Lappmark.

Ganander cites according to Sidenius that "*Junkari* was a Lapp idol who was worshipped as promoting hunting and trapping. He was invoked by a large rock or tree stump, to which in his honor, reindeer blood and all antlers from every Lapp family were gathered (NB: the intention was that the *Junkar's* image should be smeared with blood.). He was worshiped under the names of *Stor-Junker* and *Lill-Junker*." Sidenius in Ganander.

We probably cannot doubt that the *Junkars* were objects of the Lapps' worship, but where they got the name *Junkar* is incomprehensible to me. It is not Lapp. According to Lindfors' *Lexicon*, *Junkar* is supposed to have meant a *juvenus generosus* [young gentleman of noble birth, good family], perhaps even a prince, why also *the underhanded scoundrel* [?] was called *Dal Junkaren* (*Daljunkern* was a rebel leader of disputed identity who in 1527 with Dalarna as a base tried to start a rebellion called the second Dala rebellion to overthrow Gustav Vasa from the throne). But for what reason the Lapps got such a *Junker* among their gods is nowadays more impossible to decide. That the name was borrowed can be taken for granted.

§. 50.

Torneus states the following about *Junkar*: "The Torne- and Kemi Lapps know nothing about *Stor Junkaren*, scarcely also Piteå and Umeå Lapps. But, as much as I have dared here, the *Store Junkaren* in Luleå [Lapp]mark, is evident only on a mountain near Gråtræsk; what is known is that a sheriff and his party were traveling over there; when the Lapp, who was accompanying him, came toward the mountain, put the corner of his axe into the ice, and gave notice around there to the honor and service of the *Stor Junkar*, for he said that the *Stor Junkar* lived in that mountain. When the sheriff asked what good oaths to the *Stor Junkar* do? The Lapp said: when we row and fish in this lake, then he stands on the shore, has a small gun in his hand; when we row, he stands in the boat, when he sees a bird swim, he shoots it and gives it to us. He is a handsome, tall man in black *Junkar* clothing, but his feet are like bird feet. This Lapp." This story clearly reveals that both name and garb are borrowed, but for what reason? It has likely from the beginning been a swindle by the Birkarls,[18] who, through the supposed, perhaps purposely overly dressed up *Junkaren*, placed in the aforementioned mountain, wished to trick the Lapps into coming there with offerings. Gråtræsk is otherwise a name which I have not heard mentioned in Luleå Lappmark. I wonder whether Torneus hasn't mixed up Gråtræsk in Arvidsjaur which belongs to Piteå Lappmark.

§. 51.

Högström says the following about the *Junkars*: "That any nation at this time would worship logs and rocks, I have scarcely wanted to believe, before I, time and again in this Lule Lappmark, got to see such abominations with my own eyes. In the Jockmock parsonage are preserved three such idols, shaped with axe from roots, in the likeness of humans, which in the year 1738 were taken from a Kaitum Lapp in the district court who afterwards confessed how doing obeisance and worshiping, he fell at the foot of them. He called the one *Stor Junkare*, and it was the largest. Whether the others that were smaller represented his (the *Junkar's*) wife, children or servants, is unknown to me." Högström, ibid. §. 8.

There is thus no doubt that the Lapps in Luleå Lappmark actually had a *Stor Junkar* and *Lill Junkar*, but the reason why this so strange name got into their mythology can no longer now be investigated.

§. 52.

Leib olmai and *Tjatse olmai* were of a more Lapp nature. "*Leib-olmai* was a forest sprite who had charge of the animals in the forest." Jessen, p. 64.

"*Leib olmai* was the god of the hunt. To this one were offered prayers, sacrifices and genuflection, morning and evening." Anonymous in Leem.

---

[18] The Birkarls were a small, unofficially organized group that controlled taxing and commerce in central Lappmarken in Sweden during the 13th to 17th centuries.

"*Leib olmai*, one of the Lapp deities who lived on earth, a god of shooting, trapping animals and birds. The Lapps sacrifice to him that they might be lucky in their shooting and bird trapping." Ganander, according to Sidenius.

§. 53.
The name *Leib-olmai* comes from the Lapp word *leipe* (Alnus incana Willd. – grey alder) a tree that grows quite abundantly in Lapp- and Finnmark. It seems to have been a sort of sacred tree for the Lapps, because the bark from it served many of their needs. The decoction of the bark was used as medicine in various rash ailments. When the bark of the tree mentioned was chewed, it produced a brownish red juice, with which the Lapps prepared their reindeer leggings and reindeer head hides. The women spit the chewed bark juice on their husbands when they had felled a bear, and the dead bear itself was soaked too. With the juice of the chewed bark they also drew the figures on the notorious magic drum, etc. *Leib-olmai* thus actually means: the alder tree man, i.e. Alnus incanæ vir.

But the real occasion for this name's metaphorical meaning (hunting god), seems to have been taken from the aforementioned use of spraying the homecoming bear hunters and the slain bear itself with alder bark juice; either the bear hunter or the bear or both were called *Leib-olmai*, in any case: the sprayed alder bark man's spiritual representative also got to bear the same name, and thus arose *Jagt Guden* (the god of the hunt).

§. 54.
"*Tjatse olmah* were sea sprites who had charge of the fish." Jessen, P. 64.

Anonymous in Leem writes *Kiöse-almai*, and says that one sacrificed to him for good fishing. v. Vesten mentions *Gjase-almai*, and Ganander writes, according to Sidenius, *Kiase-olmai*, and adds that it is a god of fishery that sends the fish to the hook, net or seine. NB: according to Lindahl and Öhrling's orthography it ought to be written *Tjatse-olmai*, which means: Aquarius. Presumably, it was only fishing Lapps along the Norwegian coast who worshiped *Tjatse-olmai*. The Swedish authors know nothing about this god. Whether this *Tjatse-olmai* corresponded to the Swedes *Sjö-Rå* (sea sprite) or the Norwegians *Drauen* 'headless man destined to die soon' [Old Icelandic *draugr* 'dead cairn dweller or ghost'] is not so certain.

§. 55.
We now come to kinds of gods that were known over all of the Lapp area, and because they were commonly worshipped, are still present in the Lapps' memory. Among them one can first mention *Passe*, a sort of sanctuary known in all the Lappmarks, even in Finnmark, though the Norwegian authors, e.g. Leem, do not mention anything other than *Passe-Vareh* (sacred mountain).

Passe is not related to the Swedes' *Buse*, *Bjesse* or *Basse*; which Rudbeck imagined in his *Atlantica*; but the name comes quite simply from the Lapp word *passet* which means roast [North Sámi *bassit*].

In this connection, one has to imagine that there was a time when the Lapps, with a shortage of pots and pans, had to roast their food over the fire. This method is still very useful, and is used generally on trips where one cannot take pots and pans along. The Lapps probably never knew the art of processing metals; for had they for example known the art of smelting and processing useful household items of iron, then they would not have had to use a loon bill on their arrows about which their own stories give credible evidence.

They have, I suppose, the name of iron *Ruowde*; and copper *Veike*, but these words originally have reference to the ores, though they now designate both the ores and the metals refined from them.

On the contrary, they have no separate word for pot, pan or the like. *Ryto* in the southern and *Patu* or *Paathe* in the northern Lappmarks as well as *pannu* are borrowed from Swedish and Finnish.

§. 56.

Kiebne, stew-pan, seems to be the first vessel of metal that came to the Lapps. I say deliberately that these kinds of vessels came into the Lapps' hands through foreign nations; for that the Lapps themselves could have made kettles is not likely. *Skalo*, a sort of cooking vessel of metal with narrow bottom and wide mouth, is mentioned by the Lapps, as belonging to and sometimes in feuds taken from the Karelians, for which also these vessels are called *Karjel-Skalo*, i.e. Karelian kettles. *Nibe* 'knife' and *Aksjo* 'axe' are probably loanwords; *Silba* 'silver' as well; *Riggasah*, the chain from which the Lapp hangs his kettle or pot over the fire, is probably borrowed from Swedish *Ring*. *Kaskam* 'steel' seems to be purely Lapp, and is similar to *Kiebne*, the first item of metal the Lapps themselves gave a name. Yet, they knew the art of making a fire, probably long before steel came into use. *Rissja* 'sulphur' is also Lapp.

§. 57.

When the Lapp grilled his food over the fire, then it was natural that what he offered to the gods on a trip would be grilled, and thus came *Passe* which actually is the present participle of *passet*, meaning something that one grills and thus consecrates to the gods. In time even the place where the grilled things were gathered, was called *Passe*, i.e. sanctuary. And then arose *Passe vare*, a sacred mountain, *Passe ruowde*, a sacred forest, et al. Meanwhile, one found out that what had been grilled was not consumed by the gods, but rotted or was eaten by birds of prey (NB: for the four-legged predators the offerings were preserved in a place that was called *Luowe* [North Sámi *luovvi* 'hiding place, etc.']). They then began to sacrifice to the gods such things that could not rot, or be eaten up by birds of prey, namely antlers and bones: but the place at which such sacrifices were taken still managed to keep its name. That is roughly how I imagine the origin and naming of *Passe*, sed alii aliter.

§. 58.
Such a sacred place, *Passe*, the mountain Lapps had on some high mountain in the area of their fall and spring stations. The forest Lapps had their *Passeh* 'sacred places' in some excellent spots in the forests. There one gathered antlers in large quantities, both of wild and of tame reindeer. "There, wild reindeer antlers were offered in large piles, which can still be seen in many places where there has been a *Seita* [ritual site]." Torneus, ibid. p 15. Nowadays one seldom finds traces of these antler piles, because the new settlers had already boiled them for glue beginning long ago, and those that remained rotted.

Right in the middle of the antler pile, which was placed in a sort of enclosure, one usually put an image which was supposed to represent the deity. If this image was of wood, then it was either called *Stuor-Junkar*, as in Luleå Lappmark, or *Viron-akka*, as in Torneå Lappmark; but if the image was stone, it was called *Seite* or *Säite*.

§. 59.
What the wooden idols were like that were supposed to represent the Lapps' deities Högström describes thus:

"Time and again I have in several places during my travels noticed such idols on their sacrificial platforms –

NB: by "*offer lafvar*" is meant the wooden stand on which the Lapps put what was offered to the Gods. The actual stand consisted of four or more posts three to four ells in length [ell = ca. 18 inches] perpendicularly placed in the ground, on which one has laid split posts or boards horizontally, as on a sauna bench. The wooden idol either stood on the actual platform, or next to it.

– about which more will be said later on, being (these idols) nothing other than roots, generally of birch, which were inverted and carved into heads with an axe, the actual trunk or stump showing the rest of a body with the feet. These either stand continually in their places, and are annually visited with offerings, when the Lapps happen to be near them, or they are erected every year, generally in fall at the places where they slaughter their rutting reindeer (reindeer bulls are slaughtered before they have begun the rut), or are also erected on the large mountains and hills, where they are visited and honored by a large number of Lapps."

"From this it can be understood that there must have been various kinds of these idols; a number of them were seen as *LandtGudar* 'country gods' which certain Lapps on some occasions erected in particular for themselves. I have also noticed meanwhile that they do acts of violence to each other's sanctuaries, of which I saw proof during the spring of 1742 when a violent conflict arose between two Lapps, because one of them had chopped antlers and bones to pieces that the other one had erected on a stand for his gods at a sleeping place."

"Whether all prominent wooden idols are called *Stor Junkars*, I cannot be sure; but that I often saw them made in various ways during my travels, I cannot deny." Högström, ch. 11 §. 8.

"Wooden ritual sites have no particular shape, but only a stump on its roots or a post upside down, selected and sanctified for worship." Torneus, ibid. p. 15.

§. 60.
On *Seite* Högström expresses himself as follows:

"At that place in Luleå Lappmark where I was staying, their stone idols are especially prevalent and commonplace. Whether too these represent *Stor Junkar* or someone else I am also unaware. But I have not heard them called other than *Passe* by the Lapps, namely the actual places, but the stones they call *Säite*. On them I have not noticed any particular shape or any human or animal, but they have been such as nature itself seems to have made them, but generally though have an unusual shape like fossils, rippled and knotty." Högström ibid. §. 9.

"The *Sten Seiter* [ritual sites of stone] have no form or shape made either by nature or hands, but a smooth and ordinary granite, some black, unsightly, dimpled, hollow, as if taken up from the water." Torneus ibid. p. 18.

§. 61.
If I am not deceiving myself, the actual stone *Seite* consisted of shiny slate with interspersed garnets and veins of feldspar and hornblende. When such a stone type came to lie on the seashores, the looser stone types were abraded away by the water's and sand's scrubbing, whereby various hollows and figures were formed resembling traces of reindeer, sheep, horses, humans et al. Sometimes too such a hollow could resemble human hands and the like, for which the simple-minded Lapp was not able to think of some natural cause, and this provided the occasion to erect such stones and consider them as sanctuaries. It is possible that the Lapp in these hollows thought he saw traces of subterranean livestock, and so much greater reason the Lapp had to view them as sacred.

§. 62.
"A few Lapps absolutely believe that these stones are alive and able to walk, meanwhile several are erected in one place too. Commonly, they are found near mountain extremities, near headlands and marshes, on holms near cataracts, or other hallowed places; no one knows who put them there, or when they came there." Högström ibid.

The stones presumably have been around since time immemorial, and if any were erected in more recent times, then the Lapp is probably reluctant to speak about it.

"They erected such stones on highly eminent spaces, the *Seites*, which the whole village (an entire district) worshiped." Torneus, p. 14.

"They wanted to make me believe that these places were already included at the first creation, etc." Högström ibid.

§. 63.
Högström also mentions that "The Lapps did not eagerly want to show these sanctuaries to any strangers, because they feared the gods would be offended by such, and inflict something bad on them, whereupon they cited several examples, that the one who out of curiosity got too close to these stone idols, or did violence to them, was deprived of his health, etc." Högström ibid. §. 9.

It is not for nothing that a few Lapps still have a certain respect for the ancient sanctuaries. If anyone happened to get too close to them, or walked past with improper attire, and that same person then came down with an affliction, then it was a consequence of disrespect for *Passe*. Such an instance happened as late as 1814 with a Lapp child in Quickjock, who had borrowed a pair of shoes from a woman, and happened by chance to get too close to a *Passe* with these unholy shoes. Shortly afterwards he became lame in his feet, and now it is believed generally by the Lapps that it was a punishment because he profaned *Passe*. But sacrifices and promises are no longer made to *Passe*, as much as I have been able to learn.

§. 64.
Högström tells more about the same *Seite*, that "one usually estimates the power of these stones according to their abundance and the number of people who worship them. If it so happens that one abandons sacrificing to them, then they also lose their power, then are unable to do one either evil or good, and such gods who have become powerless are not difficult for one to see." Högström ibid.

Naturally, they stopped sacrificing to the gods when the circumstances came about that one got no help.

One sacrificed both living and dead things to these wooden and stone idols. When the Lapp got into some adversity, then he usually said the name of the place and the sanctuary, and promised something positive according to the nature of the adversity.

The nature of sacrifice will still cling fast to the Lapps' mind. One does not sacrifice now to a *Seite* or *Passe*, but instead one promises offerings to churches, sometimes to several at one time, as if it were to attempt to find which church had the best power to help. What was promised to the gods was unswervingly kept, and was to be obtained, no matter how expensive. Cf. Högström §. 19. Much consideration was also given to the nature of the actual offering. What was promised to churches was to be achieved in kind, though the church would be equally satisfied with the value of what was promised. Cf. Sjögren on Kemi Lappmark.

§. 65.
"As far as the stone idols or the so-called *Säite* are concerned, then it seems they have been considered much more sacred than those of wood. Around some of them they usually put fences, sometimes far around." Högström ibid. On this subject, one's thoughts go to Balder's grove. The Biarmians god, who was called *Jumala*, had a grove too. If I remember correctly, Schefferus visualizes the fence as of reindeer antlers. When the Norwegian authors speak about the Lapps' temple, then I believe, that thereby is meant nothing other than such a grove or fence with the appurtenant items, which was precisely the real *Passe*. Any other temple the Lapps have surely never had.

§. 66.
"If anyone shoots squirrels, birds or other animals within the same enclosures, that is, within the boundary of stones, then he has to take the feet as well as the head and wings and offer them to the stones; the rest he keeps for himself. At such places one usually lifts up the stones every year, and puts fresh spruce twigs under and around them, which the Lapp does with uncovered head, crawling on all fours, even when he otherwise goes to sacrifice, when he likewise from the stone's lightness or weight can conclude whether it is favorable or unfavorable for him." Högström ibid. §. 19.

Under and around such *Säites* [ritual sites], strewn beautifully and properly, they spread green spruce twigs, but during the summer green leaves. When it was pallid and dried out, they laid fresh in its place, and adorned the space all around. There they arrived at certain times, and otherwise when something went wrong, or when they experienced some misfortune, solemnized with formal clothing, made their prayers and devotions." Torneus p. 15.

§. 67.
That the Lapps in times past ascribed great power to these wooden and stone idols can be concluded from the following: "Because they make promises to these stones, when either people or animals fall ill, I conclude that they believe in them, to have health and illness, life and death in their power; but that they also expect evil from them, I conclude from a certain Lapp's own story, who acknowledged that when he some years ago came unwittingly on his migration to go too close to such a *Seite*, and passed over the headland where the stone lay, so close to it, that he came upon the actual steps or path that the stone (*si diis [deis] placet* [if it please the gods]) had along the land over to a headland opposite; when he noticed this, he pledged sacrifices of bull reindeer, reindeer cows, sheep, goats et al. But could not thereby appease him; because wolves came the same night together with his reindeer and did him considerable damage." Högström §. 10.

Högström also speaks about *Stuoramus Passe*, which means the most distinguished sanctuary, from which one can conclude that some sacrificial places were considered more sacred, others less sacred. Probably *Stuoramus Passe* was a ritual site of the entire district, because the *Seite's* power and reputation increased with the number of worshipers. The less sacred *Passeh* presumably belonged to particular families and were inherited.

§. 68.
That some of these *Seite* stones were not extremely large can be concluded from the following: "To begin with, as far as the sacrifice is concerned, it consists of three things. First, a stone, which they call *Zeit* or *Rå* (sprite). Secondly, alongside the stone a tree is set up, like the keel of a boat, which they call *Hyden venet*, i.e. *blåkulla*[19] båt, and by another name, *Lista Murit* (should be read *Liste muor*) 'tree of trust;' thirdly, of the actual service or worship, which they call *Rucce* (should be read *rukos* or *rukkuse*); it is the adoration of humility and glory, which occurs with devoted questioning or assigning by lot; for when the Lapp begins to demonstrate this his glorious service, he takes his cap off, lays this stone upon his hand and speaks to his god with formulas: Now I touch Thee with greatest humility in your sacred space, and lay my hand upon Thee and beseech from Thee (whatever it might be or be called). And when he in this his prayer mentions all sorts of things, and requests one at a time, however, he strains to see whether he can get his hand up together with the stone from the ground. If he does not get his hand up, but it becomes ever heavier, then he has no hope of what he requested this time."

"Therefore, he requests again a second, 3rd and 4th time and so on, all sorts of necessities, whether riches or something else, and he at last comes across what he wants to have from his god. Then the stone, however large it was, becomes light, so that his hand rises up from the ground; but as long as the idol does not want to answer, his hand remains heavy, no matter how small the stone is, and when he has gotten the answer that pleases him, he says: you are my god or; as you wish, my god. And when he has gotten that which the lot has provided him, then the worshiper asks the god anew whatever it is he wishes to have, saying that he will procure it, whether it be a lamb, a female deer or wild reindeer, nanny goat, billy goat, according to what he has named, whether alive or dead." Tuderus ibid.

§. 69.
One can see from this report that the ceremonies for *Seite* worship were somewhat different in Kemi Lappmark, which is a consequence of the great distance between the Lappmarks. People in Luleå Lappmark know Inari only by name, and the Torneå Lapps know the nearest neighboring Lappmark congregations in Jockmock, but no further. The Lapps seldom have any communication with each other across the

---
[19] Blåkulla is the Swedish name for the German Brocken, a peak in the Harz Mountains.

country, but rather along river courses. From that come the great differences in their languages, customs, clothing and way of living.

Odd that none of the Norwegian authors know *Passe* and *Seite*. Jessen and Leem only mention *Passe vareh* 'sacred mountain.' So, it seems as if these deities have chiefly belonged to the Swedish Lappmarks. It was probably the forest Lapps who mostly worshiped *Seite*. These in turn did not have much communication with the mountain Lapps, except that time in the year when their dwelling spaces neared one another.

§. 70.

How *Passe* came to mean sacred I have already explained above. We can add that *Passe* also means holiday, festival, really: *Passe peiwe*, the sacred place's day, on account of the sacrificing performed or carried out certain days. *Pasatis*, a festival celebrated at the end of November in honor of *Passe*, has also gotten its name from that, likewise the month of November, during which the feast or sacrifice occurred, was called *Pasatis Mano*. That this *Pasatis* should come from *passat* 'to wash' is less believable. The Lapps seldom used to wash, least of all during the winter.

It is more difficult to explain the origin of *Seite*. In Lapp there is a stem without meaning. In Finnish I do not find anything other than *siitä* 'breed,' of which the Lapp word *Säiteje* 'solitary, conceiving.' Cf. Lindahl et Öhrling *Lexicon*. Now if *Säite* should be a contraction of *säiteje*, then it would mean the 'the breeder;' but this derivation is not so certain. That it should mean *Rå* 'sprite,' Tuderus thinks not likely. Even less could it come from the Greek word *Zevs* [Zeus], as a few older authors thought. More likely it could be related to the old *sejd* 'witchcraft,' which according to Scandinavian mythology should mean the art of witchcraft (Old Icelandic *seiðr* = spell, charm, enchantment). Or have the Scandinavian people gotten their *Seid* from the Lapps' *Seite*? – Some places still bear names from the ancient idols, e.g. *Seite tjålme*, in Piteå Lappmark; also the name *Seite kallo* 'Seite's stone' is not unknown among the Lapps; they know perfectly well that their ancestors worshiped such stone idols.

§. 71.

"Among the Lapps' subterranean idols in the fourth and last class are counted first their *Saiwo*: *Saiwo-Olmah*, *Saiwo-Nedah*, *Saiwo-Lodde*, *Saiwo-Guelle* and *Saiwo-Sarwah*, all of which were supposed to stay beneath the earth's surface. For it has been an old belief among the Lapps that in the hills of their mountains which they call *Saiwo* (indicated under Nº 41 on the drum diagram) or *Passe vareh*, as well as in the kingdom of the dead beneath the earth, called *Jabma-aimo* (Nº 14 on the drum diagram) have stayed such beings as they themselves are. These (subterraneans) have carried on a sort of livelihood, like they themselves, plus had domestic animals too; but with the difference that the creatures that lived in the hills as well as beneath the earth, were in a happier state than the humans on earth; which is the reason why the Lapps viewed *Saiwo-Olmah*, who lived in the hills as a glorious and rich people, who were well acquainted with witchcraft and runic wisdom. However, the Lapps viewed themselves as poor and wretched people, who needed the former's protection. The Lapps alleged they had often been in *Saiwo*, together with *Saiwo-Olmah*, danced and *yuoikat* (yoiked/sung) with them, and seen their husbands, wives and children. They also could enumerate their names. Some alleged they had been weeks with *Saiwo-Olmah*, smoked tobacco with them, enjoyed schnaps and other refreshments. That is why every mature Lapp acquired ten to twelve of these *Saiwo* as guardian angels." Jessen ibid.

§. 72.
That this belief in subterranean beings has been, and still is just as common among the Lapps, as among neighboring nations, is no doubt subject to examination; yet it seems the doctrine of *Saiwo* was more developed among the Lapps, than the doctrine of the subterranean beings in other nations. Jessen has probably misunderstood his informants, when he mixed *Saiwo* with *Jabma aimo*, which in the people's notions seem to have been definitely distinct. *Jabma aimo* was the kingdom of the dead, but Saiwo was the world where the subterranean beings had their residence. In *Jabma aimo* were real spirits, namely the souls of the dead, but in *Saiwo* there were half spiritual and half material beings. As these play an important role in Lapp mythology, we want to present the doctrine about them, as completely as space allows.

§. 73.
"The inhabitants in *Saiwo* were men, women and children, four or five who lived in each place. In some places they were married, in others unmarried. Besides these people, there were livestock in *Saiwo* who were much more beautiful than those of the Lapps." Jessen p. 24.

"*Saiwo olmak* 'men of the hills' were of service to all people, but particularly to those who had inherited them or bought them from other *noaidis*, or had acquired them through diligence in the art of divination. These *Saiwo-olmah* gave advice on many occasions, both during sleep, also through *Myran* (divination?) on the magic drum, belts, guns, stones and horse bones." Anonymous in Leem.

This stanza by Anonymous seems to me fairly obscure. He says that *Saiwo olmah* gave "advice," i.e. oracle answers during sleep, i.e. that *Saiwo Olmah* revealed himself in the dream. Another way to ascertain *Saiwo*'s advice happened through *myran*. If I am not mistaken this *myran* ought to mean fortune-telling, or the actual act whereby the *noaidi*, by means of certain signs, marks and tricks, sought to ascertain the outcome of an affair. One cannot at any rate in any other way imagine this action, when the author mentions that *myran* happened not only on the drum but also on other things. Presumably, the *noaidi* did not always have the drum available on his trips, and he then had to look into *Saiwo's* intention with certain tricks on other things. I presume that this *myran* had to have happened, because one still has even today certain marks or tricks for investigating the outcome for example of a bear hunt, beaver hunt, etc.

§. 74.
"Because the Lapps viewed the inhabitants of *Saiwo* as real beings, they entered into alliances with them, whereby the Lapps bargained for help from *Saiwo*. *Saiwo* was supposed to become their guardians; they were supposed to bring them luck in their endeavors, such as for example fishing, etc. They were supposed to save people's lives, help find out everything, and avenge wrongs suffered by the Lapps. Whereas the Lapps promised to serve *Saiwo* with life and property." Jessen, p. 27.

"*Saiwo* was inherited, as well as bought and sold, wherefore the parents while they were still alive shifted this *Saiwo* between their children. When one received many *Saiwos* in dowry, it was viewed as a successful marriage. If the parents had died before they shifted *Saiwo* among their children, then the latter had to gain *Saiwo's* support through sacrifice." Jessen, p. 26.

How this distribution of inheritance must have occurred is not easy to perceive, since the author does not explain it. Previously, the author has carefully stated that the Lapps had names for the inhabitants of *Saiwo*. One must then imagine that the children were vouchsafed certain enumerated *Saiwo* men and women. But it seems more likely the Lapps had marked certain reindeer in *Saiwo's* name, as being of a better race, and that these reindeer were distributed among the children. Since now these reindeer were as if hallowed to *Saiwo*, and bore *Saiwo's* name, then they were seen as having a better suitability than other reindeer, and those who got such reindeer as their lot, were also seen as more closely connected to the *Saiwo* to which the reindeer were hallowed. This ought to be better understood by the following where *Saiwo-vuoigna* and *Saiwo-Sarvah* are discussed.

§. 75.
"Every Lapp should have with him in his *Saiwo* three kinds of animals, which were present as soon as he chose to call on them: namely, 1st a bird, which was called *Saiwo-lodde,* 2nd a fish, or serpent that was called *Saiwo-quolle,* or *Guarms,* (depicted under N° 45 on the drum diagram), 3rd a reindeer called *Saiwo-Sarwa* (N° 42 on the drum diagram). But all these animals are called by a common name *Saiwo-vuoign.*" Jessen, p. 24.

NB: *Saiwa-lodde* means *Saiwo's* bird; *Saiwo-quolle* Saiwo's fish; *Saiwo-Sarva* Saiwo's reindeer bull. *Vuoign* actually means the spirit or the air, that humans breathe, from which the metaphor of life, and in the end the individual, in the latter sense of which the word occurs in this place. All these names are purely Lapp, so that there is nothing to remark against them.

These animals in the *noaidi's* conception seem to have been the animal kingdom's spiritual representatives; i.e. such as belonged to the inhabitants of *Saiwo*; the *noaidi* had as a result of his close connection to *Saiwo*, gotten the right to use the subterranean animals as his personal and captured property.

§. 76.
"The birds (namely, *Saiwo-loddeh*) were of various sizes, some like swallows, sparrows, ptarmigans, eagles, swans, capercaillies, black grouse and hawks. In color some were white and speckled black, some black on the backs, white on the wings and gray under the belly; some pink, some grayish black and white. Their names are: *Alpe, Brudnehark, Habik, Fietnaalegonum, Gierkits Gisa, Molk, Gaasa, Varrehauka, Maaka, Rippo, Suorek, Staure, Paiwo, Jap, Lainöer, Paimatz.*

They served their masters by following them when they yoiked (sang their magic songs) to them, showed them the way, when they wanted to travel, and gave them hunting equipment when they were going to hunt; brought them information from distant places, as well as helped them look after their reindeer and other belongings, and when they were so constituted, they were called only *Saiwo-loddeh*, of which some Lapps had many, others few. But when a *noaidi* used *Saiwo-lodde* to harm other people, which was not uncommon, they (the birds) got the name *Vuornes-lodde*. The *noaidi* could also travel long distances on the bird's back." Jessen, p. 25.

Appendix to §. 76. "*Saiwo lodde* 'mountain bird' shows the *noaidi* the way during his travels. The *noaidi* is even in the habit of sending this *Saiwo Lodde* to harm some other soothsayer, or others he has a grudge against." Anonymous in Leem.

"*Saiwo lodde* 'mountain cattle,' who show the way where *noaidis* [shamans] intend to travel, and the *noaidis* use *Saiwio* [sic] *Lodde* to accost other people and *noaidis* when they are angry." Sidenius in Ganander.

Note. Anonymous translates *Saiwo lodde* with *Bergsfogel* [*Bergsfågel*] 'mountain bird,' but this translation fits just as little as Bergsmän (mountain men). Ganander has made the meaning even worse, when he translates *Saiwo lodde* as *Bergsfä* 'mountain cattle.' If one were to say *Trollfogel* 'magic bird' one would at least get closer to the truth.

§. 77.
It would no doubt be interesting to know which birds are meant under the names cited; but in the Swedish Lappmarks they are for the most part unknown. Leem has not taken up more than *Alpe*, which is supposed to mean *Snösparf* (*snøspurv* 'snow sparrow') in Norwegian. A large number of these names ought to be troll names, which only the *noaidis* knew. It also seems clear that neither Jessen nor the authors he followed could really comprehend the pronunciation of the words. Thus, *Habik* ought to be *Hapak*, which means *Hök* 'hawk' (*Falco gyrfalco* Lin. [jer-falcon]). *Paimats* ought to be written *Poimats* (Falco lagopus Lin). *Gaasa*, a Lapp version of Swedish *Gås* (Anser segetum Nils). *Brudnehark* seems to be Cinclus sturnus Lin. *Ki-*

erkits Saxicola oenanthæ Lin. Some of the birds probably belong solely among such birds that live on the Norwegian side for which the Lapp names are unknown to me.

§. 78.
Most nations have bestowed on birds the ability to have a premonition of the future, for which reason Augurium (Augur) was an important office in Rome. But the Lapp *noaidis* thought that the native birds were not all that wise, and therefore chose these birds' half spiritual representatives in *Saiwo*, as being of a much higher and nobler nature. It was not hard for the *noaidi* to use these magic birds in his service, since he often made trips to *Saiwo*, and was so closely connected with the inhabitants of this subterranean kingdom. These *Saiwo-loddeh* were thus not natural birds; they were fetched from *Saiwo* itself, and it was thus not surprising that the *noaidi* through them could do his enemies harm.

Since these magic birds were feared, because they were thought to herald, or even bring about one's misfortune, it was also natural that one sought some protection against these ominous beings' magic shots. One believed generally, and this belief will still cling to a few Lapps, that someone who heard for the first time the ominous spring birds crowing on an empty stomach, would unconditionally meet with misfortune, or come to suffer adversity. The one who thus was surprised by a spring bird's crowing was said to be *paikatallam*, which means shot down, i.e. that he was subjected to evil, which through the bird's sound was portended. To forestall this trouble one had to hurry to take some refreshment, as soon as they opened their eyes, and this breakfast was called *Lodde-pitta*, which means bird morsel, or the bite that would reduce the bird's ominous power to nothing.

This belief in certain spring birds' ominous sounds, is still prevalent among some Lapps, and therefore it is thought necessary not to go out on an empty stomach. Some are so cautious that they put a bit of food under their head, so it is immediately available as soon as they open their eyes.

But it is not all spring birds that are seen as ominous, nor does it make a difference if one on an empty stomach hears such a bird's sound, a second and 3rd time. It is especially the first time in the spring when such a bird appears that one must be careful not to get crowed over on an empty stomach.

§. 79.
As this opinion undoubtedly originates from the above described *Saiwo-loddeh*, who were believed to be sent out by *noaidis* to harm people, then it does not seem out of the way for the sake of continuity to mention here which of these birds were viewed as most ominous.

Among them is found first a small bird in the hawk family, which in Luleå Lappmark is called *Qvuoddalvis*, i.e. the bearer. This bird is regarded as bearing messages about, or portending a person's death, which goes like this that the bird takes in its mouth some of the dying person's property, e.g. a piece of ribbon or something from the clothing the person is wearing, whose death it is portending. (Such a relic the bird seeks in the places where the Lapps have their tents.) With this relic he flies to the cemetery (the burial spot), and imitates the dead man's voice with a wailing sound. The one who hears this sound, will not only recognize the voice, if the fey, you see, is familiar, but the bird will even be able to be induced to alight if one asks what it is carrying. However, it is not prudent to let the bird alight on oneself, but one gets under a low or tumbled tree-trunk, and lets the bird alight on it.

§. 80.
What sort of a bird it is, whether imaginary or real, is impossible for me to decide, since I could not see it either living or dead. According to the description it is supposed to be somewhat larger than a thrush, have a yellow beak and red feet. Some have a green beak and orange-colored feet. All are equipped with claws, but the color of the feathers is supposed to be variable. If it is a real bird, which my informants assure, then one must seek it among the lesser hawk-like birds of prey.

The cuckoo (Cuculus canorus) is thought to be a very wicked bird. It is believed to forebode a person's death if it sets about crowing on the Lapp's hut, and that happens on an empty stomach. If the cuckoo sits and crows on the tree under which the person sits, the person will live just as many years as times the cuckoo crows.

The diver (Colymbus septentrionalis) is also an ominous bird, if it gets the chance to crow over one with an empty stomach. The [hooded] crow too. (Corvus cornix). Swan (Cygnus), Goose (Anser segetum), etc.

§. 81.
"The fish and serpents that were called *Saiwo-quolle* or *Guarms*, were quite a number of names, sizes and colors. The stronger the *noaidi* could yoik (sing magic songs), the larger the serpent was, up to three fathoms. It served to inflict harm on his master's enemies, and on it he could travel to *Jabma aimo* (Hades)." Jessen, p. 26.

There is also a *Saiwo quolle* that is supposed to protect the *noaidi's* life when he is going to make his way into *Jabma aimo*. *Namma-quolle* 'name fish' is a sort of genius in fish shape who watches over the man's name. When the man encounters something evil, he is supposed to be rebaptized with a magic name from his grandfather or father, whose name protector is *Namma-quolle*." Anonymous in Leem.

"*Saiwo quolle* 'mountain fish' who protects the Lapp *noaidi's* life when he is going to make his way to *Jabma aimo*, either to bring up someone from his family, father or mother, who is going to be a reindeer herder 1, 2, 3, 4 years or longer; or to bring up a sick person's soul again." Sidenius in Ganander.

§. 82.
The idea of *Saiwo-qwuolle* seems most closely related to *Saiwo lodde*. For, seeing that there were birds in *Saiwo*, then fish too should have their representatives in *Saiwo*,

which were vastly superior to natural fish. As it says that *Saiwo qwuolle* is supposed to protect the *noaidi's* soul during descent into *Jabma aimo*, that probably means the *noaidi* in the spirit crawled into a *Saiwo-qwuolle*, and took on its shape. That idea also occurs in the sagas, that people were bewitched into fish. That the serpent is called a fish too is not uncommon. In the sagas, the serpent appears often under the name of *Sjuda-qwuolle*, i.e. the hissing fish, and sometimes the serpent is called *Kukkes-qwuolle* [North Sámi *guhká* 'long' *guolli* 'fish'], i.e. the long fish. It was presumably this kind of fish the *noaidi* used to harm others. In a number of places, one holds the serpent in great respect, and that belief I have heard discussed even among the Finns on Torneå River, that a few serpents are not natural, but supernatural serpents, or such that have been incited against people by *noaidis*. Hereby, the gnome serpent reported in Nordland ought to be somehow connected. The gnome serpent was nevertheless seen as a sort of protective being and was not to be molested. But a serpent who lies down near a bridge, and regards a person arriving or leaving, was thought to have been incited by a *noaidi*.

§. 83.

In connection with magic serpents it ought to be most suitable to say something here about the superstitious notion the Lapps and even the common folk in Nordland have about natural serpents. You see, one says that when the serpents assemble in a hissing throng in the spring, there is found in every larger den of serpents a 'serpent king' that is very large and white in color. This serpent king has a little smooth and white stone in its mouth with which it plays; it throws it up and down, and grabs it with its mouth, as one takes a ball, and the one that can be the possessor of this *worm stone*, shall with it be able to obtain everything it wishes. But it is quite dangerous to engage in the serpent game in order to pick up this stone, when the serpent king throws it; for as soon as the serpent king loses its stone, the entire swarm of serpents is thrown into a rage, and pursues the robber with violence, and it is absolutely impossible to escape, because the serpents bite themselves in the tail and roll around like hoops, so that not even the fastest horse can run away.

Many tales are told about this. One man, in order to get to a *worm stone* without endangering his life, had made 3 large bonfires around the serpent games; but the biggest serpents had pursued him all the way to the 3rd fire. When I was traveling in Åsele Lappmark in 1824, one of the farmers driving me showed me the actual spot where his father out of curiosity had taken hold of the fatal *worm stone*, which he found lying on a path on a wooded hill, but he had to let go of it, for though to begin with he saw no serpents, he had nevertheless been surrounded by serpents in such a hurry that he had to let go of the stone and take flight.

§. 84.

How any of this common folk belief can be based on anything real, is for me entirely impossible to decide, since I have probably seen serpent hissing, but never the reported serpent king, nor have I noticed a natural scientist speak about such. For the *noaidis* it was of course a simple matter to procure a *worm stone*, and it must have been from someone like that the deceased parish pastor Kohlström in Muonioniska got hold of one. The *worm stone* is usually no larger than a swallow egg, white with a few red dots, like fine porphyry. Presumably, one has taken some stones turned by water, and passed them off as *worm stones*.

In an old book called *Francisci Redi Experimenta*, printed in Amsterdam in 1685, there are a whole pile of stories about the so-called *worm stones*' power to cure various illnesses. The author who is said to have been a physician, has made several attempts with such *worm stones*, but found them to have no effect. The author has also provided various sketches of *worm stones* collected in the East Indies, where belief in the *worm stones*' remarkable effects were common among natives in the area of the Ganges; but he has not been able to make clear whether the alleged *worm stones* were really found in serpents or whether they were natural stones. The author mentions only that these stones, according to travelers' reports, according to some had been found in the serpents' stomachs, according to others in the serpents' heads.

It is probably not impossible that stone formation could arise in certain individuals in the serpent family, in the same way as bladder stones and pearls are formed in certain animals' bodies. And otherwise I do not know from where common people might have gotten their belief in *worm stones*, a belief spread all the way to India. I am also reminded of a settler in Luleå Lappmark and Pewawre village who had two *worm stones*; but at the time I saw them, I did not have the common sense to ask where he had gotten them. Afterwards, I heard that he was supposed to have gotten them himself from the multitude of serpents there are in the area of the same Pewawre. The man was namely a little *noaidi* who could humble serpents and wasps through some sort of incantation. It was thus no trick for him to get hold of *worm stones*. He humbled the serpent so that it later lost all power to harm. He wrapped the serpent around his hands, stuffed it into his chest, etc., just as Franciscus Redus reports about certain wizards among the natives in India. But this author claims that this wizard previously took the poison out of the serpent, by letting it bite in some shoddy tree, fungus or the like. Whether the *noaidis* in the Lappmarks use the same tricks, I do not know; nor can I say what kinds of serpents there are in the Lappmarks. But that both people and animals have been bitten by serpents and that they really had swelling and pain, that I know for sure. How one humbles wasps, that I have seen with my own eyes; and that is the only magic I have seen in my life. I was a 12- or 13-year-old boy then. It was a settler farm-hand in Quikjock (Luleå Lappmark), who had learned the art from the settler in Pewawre. He read and mumbled something that I didn't understand or pay attention to. But in short the wasps became as tractable as lambs. He tore apart the wasp's nest without the wasps being able to do him any harm. They seemed to be entirely checkmated. They crawled on his hands and couldn't even fly. What tricks he must have used are incomprehensible to me; but that it happened through an incantation he proclaimed himself.

Another belief or superstition about the serpent I also remember. It is alleged that the serpent immediately seeks water when it has bitten a person; but if it doesn't find water within a certain specific time, then its bite has no effect.

That much, one sees from the author cited above (Redus), that belief in the serpent's miraculous power was not confined to the Lappmarks. I wonder whether this belief doesn't originate in India, together with much else that belongs to Lapps' and Finns' magic?

The serpent skin is otherwise a part of Lapp medicine, and is viewed as a propitious remedy. Even the fat is used as salve for rheumatism and the like. One is in the habit of giving serpent skin in schnaps to wives in childbirth, and when one wants to enchant someone into falling in love, a bit of the serpent goes into the enchanting drink. The belief is also prevalent that the serpent does not die until sundown, even if one breaks it into pieces.

If one puts the serpent into an ant hill, then the feet it had before it seduced Eve will become visible. If a serpent's tongue blows 3 times in the mouth of someone who has a toothache, then the toothache will abate, etc.

§. 85.

Besides, as far as the *Saiwo-qwuolle* described above is concerned, there still remains some of the old superstition. You see, there are in all Lappmarks certain smaller lakes in which the fish are very timid so that they cannot be caught with a seine, if the least noise is made during the dragging. Such lakes are normally called *Saiwo*, i.e. magic lakes. The water in these lakes is so clear that one can see the bottom at 10 fathoms depth. It is cold even during the summer, but warm during the winter, i.e. warmer than other icy water, so that in shallower spots it causes blind holes in the ice. This comes naturally from the cold springs that well up on the bottom. People believe that in such lakes there is a double bottom; and the real situation is that the bottom is full of holes, caused by the veins of water that well up there because the holes are not visible everywhere.

This water, even if clearer than other lake water, is nevertheless heavier than other snow and rain water since it contains a quantity of dissolved mineral material. But from physics it is known that what is called sound is propagated more strongly and quicker through a thicker (tighter and heavier) medium than through a thinner one, and that the fish experience the effect of that noise, is generally known. It seems to be the natural reason why the fish in such lakes are so shy that they don't tolerate the least noise or sound. One can thus see the seine full of fish; one can have the wedge quite close, but at the slightest sound of a word or the like that the fisherman lets slip, every last tail disappears as if it were conjured away.

§. 86.
Such a fish so constituted that it does not tolerate any noise, is called *Saiwo-qwuolle*, and the lakes in which such fish are found are called *Saiwo*. The fish found in such magic lakes are very big and fat. There can be both whitefish (Coregonus lavaretus), perch (Perca fluviatilis), burbot (Gadus), salmon trout/brown trout (Salmo trutta Linnæus) et al.

When one drags a seine or fishes in such lakes, one must proceed carefully. No noise must be heard, not a single word may be uttered by anyone during the entire dragging; everything should happen here through signs and waves. You see, one has made the observation of real experience that proves that the fish in these waters do not tolerate any chat, wherefore I tried to explain above the natural cause; for at the slightest sound it likely goes down to its familiar secret hole at the bottom and thus disappears out of the seine.

That such are the actual conditions, I will confirm with an example. It happened not too long ago that 2 settlers here in Karesuando went to some mountain lakes to fish with a seine. One of them was old and believed in the strange ability of the subterraneans to enchant the fish away in *Saiwo*; the other one was young and did not believe anything, but only made fun of this pagan superstition. The natural reason for the fishes' silence in this *Saiwo* lake of course neither of them could comprehend.

§. 87.
Now it happened thus that the catch for these 2 fellows was quite meager in the profane waters that were not *Saiwo*. The old one said he was familiar with a little lake, where fish absolutely would be found, but uttered too that it wasn't worth the trouble of going there, since his companion couldn't keep quiet. Oh! The other said if it depended on that, he would keep quiet, he wouldn't make a sound. But the old man demanded absolute silence, and when the other one promised, then they were off to *Saiwo*. The seine was thrown out; they began to drag; they saw as soon as they got to the arms of the seine that the fish were inside, but when the wedge had gotten somewhat closer, the other one forgot his pledge of silence deliberately, and uttered an unconcerned word. Presto! The fish disappeared from the seine, and when the wedge came ashore, there wasn't a single tail.

"I don't understand that," said the old man indignant, and wanted to leave right away. But the other one who still more wanted to see whether the old folk's belief could have any reason, persuaded the old man to cast the seine out from the same haul on shore, and promised silence. Now he kept his promise until their Finn seine neared, but then let slip a word, because he thought it was impossible for the fish who could be seen inside to slip out. But the old one was right. The wedge came ashore empty.

Now the old one said that it was absolutely no longer worth the trouble of dragging with someone like that, who couldn't hold his babbling; but let himself with great reluctance be convinced to throw out the seine a 3rd time. Now not a single word was uttered before the wedge was wholly on land. It was full of large and fat whitefish, and from that time the unbelieving seine companion even had to be convinced that the fish in *Saiwo's* lake did not tolerate chat.

§. 88.
Several similar examples could be cited, but I consider them superfluous, since it is a commonly known fact, at least in Nordland and Lappland, that 1st there are certain lakes in which fish cannot be caught if some noise or sound is given rise to during dragging of the seine; 2nd that the water in such lakes is colder and fresher during the summer than the water in other nearby lakes; for which reason too the farmers in Alkula for example (belonging to Upper Torneå) fill their drinking bottles with fresh water from a brook that flows from such a *Saiwo-vesi* (magic lake). From this it follows, 3rd that the temperature in such lakes originates from the springs welling up from the bottom; 4th the water in such lakes is both clearer and heavier than the water in other lakes; 5th this is the natural cause of the fishes' shyness, because sound propagates more easily through a denser medium; 6th that the whitefish, shy by nature, can disappear from the dragged seine with a single word uttered by the fisherman has its natural cause.

But for the simple-minded Lapp this phenomenon was sufficient to put both the water and the fish under the influence of the invisible beings that lived in *Saiwo*. That the water too in such lakes was viewed as sacred the following shows:

§. 89.
"*Saiwo-tjatse* was a sacred lake that ran from *Saiwo*." Jessen, ibid. p. 29. "The women drank of Saiwo's water." Ibid. p. 44. "At the beginning, when the *noaidi* is going to accept *Saiwo olmah* in his service, he is strengthened with *Saiwo-tjatse* 'mountain water' (more correctly magic water) and later, when he is going to get into a feud with other *noaidis*, he gets a strength drink now and then from *Saiwo-tjatse*." Anonymous in Leem. "Mountain women initiated and strengthened the *noaidis* with *Saiwo tjatse*, when they were going into battle with each other and testing their strength." Sidenius in Ganander.

Even now one readily drinks water from *Saiwo* during the summer, since it is so clear, cool and good tasting. Where this *Saiwo tjatse* was gotten from, the above-mentioned authors do not say; but it seems likely it was gotten from lakes of such a nature as we described above.

§. 90.
As far as I could learn, most of the Lapps on the Swedish side have imagined the

residents in *Saiwo* as kinds of sprites, although not quite in the sense the Swedes take this word. Thus several lakes have been named after *Saiwo*, but I know few mountains that bear that name. This also seems confirmed by Högström who says about *Saiwo*:

"As mountain Lapps, and those that have reindeer, sacrifice antlers and bones, and even rub reindeer blood on their gods, so too fishing Lapps have their sacred stones, for advice and guardians by their lakes, that they call *Saiwo*, which gods they, apart from other sacrifices, often rub with fish grease, which according to their belief will cause "greased" lakes to usually have a fatter group of fish than out in others. The earlier they grease their stones, the more and fatter fish they think they get." Högström p. 193.

§. 91.
"*Saiwo-Sarwah* used to fight with other *noaidis' Saiwo-Sarwah*, and the outcome of this struggle (between 2 reindeer bulls from *Saiwo*) also decided the owner's fate." Jessen p. 26.

"The *noaidis* also have their *Sarvah*, which they acquired in the same way as *Saiwo-olmah*. These *Saiwo Sarwah*, are goaded together by the owners to fight, and this kind of duel between *Saiwo Sarwah*, is crucial for their owners. If the one's *Saiwo Sarwa* gores the antler of the other, then it is also the *noaidi*, who possessed the same one, who is the loser." Anonymous in Leem.

"*Saiwo Serwa*, a mountain reindeer the Lapps set against other *noaidis' Saiwa-Serwa*, which relentlessly gore one another. The Lapp who owns the reindeer that loses its antlers or head (in the struggle) becomes ill and in time dies." Sidenius in Ganander.

But none of these authors has explained whether the supposed reindeer bull was one of the subterranean reindeer, and acquired by the *noaidi*, or whether it was from the *noaidi's* own stock, and just branded in *Saiwo's* name. We should prefer to suppose it was the *noaidis'* natural reindeer that were gored, and that they were just sanctified to *Saiwo*, although they in the *noaidi's* imagination could be seen as descending from *Saiwo*, in the same way as the birds and the fish.

§. 92.
When we compare everything that so far has been related about *Saiwo*, it seems the main thing is the following: the Lapp *noaidi* pictured a kind of people that lived in *Saiwo*, i.e. in a world not everyone could see from the mountains or sea, or in a word, beneath the earth's surface (Ganander has surely not understood the matter correctly, when he places *Saiwo* among the sky's deities.) This subterranean people was in all respects happier than the Lapps above the earth, but they (*Saiwo's* men) nevertheless had the same kind of business as the people on earth. There in *Saiwo* there were reindeer, dogs, birds, fish, insects, snakes. In a word: all of living nature was represented in *Saiwo*; and just as no fish were as fat and delicate as *Saiwo-*

qwuolle, so too were all the other animals' characteristics in proportion to that, each according to its nature. The *noaidi* alone knew the art of catching *Saiwo-qwuolle*, and he alone could become the owner of *Saiwo-Sarwah*, and command the other subterranean animals.

§. 93.
As an appendix to the now investigated history of *Saiwo*, it cannot hurt to cite a few samples of the sort of subterranean beings that are still alive in the people's imagination.

In Luleå Lappmark and part of Piteå Lappmark there is still a sort of subterranean being that in Lapp is called *Kadnihah*, corresponding to the well-known *Saiwo-neidah* on the Norwegian side, i.e. *Saiwo's* maidens. What *Kadniha* actually means, I do not know; just as little can *Saiwo* be said to have some other meaning than the one that follows from the description of *Saiwo*; for both words are stems in the language, without further derivations. Presumably every object must have its name, and this may have come by chance.

Kadnihah are, as said, a sort of subterranean people, who sometimes appear before people in red clothing, with long hair, that reaches down to the waist, and resembles green flax. They too have reindeer, dogs, et al.; the language, song and clothing are Lapp. People have even learned their song which is called *Kadniha-vuolle*. Let us now hear on what this belief is based.

§. 94.
A youth in Luleå Lappmark reports having seen *Kadnihah* by the lake *Parkijaur*, and it happened thus, that walking up a mountain he felt himself quickly become faint, whereby he fell into a trance, and during this, heard a very beautiful melancholic Lapp song; immediately thereafter, he saw 2 *Cadniha neidah*, i.e. subterranean maidens, remarkably beautiful, and dressed in the above-mentioned red outfits. But the maidens disappeared after a few minutes into a gorge, and the song fell silent. The entire splendor was past; with delight he saw them; with indescribable regret they disappeared before his eyes, and yet several years ago he recounted the event with visible emotion. Such an indescribably beautiful impression the subterranean maidens had made on his mind. Say, was this a dream, or an ideal of feminine beauty that the imagination created before his soul? – I know the youth very well. He is now a middle-aged man, but then was a hired hand with a settler.

§. 95.
Another example: 70 or 80 years ago it happened that a Lapp village consisting of 7 Lapp tents had camped north of Tjåmotis, a new settlement, part of Quickjock parish from Luleå Lappmark. It was that time of year when district court and fair were held in Jockmock. Since all the older people had made their way to the fair, the

youth left behind let themselves go with games and races on a little lake which lay close to the Lapps' pitched tents. A single older Lapp woman who was nearby, and who was aware that the inhabitants on the mountain opposite did not tolerate such a racket, warned the youth, but in vain. Now it became evening, and everyone retired; but scarcely had it become quiet in the Lapps' tents before *Kadnihah* began to make an uproar. Rattling of bells, human voices, barking of dogs, noise of reindeer herds starting to move, was heard. It absolutely resembled a large migrating procession of Lapps with their reindeer herds. The Lapps' own dogs rushed out of the tents, and began to howl, roar and bark. Fright and terror occupied everyone's mind. The previously mentioned older Lapp woman got up from her bed, and looked out the tent door. There she was able to see the subterranean horde in the moonlight, raising dust straight toward the Lapps' tents. There was no time to lose now. She wrapped herself immediately into an awkward sheepskin rug, then went to meet the subterranean horde and began to come to terms. She promised penance and improvement on behalf of the noisy youth. With great pains she prevailed upon *Kadnihah* to turn back, and thus averted the danger of being trampled. But it became silent from that day, and the youth kept quiet. Nothing further was heard. – The account of this misadventure is common in the entire district, and the Lapp woman who came to terms with *Kadnihah*, I saw as a child in Quickjock. It was the mother-in-law of Erik Ersson Alstadius in Njawe.

§. 96.
In the Torneå River area the Finns' subterranean beings are called *Maahiset* (plural), *Maahinen* (singular). NB: *Para* which Andreas Faye in his *Norrske Sagn* (*Norwegian Legends*) regards as the Finns' subterranean beings, is an entirely different object). *Maahinen* comes from *Maa* 'earth,' and means terrestrial, or being in the earth. This object is completely different from *Maanalainen*, about which more still to come. *Maahinen* appears to the Finns in the same attire as *Cadnihah* for the Lapps, with the difference that the Finns' *Maahiset* has cattle and Finnish clothing. An example belonging here is told in the following way:

A settler in Kuttainen By from the Karesuando parish in Torneå Lappmark, made his way some 30 or 40 years ago to a fishing marsh by the name of Paitasjärwi to drag a seine as usual. During his stay at this marsh he went to the woods to cut a few poles on which he planned to hang up fish to dry. But just as he was busy with this task, 2 red-clad girls appeared who came quite close to him, and bade him follow them home. He asked who they were, and where they had their home. They said they lived quite close. As they repeated their request that he follow them home, the old man answered: "No, wait a bit, I don't have time yet, I first have to trim my poles." Thereupon, the 2 girls disappeared, and only then did the old man notice that they were not natural young girls. This old man who one usually called Jatko Ejä died a couple years ago; but I knew him very well. He was a slow and gentle man in his entire being.

§. 97.
Another incident belonging to the same topic was reported to me by credible persons, though I was not in a position to consult with the witnesses themselves.

It happened about 10 years ago that a Lapp family which as usual moved out onto a mountain headland jutting out into the Norwegian sea, lost an 8-year-old child. The child had gone out of the tent and disappeared very suddenly without being able to be found again, although the parents had taken great pains to find the child. The parents had finally given up all hope of getting to see their child again, either alive or dead.

But after a week had passed, some herders had found the child on the other side of the fjord. It was already frightened by people, and the herders had trouble getting hold of it, since it ran like a hare between the bushes. They even had trouble inducing it into taking some food after it was taken back to the farmhouse; but since it had been somewhat restored, it had said it had been in very good company with such fine-looking and beautiful people, that it had been very well kept, and seen many strange things, etc. But how it got to the other side of the fjord it didn't know.

§. 98.
We probably cannot doubt this information entirely, since it is borne out by several eye witnesses, namely that the child disappeared on one side and was found on the other side of the fjord; but how the child could get across the fjord without human help, that seems more extraordinary. The one who knows the circumstances in these fjords must consider it a physical impossibility that an 8-year-old child could escape with its life over all the torrents and precipices lying in the way. The only thing would be if some large eagle could lift the child over the fjord, because this king of the birds has enough strength to carry a considerable weight. Maybe the child just got dizzy from the high speed through the air, and so became bewildered. The eagle however could have let go of his prey very nicely on the other side of the fjord when it became aware of people. That a Lapp child can live for a week on berries, common sorrel and the like I do not consider impossible. This explanation of the story is nevertheless just a guess. The general belief among the common people is that the child was spirited away, and thus found on the other side of the fjord.

§. 99.
Yet another story to illustrate the common people's belief in subterranean beings.

Schoolmaster Emanuel Kohlström, missionary in the imperial Russian section of Enontekiö Lappmark has given the following report. In Jerisjärwi, a large and good fishing lake within Muonioniska parish there is a holm on which fishermen usually dry their nets. Close by this holm lies another little holm, which in a historical and physiological respect is not without strangeness. One fine day Schoolmaster Kohlström together with some other fishermen from the Finnish nation went ashore on the larger holm to dry their nets, and get some rest in a fishing shack erected there. While he and the other fishermen lay in the shack, they all heard instantly the rattling of reindeer bells which they thought came from the little holm; but as they knew there were no reindeer in the entire district at this time of year, they all went out to see what it could be; but they saw nothing, nor heard the rattling any more. One of the fishermen noticed then that it had not at all been natural bells they had heard, because the little holm had already been haunted for some time. (NB: *oknytt* is said in Västerbotten about such little ghosts that are heard. *Oknytt* means that something strange has been heard or seen, i.e. it is haunted.).

It had accordingly been subterranean reindeer bells.

§. 100.
But at the time when Kohlström and his companions heard the reported reindeer bells, one didn't know what there actually was on the little holm. They discovered later on that there was an old burial place about which the tales had nothing to say. The incident was such that one was forced to bury a corpse on this holm, which in this sparsely populated district is very common when someone dies during harmful conditions. When they began to dig on the little holm to bury the corpse, they found a large quantity of bones in a properly built grave. When neither the tales nor old deeds provided any guidance about it, that here there was supposed to be a burial place, it is likely to have come before the introduction of Christianity. What connection the reindeer bells that were heard might have with the burial place, we will try to explain later on.

§. 101.
In the account of the reindeer bells I can still add a few anecdotes which have reference to the subterranean beings. Old county Sheriff Granström in Jockmock, Luleå Lappmark often recounts having been misled by that sort of rattling when he was going to look for his cows. He said he heard the bells very close, but when he went there, there was nothing.

That the subterranean creatures can have cows, and that one can also become an owner of them is a fairly common legend in Nordland. In Tåsjö (uppermost parish of Ångermanland) people said they had stock of *Vitterkorna* 'the vitter cows.' Such infernal livestock one can acquire if one throws steel over them. But one cannot milk a *Vitter* cow more than 2 staves in measure [on the bucket]; otherwise it will be spoiled. The so-called whitlow (Panaritium 'acute inflammation of a digit'), or as the common folk in Norrland say "meet with evil" believed to be an effect of *Vittra* (as the subterranean folk in Ångermanland are called). I have talked with several farmers in Ångermanland about *Vittra*, and thereby found them firmly convinced not only that *Vittra* existed, but that it could even harm people, if you got in its way. That horses and cows stumble or otherwise pine away, is also believed to be caused by *Vittra*; some call it *Trollskott* (magic shots).

§. 102.

In Westerbotten [Västerbotten] the subterranean people are called *Underboni[n]ga* [forest sprite living underground], about which in my youth I heard countless stories, how people had become enchanted, etc. But I am not entirely certain whether *Trollkäringa* [female troll, witch] is the same creature as *Underboninga*; at least there seems to be a little difference between them, since *Trollkäringa* is always pictured as an angry and malformed creature in human shape; she is depicted as a real Fury. But the *Underboniga* does no harm to people, as long as she is not molested, which can also be seen in the following story.

An old peasant woman in Luleå parish (if I remember correctly, the incident occurred in Sunderbyn) was called during the night one time by an unknown man to assist his wife in childbirth. The old woman followed the man, and when they had come a little way from the farm, they went down some steps, and before long they were standing in an underground house where a woman lay going through the agonies of labor. The childbirth proceeded properly with the terrestrial woman's assistance. A while later the old woman headed home with gifts the subterranean man laid in her apron. Furthermore, he requested that the old woman move her cow barn since it stood directly above the subterranean people's abode and caused them a great deal of harm, etc. Finally, he accompanied the old woman home and disappeared. She tossed what she had in her apron into the stove because she thought it was coal. But in the morning when the old woman's husband got up to make a fire, he became not a little astonished to find a whole pile of silver coins in the stove, and asked the old woman whether she hadn't been out stealing during the night. But she now related the circumstances, and the cow barn was moved. This incident is supposed to have happened a rather long time ago.

§. 103.

I've heard several similar stories about *underboninga*, but I just haven't remembered all of them. The main thing in all of these stories is that *underboninga* cannot stand the sign of the cross (thus they cannot tie the swaddling clothes in a cross over the subterranean child). The subterranean people have a sort of ointment which makes them invisible, but if put on mortals' eyes, makes them clear-sighted, so they are able to see the subterranean people. If one is called as a midwife (which happens not so seldom), one probably ought to help the needy, but accept no food, because then one has trouble getting back up again. If someone becomes enchanted, one must be careful not to accept anything offered. The subterranean people in that case have to release the enchanted person within three days. Where the subterranean people originate I have not investigated. Nevertheless, I seem to have heard that they were created by our Lord. According to Faye's *Norrske Sagn* [*Norwegian Legends*], it is believed in a number of places in Norway that the subterranean people are fallen angels. Others believe they are descended from Adam. "Eve was busy bathing her children one fine day. Suddenly she was called upon by our Lord. Now she hurried to hide away those children that were not yet washed. Our Lord asked whether she had all her children. She answered yes. Then our Lord is supposed to have said: *what you have hidden from God shall also be hidden from mankind*. The children hidden away became the subterranean people." Faye, ibid. The story is of good enough quality, and shows how resourceful the common people are at feigning.

§. 104.
I've also heard another story about *Trollkäringa* (the female troll), which is competent enough in its way, and seems to prove that this being is different from *underboninga* in the people's conception. An old soldier in Skellefteå parish had one time gotten lost on a squirrel hunt, and couldn't find his way home. He finally came to an old cabin in a mountain pasture, and camped there for the night. He made a fire, and began to boil some of the day's catch in a kettle he had with him. Now the *Trollkäring* steps into the cabin, and asks the soldier: "What's your name?" "My name is Self," the soldier answered. But at that very moment he took a ladle full of hot broth, and smeared the ladle right in the middle of the crone's maw; now she began to shriek and wail quite wretchedly: "Self burned me, Self burned me." "If you yourself burned, you yourself will hurt," answered a voice from the nearest mountain. It was the female troll's companions. Through this ruse the soldier had indeed frustrated the trolls and diverted their revenge from himself, but the female troll nevertheless said as she left: "Self sensed me, and Self burned me, and Self shall sleep to a year," (i.e. until next year).

The soldier lay down to sleep after finishing supper. But in the morning when he awoke, and began to dig in his food bag, he found it completely full of mold, but could still not understand how that had come about, until he found his way to people. Only then did he know that he had been gone an entire year.

§. 105.
If I were to remember all the stories I heard as a child about *underboni[n]ga* (forest sprites living underground), *Vittra* (sirens) and *Trollkäringa* (witches), several books could likely be filled by such true stories; but the samples I've now cited should be sufficient to demonstrate the identity between the Lapps' *saiwo-olmah, saiwo-neidah, kadnihah*; the Finns' *maahiset*; Västerbotten's *underboninga, trollkäringa* as well as the Ångermanlender's *vittra*. The transformation of humans into animals, birds or fish is often spoken about in Norrland, and that this metamorphosis is not entirely unfamiliar in Lappland the following story shows.

A man had once caught a salmon in such a magic lake as described above. The salmon lay still a while in the boat, but all at once he heard a voice from the nearest mountain: "Carin, what are you doing there?" And presto the salmon jumped into the lake. It was thus an enchanted woman bewitched into a salmon. Running wolf was nothing unusual in the Lapps' mythology. It wasn't the least trick one *noaidi* could do to another, to let him run wolf, i.e. the entire man was transformed into a wolf, and such people in wolf form were viewed as seven times worse than other wolves. This belief has still not been entirely wiped out among the Lapps. Even in 1823 I heard the Lapps in Arjeplog speak about a *Piellokis*, i.e. a bell wolf or a wolf with a bell around its neck. It was, in their way of thinking, no ordinary wolf, but a bewitched human in wolf guise. Everyone feared it, worse than death.

A Lapp had told Högström that he had killed and skinned a wolf that had a belt knife and tobacco pouch under its skin. It was thus a bewitched Lapp who had run wolf. Not too long ago a Lapp here in Enontekiö was on the way to becoming a wolf. He had run naked from Enontekiö to Maunu 5 kilometers in the middle of the coldest winter; and upon his arrival in Maunu he jumped in bed between a couple. "If I hadn't slipped between you," he said, "I would have soon become a wolf. If it wasn't that true, then it was funny at the time!

§. 106.
Another well-known mythological object in Norrrland and Lappland is *Bytingen* or *Bortbytingen* 'the changeling,' which can be placed here most conveniently, since it is thought to be connected with the subterranean beings. *Byting* is called in Lapp *Målsotis* [North Sámi *dear'ri*], which means changeling. One imagines that the underground people swap human children from above ground with themselves. But since the underground people can't tolerate the sign of the cross or its name, the danger of swapping is greatest before baptism. To forestall such an exchange some people usually lay an ABC book under the child's head; others put steel there. Yet, it seems the belief in *Målsotis* is not very ancient among the Lapps, nor is it so common. Very likely the Lapps' concept of swapping is borrowed from neighboring nations. But among the Swedes the belief in this subject seems to be very old.

The cause of this belief seems to be that more delicate children subject to drafts or laid on the cold ground, got cramps, whereby the facial muscles became deformed. One then imagined that the underground people swapped the right child, and put their own malformed child in its place. Such an incident is supposed to have occurred not too long ago in Arjeplog, where a careless nursemaid had put a child down on the ground, while she herself picked berries. When she came back, the child was already changed. A changeling cries almost constantly, appears quite anxious and doesn't live long.

§. 107.
The widely known *Maran* "nightmare" (in popular belief: a being – usually female – who is thought to torment sleeping people – to sit down on their chest – "to ride them") is not entirely unfamiliar in Lappland either. It is called in Lapp *täddalmis*, i.e. the oppressor; and the one who is "ridden" is said to be *täddatallat*, i.e. oppressed. In Finnish *Maran* is called *Painiainen* [*painajainen*], i.e. nightmare. The

Sámi camp

Lapps naturally imagine that it is a result of wicked witches, who either in their own shape, or in the guise of other things, accost people who are asleep. Some people swear it happens when awake. They say they obviously see and feel the repugnant hag, how she comes in through the door, and sits astraddle one. If one can move a finger, or get out a word, then one is immediately rid of her.

But it is not just people who are harassed by *Maran*, even horses are vulnerable to her. Once a man whose horse was often "nightmare ridden" decided to ambush the witch. She came right into the stall, and the man who was lying in ambush gave her a blow of the axe. The *Maran* made off, and the following day it was learned that a neighbor woman had gotten a nasty wound. So the story goes. The doctor says that *Maran* is nothing other than pressure on the brain.

§. 108.
Another monster that has not entirely disappeared from the people's imagination is the so-called *Baran*, which is also called *Bjäran* or *Bäran* [the bearer]. In Finnish it is called *Para*, sometimes *Voi kattu*, i.e. "butter cat." Among the Lapps this monster is not unfamiliar. Yet, the idea seems to be borrowed from the Swedes. *Baran* was made of rags (to Zetterstedt people mentioned 9 kinds of wood). The old woman who makes this monstrosity, becomes engaged to the Devil, during which she pricks her left little finger and lets a few drops of blood drip onto her bundle, with the words "May the Devil give you life." And so the monstrosity is ready. Now the old woman is also supposed to say what *Baran* should bear [bring], e.g. butter, milk, etc.

Once upon a time it happened an old woman was busy with this task, and had meanwhile asked a farm-hand, who was with her, to go out of the room so as not to witness what was going on. But the hand had understood the ruse, and therefore climbed up into an attic that was above the old woman's room, so as to lie in wait and find out what was going on down there. When *Baran* was ready and had already gotten life, it asked what it should bring. Then the farm-hand who heard the question answered: "Shit." *Baran* then hauled home so much of this sort that the old woman nearly must have drowned in excrement. *Baran* leaves some refuse behind that resembles beastings, and in Norrland it is called *Bärar dynga* 'bearer dung,' but farther south is called troll butter. If one burns *Bärar dyngan* in 9 types of wood, then the old woman has to come forth no matter how far away she is.

Troll butter is otherwise a kind of mushroom (Æthalium flavum 'Fuligo septica' or Mucor unctuosus Lin.) that grows very rapidly on the musty floor of a cow-barn, rotting tree stumps, and other places. Country folks who cannot understand the reason for the mushroom's rapid growth, have taken the occasion to imagine that same thing as the excrement of some troll creature. On the other hand, envy has been thought of – that blessing in the barn, which through sensible management exists in one but is missing in the other neighboring woman – as the result of secret troll tricks. But the actual structure of *Baran* seems to be as old as the papacy. The name is likely taken from the Swedish word *bära* (*portare* 'carry'; *transferre* 'transfer), because *Baran* was thought to bring butter, milk and other blessings from the neighbors. Finnish *Para* was probably borrowed from Swedish *Baran*. Although the Lapps have the concept *Vuoja kattu*; all the same, it does not seem originally to be familiar to them. In Schefferus there is an illustration of *Baran*. It consists of a bundle of rags the size of a fist. Some even give the bundle a tail.

§. 109.
The Swedes' so-called *Sjö Rå* (water-nymph/naiad), *Skogs Rå* (forest nymph/dryad), *Tomte Gubbar* (gnome/brownie) and more such, actually have nothing really corresponding in Lapp mythology, to the extent these things are not exactly synonyms of *Underboninga* (underground forest sprite), *Vittra* (sirens) or *Trollkäringa* (witches). If I have understood the country folk of Norrland correctly, they distinguish between *Skogs Rå* and *Vittra*. Namely, one ascribes *Skogs Rå* greater power and authority in a more far-flung area, etc. The Swedes' *Sjö Rå* seems to be exactly the same entity as the Norwegians' *Drau[g]en* 'headless man destined to die soon,' and the way I have understood the matter, then *Necken* 'evil spirit of the water' too is a sort of *Sjö Rå*, i.e. a far more powerful being than *Underboninga* and *Vittra*. Corresponding to *Skogs Rå* and *Sjö Rå* are probably the Finns' *Maanhaldia*, *Vedenhaltia*, even the Lapps' *Ädnam-halde*, which word, although borrowed from Finnish, still occurs in the northern part of Arjeplog. The Finns' *Tonta*, which word the Lapps imitate too, presumably comes from Swedish *Tomt*, *Tomte Gubbe*, a creature believed to live in old building sites. The Finns on Torneå River make *Tonta* nearly synonymous with the Devil, and almost the same idea the Lapps seem to hold about this entity. That both the Finns' and Lapps' *Tonta* is borrowed from the Swedes' *Tomte* seems to be more than probable. The description Zetterstedt has of *Tomten* is not genuine, but sooner borrowed and somewhat reshaped from the Lapps' *Pädnak njunne*, which even has an eye in its forehead.

§. 110.
That part of Lapp mythology that treats the souls' immortality and a life after this one, constitutes an important item in common folklore. It will show us that the old Lapps not only believed in the soul's immortality but also the dead's resurrection, or the body's renewal after death. – The Norwegian authors have the following about this:

"The Lapps recognized 2 states after death. The one or happy state was called *Saiwo-aimo*, *Jabma-aimo*, or *Sarakka aimo*; the other was called *Mubben aimo*, *Rut-aimo*, *Fudnos-aimo* and *Tjappes aimo*." Jessen, p. 29. "A 3rd place too was called *Radien aimo*." Jessen, p. 30.

"The Lapps believed they went to *Saiwo* after death, and enjoyed great happiness, the more they honored them in life with yoiking (song) and drumming." Jessen, p. 28.

"At a certain distance below the earth is the kingdom of the dead, *Jabma aimo*. There rules death's mother *Jabma akko*; there they will get a new body in place of the decayed one above ground. They will also have the same power and esteem they had in life on earth. But those who are deep down in the earth or closer to the abyss, reside in *Rota-aimo*. They will never get away from there to *Radien* or *Allfadren* [All-Father] in the firmament as will the other dead." Anonymous in Leem.

"*Jabmi aimo*, the Lapps' Valhalla or Gripnir's halls, the Finns' *Tuonela* and *Maanala* or death's abode were some distance down in the earth. When someone dies, the Lapps say that the soul has gone to *Jabma aimo*. They also think that the soul has gone to *Jabma aimo*, when one has become ill, which is why they conclude that the body wants to follow along and die. All the dead in *Jabma aimo* are equally mighty as they were here on earth, and they get a new body in place of the one that has decomposed here on earth." Ganander according to Sidenius.

§. 111.
Aimo actually means state, "state of time and place, on this side, and thereafter, weather, distance, state, life, etc." Cf. Lindahl and Öhrling, *Lexicon*.

Saiwo aimo should thus mean "*Saiwo's* or the underground beings' world"; *Jabma aimo* "the world of the dead, i.e. Hades." *Sarakka aimo* "*Sarakka's* world"; *Mubben aimo* "the other world"; *Fudnos aimo* "the Devil's world"; *Tjappes aimo* "the black one, i.e. the dark world," etc.

The other world is also called *Tuonan ilme*, from Finnish *Tuonela*, or perhaps Finnish *Tuonela* comes from Lapp *Tuonan ilme*.[20] According to my way of thinking, the Lapp word *Tuonan ilme*, a compound of demonstrative pronoun *Tuoi*, genitive *Tuon* "evil" and *Ilme* (Fin. *Ilma*) "air, climate, world, etc." from which *taan ilmen* "in this world," *tuon ilmen* "in the other world", *kåbban ilmen* "in which world?" *Tuonan ilme* is thus a paragogic form from *Tuoi ilme* "the other world." Finnish *Tuonela* could also have come from the locution: *Hän meni tuonne alla* "he went down there, i.e. under the earth," which through rapid pronunciation became *Tuonela*, and through habit finally became a permanent word, i.e. a substantive. That *Tuonela* arose in this way seems much more probable, since the Finnish word *maanala* is obviously a compound of *maan* and *alla* "under the earth" which also via rapid pronunciation became one *Maanala* "the kingdom of the dead" etc.

§. 112.
What concept the old Lapps made for themselves for the world edifice can no longer be ascertained entirely since the pastors gave them a vague notion of the Copernican system. However, the idea, as it were, seemed to take root in their notion that not only Scandinavia, which they now inhabited, is an island (which Seveåsen calls *Suolo-kårå* "the island's hill" or *Suolo-tjelke* "the island's back," but the entire earth

---

[20] From this point in the text to the end of *Gudalära* comprises the last part of *Fragmenter* discovered in 2001.

is even thought by them to be an Island, that lies and floats on an immense ocean. Their idea of the Flood is also based on this, about which a rather interesting, and, as it seems, a real Lapp story, is recorded in Högström, p. 57. This story runs as follows: "While I asked them if they knew how their ancestors came to live in this country, and whether any people lived there before they arrived, they answered they did not know before, but they were of the opinion that there as well as in other places people had lived, before God overturned [*stjelpte om*] the world. I asked how that came about? They replied: There was in days of yore a time when God turned [*hvälfde om*] the earth upside down so that the water from the marshes and the rivers climbed up onto the land, and drowned all the people, except 2 siblings, a boy and a girl. God took them under his arm to a high mountain called *Passe vare* "the holy mountain," which since the danger was past, and God had let them go, they separated from each other and went each their own way with the idea of finding out whether there were other people in the world than they. After they had thus wandered around 3 years, they came back together, and recognized each other again. Hence, they separated again, and went another 3 years, until they met and recognized each other again. But when they met a 3rd time after another 3 years, they could no longer recognize one another. Therefore, they agreed to accompany each other, and produced children, from which later on all humans who now live on earth have come."

So far Högström.

§. 113.

This story is strange not only because it agrees with all nations' stories about a universal flood, but chiefly because it shows us the Lapps' notion of the world edifice. The very word *omstjelpa* "overturn"/*omhvälfva* "turn upside down" is in Lapp *kåmetil* [North Sámi *gomihit*?], and cannot be said of spherical objects; it is said of plates, concave or horizontal things. From this as well as from other stories it seems the Lapps visualized the earth's surface as flat. They imagined the entire earth as surrounded and resting on water. Nearest beneath the earth's surface lived the underground *Saiwo-olmah*, *Saiwo-neidah*, etc. who were neither *Alma-ulmuh*, evident, i.e. visible people (the real people were called *Alma-ulmuh*) nor human spirits (*Jamikahah*, Fin. *maanalaiset*), but something between body and spirit. Farther down beneath the earth's surface was *Jabma aimo* (the kingdom of the dead). There death's mother *Jabma-akko* reigned; still farther down beneath the earth's surface one came across *Tjappes aimo* or *Ruott-aimo*, about which v. Vesten says in his letter the following: "They did not believe in resurrection of the dead, but awaited a body in *Mubben aimo* (the other world), and from there expected to go to the world of eternity. Their spirit and that of the animal would travel from the body to *Radien*, *Ratskin*, but the bodies they had now were readied by *Madder akka*, and therefore since they died they (the bodies) would always remain in the earth. They believed no one was damned or came to *Ruott-aimo*, (in the original it stands incorrectly:

Roth amme), except those who have stolen and been malicious. But the greatest *noaidis* (shamans) lived best in *Mubben aimo* (in the original it stands incorrectly: *Mublen aimo*), and *Ibmel aimo* (incorrect in the original: *Ibel-aimo*)." v. Vesten, ibid.

§. 114.

From v. Vesten's, Sidenius' and Anonymous' concurring information it seems that *Saiwo* was not the same as *Jabma-aimo*, which even now, as far as I have professed, are distinctly separate in the people's conception. Thus, Jessen has either himself, or because of differences in the manuscripts, made a mistake when he mixes up *Saiwo* and *Jabma aimo*. Probably no one could get to *Saiwo* except for someone who was enchanted and thus disappeared from the land of the living; but everyone had to come to *Jabma aimo* after death. Very likely even those, who were condemned for eternity, had to pass by *Jabma aimo*, inasmuch as those who later on were moved to *Sarakka aimo*, or *Radien* in the starry sky had to stay a while in *Mubben aimo*, or *Jabma aimo*, to get new bodies. Otherwise, it seems that the *noaidis* in different Lappmarks were not very much in agreement in regard to the humans' state after death. From that it also seems the authors' different statements originate. Asking today's Lapps which of the authors' information is correct is not possible. Anonymous in Leem is brief and precise, displays excellent consistency in the flow of ideas, and I should think therefore that his information is most in accordance with the popular belief at that time; however, Sidenius and v. Vesten nearly agree with him.

The main content of the Lapps' conception of human beings' situation after death is then that there were 2 *aimoh*, i.e. worlds or spaces beneath the earth where the dead souls could go; namely, first: *Jabma-aimo*, which is also called *Mubben aimo* and *Tuonan-ilme*. There the dead would get a new body, (accordingly, not the same as they had in life on earth); and from there those who lived virtuously on earth, moved to *Radien* (according to Anonymous), or to *Ibmel-aimo* (according to v. Vesten) in the starry sky, and there enjoyed eternal bliss. But those who behaved badly here in the world, would sink deeper down to *Ruott-aimo*, and be tormented there for all eternity.

§. 115.

In this theory about man's state after death, as far as I am concerned, I find nothing unreasonable or offensive about the idea, nothing incompatible with other nations' common ideas on the same subject. We find again in *Jabma-aimo* the Hebrews' Sheol, the Greeks' Hades, the Romans' Orcus or Inferno; we see in *Ruott-aimo* the Jews' Gehenna, the Greeks' Pyriflegeton [tributary of Styx] and the Romans' Tartarus [abyss used as dungeon of torment]; we find in the Lapps' doctrine of resurrection an important article of Christian faith affirmed, though presented in another way. That this article in Lapp mythology is genuine, we could hardly doubt, when so many other circumstances testify that the Lapps had the same belief about dumb animals: their bodies too would be renewed in another world. In this article, the

Lapps stand far above Greeks and Romans for whom resurrection of the dead was inconceivable. And if one may assume the theory about moving to the starry sky as genuine (to the extent this idea is not borrowed from Catholicism), then we also find there one of Christian faith's most important articles affirmed, or mirrored. This last article I do not quite dare rely on, since the idea seems to be too exalted to be entirely genuine; although an exalted idea can nevertheless arise in the mind of the uneducated, as in that of the very wise. But the authenticity of the other articles one has no reason to doubt.

Since the doctrine of man's state after death is the most important item in every nation's mythology, then it does not seem to be out of the way to investigate and explain in greater detail the old Lapps' ideas about that, especially as some of their ancient ideas still cling to them. That mankind's conduct after death was an ancient folk belief among them, I do not doubt; but that the views were somewhat different in what concerns the actual nature of this life, is not surprising, when the actual revealed religion rather little satisfies human curiosity in what concerns mankind's state after death.

§. 116.
It is a common belief among Lapps and settlers that murdered children are around a long time in forest and field in order to discover their murderers. (Zetterstedt was told 7 years was given for the ghost's transmigration). Such a weeping spirit is called in Lapp *Äppar*, in Finnish *Äpärä*, in Swedish *Utböling* (outsider) or *Skratt* (laughter), because one alleges that the child sometimes cries, sometimes screams and sometimes laughs. It's correct name in Swedish should be *Gast* (ghost). When one hears a ghost scream, one ought to give it a name, because superstition alleges that it has no peace, until it gets such. The ghost can even discover its murderer if one gets into a conversation with it, etc.

Owing to this common folk belief, occurred an incident, both comical and unpleasant, in Piteå parish, in 1823 if I remember correctly. At the least, I heard it when it was told as recently happened. A Lapp girl had murdered her child and kept it secret, but it was discovered. The tongue of the dead fetus had been cut off. This the murderer had done with the aim of forestalling its crying after death. So superstition was stronger in her, than religion, kinship and motherly feelings. This is a psychological phenomenon to which we later on want to draw the reader's attention.

§. 117.
The stories about the outsider are almost innumerable in Norrland. There is hardly a parish in all of Norrland and Lapland where no one has heard of him. Some of my informants have not only heard but seen him. But what sort of beast it actually is that cries, is not so easy to decide, since everyone who has heard the strange sound, assures that it cannot be distinguished from the sound of a child crying. I have never

Fellow botanists – Lars Levi Læstadius
Bergveronika, Veronica fruticans
Found in Kåfjord in Alta in 1838

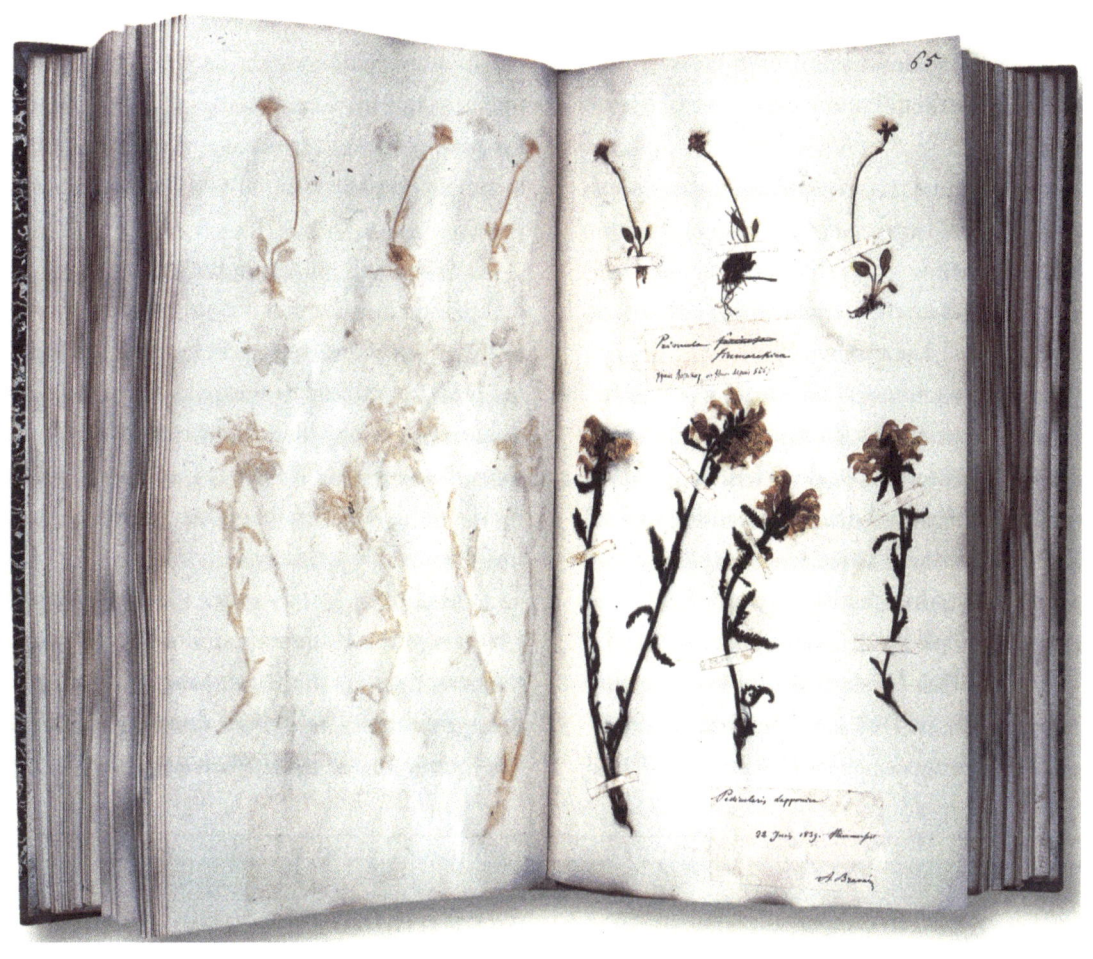

Fellow botanists – A. Bravais
Primula finmarchica from Bossekop and
Pedicularis lapponica from Hammerfest
1839

heard any such bawling of a child, for all the hiking I've done alone in the forest, winter and summer. But I have indeed heard the hare (Lepus borealis Pall. Secund. Nilss. Faun. Sv.) cry like a child, when it had been wounded, or otherwise fallen into distress. In the autumn, certain members of the owl family are in the habit of emitting a sound that resembles a child crying.

One generally hears the outsider during the autumn, before the fields get covered with snow. It is then heard crying for a long time during the evenings. It's not long ago that folks in Upper Torneå or Alkula heard such an outsider, and even Schoolmaster Em. Kohlström, who at that time was assistant master in Alkula, when one evening he was rowing with a friend past a mountain close to the river, heard a strange sound, but without knowing what it might be. When they got back, they told their hosts that they had heard a strange sound at that mountain. "Oh! the hosts answered: "Doesn't the schoolmaster know that *Utbölingen* (*Äpärä*) has been making itself heard at the mountain for a long time?" Kohlström thought it was an owl or hawk at the time, but afterwards he had found out that it may have been a hare, because he had heard precisely the same sound from a hare, which on a later occasion was wounded by him.

§. 118.

A longer time ago, or in the 1780's, Lapps who came to Quickjock to attend the so-called Larsmess Böndagen, in the middle of August, were frightened by the previously mentioned *Äppar*. Dean Öhrling, who at that time was pastor in Quickjock, had to travel to the place to investigate what sort of strange beast it might be; but since none of his companions dared go near the place from which the shriek came, he had to go there alone, and had upon his return said to his companions that it was a bird, presumably a small owl or also a great grey shrike (Lanius excubitor?). Such stories naturally circulate among the simple masses, although the occasion is most often entirely insignificant.

Thus one time a lad tending the animals for that same Dean Öhrling came and said with a serious mien: "Do you know, Father, I have seen the Devil." "Nah!" said the unbiased man, "since you have seen the Devil, then you can also probably tell us what he looked like?" The boy then began to describe that he had large claws, projecting ears and feathers on his body. Then the Dean said: "Take the gun now and shoot him to death. The boy did as the Dean had asked; he shot the Devil to death, and came quite boldly draggimg him back. It was a large eagle owl (Strix Bubo Lin.).

Such ludicrous mistakes could probably most often be the occasion for the strange tales that circulate among the masses. But one must not therefore reject or laugh at everything that occurs in common folk belief: for it is never the case that there is not something as the basis. It deserves in any case an investigation; if for no other reason, it should happen to shed some light on the matter.

§. 119.

I have another story about *Utbölingen* (the stranger) from Umeå Lappmark, but I didn't commit to memory where the incident is supposed to have occurred. One Saturday evening some young people had organized a dance in a church village house, which often happens in Norr- and Västerbotten's so-called church towns. When people had danced there well into the night, a very thin and clear voice was heard singing the following stanza under the floor: "If there wasn't a scissors, if there wasn't a scissors, I would probably have danced along." One of the girls dancing had then fallen to the floor in a swoon. They eventually began to investigate the circumstances, and they found under the floor a child's skeleton with a scissors over the neck. Everyone suspected the one passed out of being the mother of this child; and people found it likely she had murdered it with the scissors left behind. Whether the matter was further investigated is unknown to me, since it is supposed to have occurred long ago.

However, one sees from this story on what the common folk's belief about *Utbölingen* rests. If I understood the common folk's views correctly, then this and similar tales about childlike revenants deterred many a person from child murder. How easy is it for the Lapp girls for example to conceal their pregnant condition beneath their thick reindeer fur coats, and what sort of a trick would it be for them to hide their children? Nevertheless, I think that sort of thing seldom happens. And I think the common folk belief just described was besides very contributive; for the idea of hearing one's own child's shrieking after death, naturally had to have a great effect on the mother at the decisive moment; what good is it to murder one's own child, when the murderer in any case is sure to be discovered, through this unpleasant bawling? Rather she endures the shame than exposing herself to the double danger of being discovered in a supernatural way.

§. 120.

Anonymous in Leem mentions *Epparis* very briefly. He says: "*Zhikkalaggah* were thought by some to be ghosts in the shape of young. But he has heard, which is no doubt related, that they were a kind of animal that resides in deep springs, and resembled young without hair and voice. They were caught by a person at the edge of the spring where they resided, by putting butter in a dish or other vessel. When these animals came up to eat it they were shot. Their meat was very tasty. This animal (the author finally says) deserved to be held in a royal museum;" but I am almost afraid that Anonymous who otherwise is usually very careful in his remarks, let himself be duped a little in this case. If such an animal actually existed in nature, then it would probably have come before more sensible people's eyes. Presumably, he has heard from Lapp fishermen stories about the same creatures, which Norwegians call *Marmæler* (little mermen who can speak with people and reveal hidden things), which even could be caught, and were thought to be children of the mermaids (sirens) mentioned; but Gunnerus thinks the so-called sea people were seals (pinnipeds, manatees, sea cows). Likely they are the young of these, in themselves curious animals, which were sometimes caught by Norwegian fishermen, and were considered to be the young of fabulous sirens. Concerning the so-called *Marmæler*, Pontoppidan relates (according to Faye *Norrske Sagn*): "They are seen in various sizes, some like a child of a half year, others of a year, and again others of three years in age." Faye, ibid. p. 62. Oddly, even the Finns on Torneå River have a notion of a sort of water spook that resembles a child. It is called in Torneå Finnish *Vesi näkki* (water spirit). A settler in Kuttainen village in the Karesuando parish in Torneå Lappmark is sure he has seen such a child-like spook, swimming like a naked child on the bottom of the river. He saw it while spear fishing on a beautiful autumn evening, but became so frightened by it that he immediately went home. The man is still alive. But this so-called *vesi näkki*, i.e. water spirit (I wonder whether it is from Swedish *Näcken* "[evil] water sprite"?) is considered to be a supernatural creature, and can thus not be the same as Anonymous' *Zhiggalaggah* whose meat one presumably tasted, since it was supposed to be savory. If it was the young of the above-mentioned really extant marine animals (manatees), then they should not be found in deep springs as Anonymous stated. – We must consider all such stories as problematic, until some natural scientist, who can judge the circumstances impartially, gets hold of a *vesinäkki* or *zhikkalagga*, *marmæler* or other such child-like water creatures. Only then can one say that it was caught. And if sometime such a strange creature gets into a museum, then it presumably will not so easily get away from there.

§. 121.

It seems strange to us that Ganander did not include *Äpärä* in his Finnish mythology, since the object is generally familiar at least in Northrn Finland. Renvall does not have *Äpärä* in its mythological sense either. It only says that *Äpärä* means a "side-kid" or an illegitimate child. In view of that, one might presume that the Finns' *Äpärä* was borrowed from the Lapps' *Äppar*. Lindahl and Öhrling however have correctly understood the meaning of *Äppar*. They adhere to the same idea I have described above. Högström only mentions *Äppar-låkkusah*, a kind of incantation formula against such child-like ghosts. Which of these it may have been, is absolutely unknown to me; but that one used some sort of reading or incantation against such ghosts is quite probable.

In Norway according to Faye one even has the same idea about "*Utburder*" (ghosts of dead children) as they have in Swedish Norrland about *Utbölingen* (the outsider). "That such places are haunted where children are concealed and murdered, is a fairly common superstition among the common folk." "The Norwegian Lapps believed a similar creature, *Epparis* or *Shjort*, which was believed to live in those places where children who hadn't gotten a name were murdered (Leem, p. 426)." "The belief in *Udburrer* seems, as well as the name alluding to the pagan custom, that parents used to put in the forest children they could not or did not want to raise." Faye, ibid. p. 84.

How widely the Lapps in ancient times also used to expose children, is not known: at the least, it is less believable.

§. 122.
Real country folk's convictions of the human soul's immortality, and the existence of various other spiritual beings, do not rest, as is well known, on metaphysical grounds, but on multiple reports of visions, which circulate among the people. That the Lapps are not unfamiliar with this subject, one can easily imagine. We have already spoken about child-like ghosts (*Äppar*) above; we also ought to mention larger ghosts to show the reader samples of the common folk's conception of the spiritual world.

Some 20 years ago it happened that county Sheriff Granström in Jockmock (belonging to Luleå Lappmark), including his household, heard several evenings in a row a cry of distress on the other side of the marsh *Maitum*. This cry of distress they heard a long time, almost every time they were busy dragging the seine on the marsh mentioned. Granström, who already previously on several occasions had heard the underground *Boskapens Skällor* [cattle bells], and besides had seen one thing or other belonging to the spiritual world, heard this cry of distress with indifference. But the servants, who were a part of the dragging, could not hide their dread and fear at this cry of distress, because they knew well that no living human needed to cry at this marsh, without becoming visible at the same time. The cry continued one time after the other, and everyone who was dragging heard it. To give the servants courage against this haunting, old Granström every so often came out thoughtlessly against this constant crying, and said it could cry as long as it chose to, etc. In a word: he made fun of the crying.

Now the servants reported to their master the young C. M. Granström that his father, old man Granström was making a fool of the ghost that was crying on the other side of the marsh, from which in the opinion of the servants no good outcome could follow. The servants said besides that they didn't dare in the future help the old man, because they feared with the dragging he was probably irritating the ghost, and thereby bringing misfortune on himself and them.

§. 123.
One evening when the crying was again heard several times and more pitiably than before, young Granström decided to investigate the cause of this crying more closely. He took a maid with him, and rowed to the shore from where the crying came.

There he climbed on land and then, after he put a cross of branches in front of himself, he began to address the crying, which had been heard several times, before Granström put the boat ashore. He asked the one shouting to come forth and reveal its distress, etc. Then they both got to see a transparent human shape appear. The girl fainted immediately, and lay unconscious in the boat; but young Granström bade the ghost stop at a proper distance.

Granström now asked what the cause was of the ghost's constant crying. The ghost answered that he had been murdered on this spot a long time ago, and then points to a thick pine tree, saying: "it's been such a long time since this pine tree grew up on my grave. Yet, the ghost added, this does not overburden me so much. But last winter a thief slaughtered a stolen reindeer by this pine, and poured tannic acid against my legs; that I cannot endure. The same thief will come back next winter, and get a licking. Your father has made a fool of me, but he will very likely pay for it." Finally, the ghost asked Granström to read a benediction over his grave. Granström who at the beginning of the conversation felt a cold shudder go through his limbs, took heart, and read the benediction over the grave. The crying stopped then, and the named thief really got a licking the following winter. But old Granström paid dearly for his irresponsible behavior. You see, some time after this incident, he had run a perch bristle into his thumb, which thereupon became swollen, because the wound turned into so-called whitlow (which the Finns call *vanha mies,* i.e. the old man, with reference to the supposed cause of this illness). And old Granström had to lie ill half the summer with this affliction. He got it for making a fool of the ghost. That was the myth among the folk.

§. 124.
In this story, the remarkable circumstance is again presented that several persons at one time were witness to the plaintive and often repeated crying. How should one explain this? – Old Granström behaved rashly in several respects; for even if the crying was no more than an illusion (which is nevertheless difficult to assume, since it revealed itself to everyone in the same way), then it was nevertheless not a matter for jest. On the other hand, young Granström behaved in all respects sensibly. Investigating a strange phenomenon is something that each and everyone ought to do. He even displayed a rare self-control with the actual disturbance. Reading a prayer over the grave of the dead is, according to my way of thinking, no mean deed; there is more religion than superstition in that; for if the entire disturbance was also a figment of the imagination, then the prayer served to calm him down. He left the place with the reassuring conviction that he had done a good deed. I know Granström and his family very well. He is according to his level of education a sensible man, and not at all superstitious as far as I know him.

§. 125.
In general, it is quite difficult to explain away such a phenomenon as this, and if one doesn't want to do violence to one's own mind, then one has to acknowledge that there is a spiritual world. But that it does not reveal itself to everyone, can be due to circumstances we do not know. We know in general far too little about our

own mind to be able to determine its relationship to the spiritual world. The human soul's strengths, actions and characteristics are far too little investigated to be able to determine their relationship to either world. We see the phemomena of madness, somnambulism, Crapula, etc. But no one has yet been able to explain precisely what these phenomena actually consist of. We see how acutely emotions affect the organism, so that people could die from acute sorrow, joy or fear. We see the suffering organism stimulate the intrinsic spirit, so that a fever can cause dizziness; long usage of alcoholic drinks can cause Crapula, etc. Nevertheless, no one yet, neither physician nor psychiatrist, has been able to tell us of what the relationship of body and soul consists, or in what way these are connected. So much less has the selfish researcher succeeded in casting an inquisitive glance into the absolute spiritual world whose obscurely wonderful distance appealed to the eternal one to conceal behind the veil of time. It is also of little avail to mankind to know what takes place behind this veil, since the unequivocal proof we have of the soul's immortality, could not put the slumbering multitude's spiritual nerves in motion, to attain this higher goal to which everyone strives, but most seek within the boundaries of time. This word stands firm: If you don't believe Moses and the prophets, then nor do you believe whether any of the dead arose.

§. 126.
Before I permit myself an observation on this topic, I would still like to quote a couple stories that could serve as guidance for the reader's judgment. In Pewraure settlement, part of Quickjock's chapel congregation in Luleå Lappmark, lived a family about which something has been written in the first part of Petrus Læstadius' *Journal*. This colony lies right on the Lapps' migration route, and since the Lapps themselves do not have the opportunity to make coffins for their corpses, then the farm tenant in Pewraure, Olof Errson Alstadius was always called upon to make coffins. This work he always carried out in a woodshed that lay near the farm. But the strangest thing was that the domestic servants were usually informed beforehand when a body was going to be brought to the farm, to have a coffin made. This happened through hewing, whittling and planing in the woodshed. It was often heard late in the evenings by all the people who were in the house. They were so used to this that they paid little heed to it. They were certain that a corpse would soon be brought to the farm, when this whittling and planing was heard, and it was seldom mistaken. Old man Olof Alstadius had to begin on the same work a couple days later, which had beforehand been foreshadowed by his neighbor's wife, for it was a woman who assured him, because he had seen her a couple times during the day in the same woodshed.

§. 127.
Another example. The year 1840 in the month of February, 4 Lapps had taken lodg-

ing for the night with a settler in Karesuando parish of Torneå Lappmark. These together with the domestic servants heard in the evening a moaning sound outside the house. The housewife, who thought that a cow was choking in the barn, ran out to have a look, but there was nothing. After a while the same sound was again heard, and the dogs, who at that had rushed out the door, made a dreadful noise outside the house. At last they saw a strange man step into the room with black boots and grey frock-coat, a broadcloth outfit, which no one in the district uses. The landlord became so frightened that he rolled out of his bed above the Lapps who were lying on the floor. The stranger took several turns across the floor with his frozen boots and disappeared. No one in the place had seen such a traveller, nor at the time had anyone heard mention of a strange traveller passing through the parish. It should be noted that no travellers at this time of year can pass through these sparsely populated places without being noticed, since each and every one who wants to make it through and remain alive, must seek lodging either with Lapps or settlers. So much more unusual did it seem to those present in the house to see at this time of year a stranger with black boots which absolutely could not protect anyone's feet against the climate's severity. The Lapps had more closely observed the unknown stranger by the blazing fire still burning in the cabin. He had been a rather large man, with a large hook nose. When he so rapidly disappeared from the room without having said a word, the Lapps thought it was Gamel Erik [the Devil] himself, but this man just has no interest in showing himself in public. Rather one might think of a specter from the old Rechardian family, which a long time ago had been a mighty trading house in Torneå. The housewife, you see, was born Rechardt, and who has probably often been near death for her intractable mouth in her equally harsh-minded husband's claws. The moaning sound that was heard, she is more than once supposed to have emitted during similar thrashings, and probably still was emitting the same moaning, because harmony in the house did not seem to want to return with age. It was probably something like that the unknown guest wanted to mirror.

§. 128.
This is the fourth example now where several people at the same time have been witness to one and the same phenomenon, and this can suffice to show on what common popular belief is based. I skipped on purpose the individual cases where only one person at a time believes they have seen or heard something strange. The stories of that sort are many, but I consider it unnecessary to repeat them here. It is not very important whether they saw something or not. Here it is more a question of the way in which common popular belief perceived the object, and the effect this belief has on people's morality. This is a subject that truly deserves reflection, on which I may later on ask for the reader's attention.

That one often hears bells and rattling outside the house, when a beloved person is expected, although the person does not come until several hours or even a day later; that many women can predict a traveler's arrival sevseral hours in advance, etc. is not an unfamiliar thing even in Lappland. The Nordland women say: "att det tegas folk," i.e. they have a feeling about people, that strangers are going to come, etc. What this ability to have a feeling consists of, they are unable to explain, but that their predictions come true, is more common than unusual.

§. 129.

In the world, *Jabma aimo*, which the Lapps visualized as beneath the earth, reigned the mother of death, *Jabma akko*, who was thought to torment the lives of the living. The Norwegian authors have the following about this:

"Sacrifices are made to *Jabma akku*, because she as well as the dead are generally thought to torment the lives of the living. In particular, the dead wish soon to be able to fetch to themselves their relatives and family." Anonymous in Leem.

"The *noaidi* has to sacrifice to *Jabma aimo*, either to bring up a dead relative to take care of the reindeer, or to appease the dead so that they not covet the soul of a sick person." Jessen, ibid. p. 30. "If the sick person should recover, then his dead family must be satisfied by sacrifice, which the *noaidi* promised on behalf of the sick person. If the dead did not begrudge the sick to live, the *noaidi* should in any case notify the sick person." Jessen, p. 32.

"The Lapps sacrifice to *Jabma akko* so that the people who are alive might continue to live; for *Jabma akko* and the dead themselves strive to get those who are related to them down to themselves from the [world of the] living, such as children and grandchildren," etc. Sidenius in Ganander.

"They admit they have put their faith in their own deceased or dead, and canonized them into their own *Deos manes* [good gods]; so that they sacrificed to them, worshiped them and feared them. For example, a son, his father or paternal grandfather's siblings; a daughter, her mother or maternal grandmother's siblings." v. Vesten ibid. NB: The publisher of v. Vesten's letters has written: "His best father's, his best mother's siblings," etc. He did not understand that the Norwegian words Bäste Far and Bäste Mor mean Farfar and Farmor in Swedish [grandfather and grandmother].

§. 130.

The belief that the dead torment the living, has not been entirely rooted out. Even the Finns on Torneå River, and for as long as I have known them, are under the same delusion. As soon as someone is affected by symptoms of spasms, epilepsy or crapula, then it is straight away *maanalaiset* [subterranean trolls], or *jamikiaiset*, that assails him. Usually, on such occasions one seeks a remedy from some *noaidi*, who passes himself off as knowing more than others. The dead must be driven away, either through an incantation, or by way of a drink made in his own way, that the sick person must ingest, etc. It is maintained that evil persons stir up the dead against people. Thus one can often hear that a particular person did not die a natural death. She was destroyed by trolls, etc.

The belief in the supernatural is still like a consequence of the ancient superstition so deep-seated that it is not possible to wipe it out. Nevertheless, they do not dare to reveal such to the pastor, who as a consequence of his office, must counteract the prejudice. In his presence they pretend there is nothing; but via the usual backstairs one likely hears how this or that supposed *noaidi* is turned to by various patients.

It is not much to wonder at, if Lapps and Finnish Lapps, who have the dismal paganism so near, still believe in *Nåidat* and *Manalaiset*, since even Norrland's enlightened country folk speak about how such and such a person has seen 'churchgoers,' i.e. the dead; how he became haunted by the Devil, etc. Even among the educated classes in Southern Sweden one does not need to be more than a Lapp to arouse attention, and inspire respect, particularly among women, if one just passes oneself off as a *noaidi*, and threatens or does some hocus pocus.

§. 131.
The belief that ghosts torment people has probably not only belonged to the Lapps. The disreputable people among the Jews, generally believed that the evil spirits caused certain illnesses, such as for example insanity, epilepsy, monthly raging, etc. If only this notion had been incorrect, it would just have been superstition and blind faith; why then did the Christian Religion's eminent founder allow such a mistake to continue; why did he not rebuke the innocent Father who told him how the spirit cast his Son sometimes into the fire, sometimes into the water? That, he did not do; on the contrary he said to his disciples: this kind of ghost does not yield to normal incantations without much fasting and prayer. I know well that the later era's deists and naturalists who readily wanted to clear away all ghosts, pretended comically enough that Our Savior did not want to get on the wrong side of popular belief, but rather allow superstition to continue, in order to gain a footing in the people's heart for their teachings. But this sort of popularity seeking, worthy of a Robespierre and his ilk, must have been a rather wretched way to gain a following among the people. About Robespierre it is said that in order not to get on the wrong side of people, he restored through a long speech in the convention: "the origin of nature, existence and immortality of the soul." But that the one who sealed his teachings with his own blood, should take advantage of the same poor remedy to win popularity, is not conceivable for anyone other than the one who has no religion. The belief in ghosts, and their influence on the people continued even among the first Christians, and I do not know whether there was more religion or superstition in that. The Norrland country folk probably do not believe, as Lapps and Finnish Lapps, that the dead, *Maanalaiset* and *Jamikiaset* torment the living, yet one often hears mention that the dead pinch people who are asleep, wherefrom bruises appear on arms and legs. The Norrland country folk have more to deal with, the underground sirens, witches, et al. of which the phrases 'meet with misfortune,' 'magic shots,' 'siren stitches' etc. have their origin. The Finns say about such sudden illnesses: *Kohtaus* 'attack,' and

the Lapps say: *Ådtjotalai*, i.e. he was attacked; all of which suggest a fairly common belief among the country folk that certain ghosts could harm people.

§. 132.

So as to even more closely make clear or explain the old Lapps' idea about the dead, it cannot hurt, to adduce a few more citations from the Norwegian authors. Jessen has the following on this:

"Non-Godfearing human beings, and especially thieves, are supposed to come to *Fudnos aimo* (the Devil's world), but the others to *Jabma aimo* (Hades). There they will get new bodies and live with *Saiwo* and *Saiwo-neid*; but they believed the same about reindeer and other animals (namely, that even they would get new bodies in another world). In *Jabma aimo* they would have far more perfect pleasure than here, but the same kind of work as in this life. When they have been in *Jabma aimo* a while, they would then get to move to heaven to *Radien* or God." Jessen, p. 70. This last-mentioned idea the author (Jessen) believes they have gotten or borrowed from the Papists' purgatory.

"[*Deos*] *manes* (good gods) were believed to take good care of the Lapps' reindeer, as long as one held sacrifices as agreed." Jessen, p. 32. It is thus clear both from this and from v. Vesten's information cited above that the Lapps also sacrificed to the ghosts of the dead.

"To Jabma aimo, everyone came, except those who swore, stole and murdered. They came to *Tjerro-mubben-aimo*" (the other world of weeping). Jessen, p. 32. – This information agrees closely with the previous.

It should only be noted that *Fudnos aimo*, which here and a few other places is discussed by the Norwegian authors, is not genuine, since *Fudno* is presumably borrowed from Swedish *Fan* (the Devil).

§. 133.

We now come to that class of mythological things that are thought to live deep down in the earth. They were thought of as evil, and for humans highly harmful beings. Among them the renowned *Ruotta* is placed in the first room, about which Norwegian authors say the following:

"To hinder the Lapps' life that fell to *Rutu*." Jessen, p. 66.

"The human spirits that are deep down in the earth or closer to the abyss stay in *Rota aimo*, or *Rota's* land. These never come away from there to Radien or to the Father of All in the starry sky, like the other dead who live in *Jabma aimo*. There in the abyss lives *Rota*, and the Lapps sacrificed to her when they had no help to expect from other gods. This *Rota* is often found tormenting humans and livestock. Then she must be bribed with sacrifices. But they do not prepare the same kind of sacrifices for *Rota* as for other gods, but they have put an entire dead horse down in the earth, with which *Rota* will ride away from them down into *Rota aimo*. *Rota's* image is made like a human, and the legs of the sacrificial animals dedicated to her are laid on the sacrifice altar, since *Rota* like other gods was thought able to create new flesh on these legs." Anonymous in Leem.

Rota, the Lapps' Rodaman? The Greeks' and Romans' Proserpina [Persephone], the Finns' *Tuoni* and *Maanalan matti* have their refuge very deep down in the earth in their *Rot-aimo*, where those persons come who did not live according to their gods' will. Those who are in *Jabmi aimo*, come to *Radien* after they have been there a while; but those who come to *Rotalanda* do not get away from there, but are tormented there as in Hell. – The Lapps have sacrificed to *Rota* and sought help there, when no help could be expected from other gods. The Lapps have found that *Rota* brings illnesses and torments people and reindeer. Then they haven't known any other way out than to buy her off with sacrifices; yet they haven't sacrificed to her in the usual manner but put down a dead horse that Rota might ride on him away from them." Ganander, according to Sidenius. Compare v. Vesten's information cited above on Rothamme. (§. 113).

§. 134.
One sees from what has now been quoted that all the Norwegian authors knew about this queen of the abyss, though they spell the name differently. Högström writes *Ruotta*, which is the correct version in all Swedish Lappmarks; but he believes though that it ought more correctly to be written *Druotta*, and in that respect, without a likelihood of the Swedish word *Drott*, which in Old Geatish [people from Götaland] meant a prince or sovereign. "*Ruotta* is probably one of their or our ancient rulers who did them harm, because one sees from what is still to be fully recounted, that he was still worshiped by them as another *averruncus* [Roman god of averting harm]." Högström, p. 180. This connection to the Lapps' *Ruotta* I am very willing to approve of. Högström as well as Anonymous in Leem wants to consider *Ruotta* as masculine, but if I have understood the Lapps' meaning correctly, then *Ruotta* is feminine genitive [?]. Högström observes *ibid.* that Christmas Eve is called *Ruott-ekked*, which today too is the correct relationship. Where would the Lapps have gotten this holiday, if both the name and the occasion for the holiday hadn't been borrowed? That the Lapps later on made *Ruotta* into a queen of the abyss, that she was seen as being the cause of contagious and deadly illnesses, that plague in Lapp is *Ruotta*, plus that everyone who swore, stole and murdered would after death come to *Ruot-aimo* or *Rota landa*, all this shows that that queen who first made herself known to the Lapps, must have been a real evil spirit. Swedes are called even today in Lapp *Ruottalatsch*, in Finnish *Ruotalaiset*; Sweden is called *Ruota Ädnam*, or *Ruota landa* in Lapp; in Finnish *Ruoti* or *Ruotsi*; the Swedish language is called in Lapp *Ruota kiel*, and in Finnish *Ruotsin kieli*. All this connected to the mythological *Ruotta*, which too means plague, does not make a favorable notion of the *Drottar*, *Drotser* or *Rutsor* that first come in contact with the Lapps. According to Gejer even

the name *Ryss* is supposed to have its origin in this *Ruotsi*. This I have nevertheless only seen cited in some issue of Gejer's *Litteraturblad* [literary magazine].

"The Lapps sacrificed to Ruotta, so that he, according to their alleging, not harm their women in a particular way (*ne ventrem illarum terebret seu perforet* "not pierce or perforate their stomach"?)." Högström p. 189. The above belongs to the doctrine of sacrifice of which more later on.

§. 135.
One can say the same thing about the Lapps' *Jåulå-Herra*, that it is like the Christmas festival (*Jåulå*) borrowed from the Geatish people. Högström tells that the Lapps have a deity for the Christmas festival who is called *Jaulo Herra* (the Yule man). "What sort of person *Jaulo-Herra* is I cannot say for certain, inasmuch as they do not understand our Savior from a pagan *Kakozælia* [cacozelia] "throwing in foreign words to appear learned, bad taste in words" Högström, p. 180. With what sacrifice this Yule man was honored, Högström describes on p. 188. This will appear in the Doctrine of Sacrifice.

The Norwegian authors do not have much to say about this Yule man. On the magic drum, which Leem describes, there is a figure that is supposed to represent *Joulo-peive-Herra* (Yule Day man). But he does not explain which characteristics and functions this Yule Day man is believed to have. Leem also mentions *Joulo-Gadze*, which he believes to be sort of devils or demons to which one sacrificed on Christmas Eve.

This *Joulo-Gadse* seems to be borrowed from the Swedes' *Julkuse*; what sort of being this may have been, I do not know, since it is not discussed in the compendia that concern Scandinavian mythology. It is generally known that in Sweden for Christmas Eve one bakes *Julkusar* for children. These buns/cakes are made in various shapes, representing crayfish, dragons, roosters, ram's horns, etc. That this custom stems from time immemorial and is connected to *Odens Galt* (Odin's boar) seems likely; and that *Julkusen* was not a good being is intimated by the name itself and the concept that one usually attaches to it. From this *Julkuse* it seems the Lapps have gotten *Jåulåherra* and *Jåulå Gadse*. That moreover both Lapps and Finns were able to celebrate Christmas with some sort of sacrificial service, even before their contact with the Scandinavian or Geatish people, is surely both likely and true; but the name of such a sacrificial holiday has not been borrowed from Swedish *Jul* (Yule). That the Lapps' *Ruotta Ekked* is also borrowed, I have already mentioned; however, this idea seems to be older than *Jåulå herra*. Among the Lapps there was originally no *Herre* (Lord).

§. 136.
Another lesser known object is *Kuowa*, which actually means image, likeness, from the Finnish word *Kuva*, which also means image. The phrase *Pardne-kuowa* "poor

child"; *Pådnje kuowa* "poor old man" is a metaphor that actually determines the previous subject's poor or pitiable nature. *Pardne kuowa* "the son's image," *Pådnje kuowa* "the old man's image," i.e. the denoted object is just an image, a shape, which is even said in Swedish about a person gaunt from illness or sorrow. *Kåwå* "image" is only a variation of this. We do not then with Högström need to accept *Kuowa* as a special deity for the month of February, although *Kuowa mano* "the month of February" has surely gotten its name from that. Rather the name should be translated as image month, which suggests a usage customary in antiquity of making idols during this month. From this also followed a sacrificing to the images made, about which Högström has the following: "As far as *Kuowa mano* is concerned, an old housewife told, that her parents a certain time in February usually tied hay and grass, like they had in their shoes and mittens, by the antlers of their reindeer; then later on with ringing and other rattling, plus pounding on the sleds bade *Kuowa manna* eat. From which it is also seen that they held this entity not only as a living creature, but also such that could live on hay, plus needed to be called through all sorts of noise and din." Ibid. p. 188. From this it seems that the notion of *Kuowa manna* as a living being cannot be further analyzed.

§. 137.

That the Lapps had a conception of more evil beings than those the authors could discover, can be seen from some names of mythological objects occurring in the language that not even the lexicographers Lindahl and Öhrling got hold of. *Kaitne* is a frequently occurring curse formula in Luleå Lappmark. For example, *The lii Kaitne* "Well, I'll be damned." That *Kaitne* was thus an evil object is certain, but as to what it was like, the myths give no information.

Vabda probably originally designated an evil being too, although Lindahl and Öhrling translate it as *omen sinistrum* "bad omen." The actual phrase *Vabda qwuolle* "piscis portento sum – I am an ominous fish?" seems to prove that *Vabda* was a monster. *Kabnja* does not actually mean *umbra* "shadow" as Lindahl and Öhrling think, but a scarecrow which the Lapps set up on a migration route to keep the reindeer away from a certain area. It seems originally to have been an object arousing terror, an unpleasant spook or the like. *Kunka* also designates some dreadful and ghastly object that the imagination brings about; it is now almost synonymous with the Devil. The phrase *Kunka valda to* "may the *Kunka* take you" proves that one was here thinking about something unpleasant or dreadful. *Hiita* or *hiida* is probably borrowed from the Finns' *Hiisi, Hiidet*. With *Hiisi* the Finns meant, according to Ganander, and *Runor* 'Finnish epic poems,' a very nasty witch, almost corresponding to the Swedes' *Hel* 'Hel, a giantess daughter of Loki,' and the Lapps' *Ruotta*. From the Finnish phrases *Mene hiiteen* 'go to Hiisi's dwelling' [go to the Devil] and *Mistä hiidestä* 'from where Hiisi's dwelling?' the Lapps too have acquired their swear words: *Mana Hiitui* 'go to Hell' and *The liiäska hiita* 'that was Old Nick.' But any further worshiping or sacrificing the Lapps probably did not show this infernal spirit, nor have they on this subject made themselves any clear notion. *Läbbo*, only customary in the northern Lappmarks, is likewise borrowed from the Finns' *Lempo*, which Ganander calls a flying evil spirit, *Helvit-tållå*, *Helvit Geune*, *Helvit tarwe*, which Leem takes up as depicted on the Lapps' drums, are all borrowed concepts. *Helvit-tållå* 'Hell fire,' *Helvit-Geune* or *kiebne* 'Hell's kettle,' *Helvit-tarwa* 'Hell tar,' all bear a clear stamp of the papacy.

§. 138.
The Norwegian authors speak of kinds of demons, or underground beings, which they call *Gadse*, for example, *Saivo Gadse*, *Nåide-Gadse*, et al. Some spell this object with *z*: *Gadze*, but rightly it ought to be written *Katse*, from the Lapp word *katset* 'invidere or envy' and *katsem* 'envy.' The Finnish noun *katset* 'looking' which actually means 'vision,' also acquires the meaning of a magic vision in certain cases, for example, *haavan katset* means according to Renvall 'examination of the wound, magic, and medicine, examining the art of magic preparation.' The Finnish words *kadet* and *kati* mean also according to the same Renvall in *Runorna* 'kinds of mythological jealousy?' Thus, *Gadse* or *Katse* on etymological grounds happens to mean a servant of the abyss or the personified abyss, with which the *noaidis* had much to do. It was not alone their teacher in the art of prophecy, but also their assistant and obedient servant. With its help, illnesses both could be cured and humans damaged for life.

Although the story about Katse and its use in the art of prophecy actually belongs to the doctrine of prophecy or the Lapps' magic, we ought to describe here however this mythological object as it is described for us in the Norwegian authors' writings.

"The young *noaidis* got revelations from kinds of spirits called *Saiwo-Gadze*. – These usually themselves taught the young *noaidi* candidates in the art of prophecy. – After the young *noaidi* was initiated, and recognized as a *noaidi*, *Nisserna* 'supernatural beings, goblins' or *Saiwo Gadze* began more intimate dealings with him. The *noaidi* could select from them as many as he liked as guardian angels. They often revealed themselves to him, sometimes in the form of young Lapps, sometimes in the form of women *Saiwo-neidah*, who were hard as rocks to lie with. – These their guardian angels the *noaidis* called their *Tonto*." Jessen, ibid. p. 54.

This last epithet, which should be read *Tåntå*, proves that *Saiwo-Gadze* were not good spirits. We have already shown above that *Tåntå* was not a good term. (§. 109).

§. 139.
"When a *noaidi* was called upon for help by a sick person, then he bade his *Nåide Lådde* go after his *Nåide Gadse*. – Since *Nåide Gadse* was sent for via the Trollfogeln 'magic bird,' they assisted through prophecy," etc. Leem, p. 475.

"Finnmark's Lapps mention *Juolo-Gadse*. – These are devils or demons to whom one sacrificed on Christmas Eve. – *Nåide Gadse* 'prophesying devils' who were the *noaidi's* teachers and servants. – With the assistance of these spirits they would cure the illnesses of people and livestock. – Such a demon, revealed to the Lapp, sought to persuade him, the Lapp, with all sorts of reasons to take him in his service. – If he would not voluntarily accept the demon's service, he was compelled to do so through threats and torments."

"Such *Nåide Gadseh* were of 2 types, namely, *Puoreh Gadseh*, good demons or geniuses. – Others were called *Perkel-Gadseh* who assisted in doing harm. These latter were also called *Pårråm-Gadseh*, because they consumed everything like a fire." Anonymous in Leem.

From this description, one can roughly conclude what concepts the *noaidis* made for themselves about *Katse*; they were spirits or real mythological objects, almost corresponding to the Romans' daemons, of which there were also 2 types, namely, good and evil. *Saiwo Gadse* was thus the *noaidi's* good, and *Perkel-Gadse* his evil genius. *Nåide Gadseh* were the *noaidi's* good and evil demons; *Juolo Gadse* 'the evil demon of Christmas,' *Julkusen*. (§. 135).

Attje Gadse, a name for the god *Tordön* 'thunder/Thor' (§. 34), is to be viewed as a demon of *Tordön*, and *Saragads*, which Högström mentions on p. 179, is together with the opinion now given, a demon of *Sarakka*. The doctrine of the functions and relationships of these demons to the *noaidis* will be found in more detail in Doctrine of Prophecy, about which more to come.

§. 140.
Another very evil object, used by the *noaidis* to harm people, was an insect which the Norwegian authors call *Ganflugor* 'gan flies.' About this infernal insect the Norwegian authors have learned the following:

"The Lapps speak of the so-called *Vuokko*, which in the shape of a large holy bird, procured the poisonous *Ganflugorna* for the *noaidi*. A so-called *Zhiokkush* the Lapps imagined caused an illness occurring vehemently." Anonymous in Leem.

"Gand flugor were also their servants. Certain so-called *Vuoko* or *Väros Lodde*, called by the *noaidi*, which shook out of their feathers a sort of insects, like *Löss* 'loess.' These were very poisonous. They were collected very carefully by the *noaidi*, yet not with bare hands, and preserved in small boxes. With these the *noaidi* could inflict great harm on humans and animals. When a *noaidi* wanted to inflict harm on someone and had lost his *Gandask* 'Lapp magic box,' then he borrowed one from another *noaidi*, and then paid with the same article. It was not always necessary that the *noaidi* got his *Gan* from *Vuoko*, for *Nåide Gadse* could instead get him a *Ganstaf* 'Gand stick' in the shape of an axe that was quite poisonous; and what the *noaidi* struck with it, whether animals or humans, immediately became ill and could not be restored to health until, another *noaidi* reversed, or cured the damage with an obstructing troll." Jessen, p. 56.

§. 141.
"*Gandflugor* 'Gand flies' were small flies that the Lapps kept in a box. These could be inherited by the father if he was a *noaidi*. Otherwise, they were procured by a devil in the shape of a bird that is called *Vuokko*. With these flies the *noaidi* could do harm to people, when they were sent out by him, but the flies came back to the owner after an errand carried out." Leem, p. 483.

"If someone was exposed to an eruption of scabies, which seemed to spread between flesh and skin, then he had been bewitched by the *Gand* flies of some *noaidi*. Such symptoms have attacked many in Finnmark, and brought about insufferable pain. If the belly on a person became swollen, or if someone coughed up blood and died from it, then such a person had been poisoned by the *noaidi's Gand* flies.

A sick person who imagined she/he was bewitched by such *Gand* flies, depended on the *noaidi* to make her/him whole, or drive them away with stronger sorcery. A *noaidi* attacked by such Gand flies could enchant himself back to health." Leem, p. 484.

As an example, it should be mentioned that *Vuokko* means a variation in respect to illness and temperament [Nielsen *Lappisk (samisk) ordbok* has under *vuok'ko* 'paroxysm, fit (speaking of an attack of illness)'], which the phrase: *Kotatt Vuokko påått* 'when it comes quickly' or 'when it occurs to him.' *Vuokko* is even said about a current illness that afflicts several at one time or one at a time, without therefore being contagious. *Tatt lä vuokko* 'that is a current plague,' or as one says in Norrland, 'it is a plague.' Here can be compared the Finns' *Vuoro*, for example, *Silmen vuoru*, a current eye sickness, whereby even *Vuornis Lådde* is probably related. It is possible that the Lapps with their *Vuokko* were thinking of an infernal spirit, as a cause of a current illness, for which no natural cause could be thought of; and that this demon revealed itself in the shape of a bird, was so much easier to imagine, which the *noaidis*, according to what we have shown above, had several underground magic birds in their service (§. 76).

§. 142.
What else concerns the so-clled *Gand* flies the *noaidi* was supposed to get from the infernal bird's feathers, and then keep in a box, I can observe that it was no doubt a venomous insect, with which the old Lapps were acquainted, although the authors cited above did not learn this insect's Lapp name. Anonymous in Leem, to be sure, cites a Lapp name, *Zhiokkush*, but I cannot really understand whether this is supposed to be the name of the Norwegians' *Ganfluga*, or whether thereby is meant some other object. Pastor Lindahl in Åsele from Umeå Lappmark says he was once bitten by an insect, from which his arm became swollen, and he had to lie sick for 3 weeks. The same thing has also happened to a few other persons in the Lappmark areas.

Lars Levi Læstadius' *Fragments of Lappish Mythology*
Part of the last discovery of the manuscript in 2001 by Nils Magne Knutsen and Per Posti in Pontarlier, France.

Verso-recto spread from §. 141 "finnarnes" [the Finns] to §. 142 "veckor." [weeks].

In this connection one cannot help but think of Linné's *Furia infernalis* 'infernal fury,' about which he says in *Fauna Svecica* N° 2070: "habitat in W: bothnia et O: bothnia inprimis supra kemi in vastis paludibus cæspitosis, unde nescio qua ratione æthera petat et in corpora animalium, ipsiusque hominis decidat, momento citius atrocissimo dolore jugularis" (habitat in West and East Bothnia, especially in the vast marshes above Kemi tufted, so I do not know the reason why he made claims, and in the bodies of animals, and of man's demise, a little faster than most atrocious jugular pain) [Despite the many accounts of this purported animal by respected authorities, including Daniel Solander and Linnaeus himself, it is now accepted that no such animal exists]. This insect he says he has never yet seen alive, and some entomologists have told me that no one knows any longer what is meant by Linné's *Furia infernalis*. If I remember correctly, Linné himself discussed in his *Skånska resa* that he had been bitten by an insect, which he thought was *Furia infernalis*, from which he had to lie ill for several weeks. For me it is absolutely impossible to decide whether such a poisonous insect actually exists, since later times' entomologists who have traveled in the Lappmarks know nothing about it. Nevertheless, it does not seem unbelievable to me, since Linné presumably got definite information about it in the district of Kemi, before he could include such an object in his *Fauna*. The testimony of those persons who themselves had been bitten by such a venomous insect, which is mentioned above, ought to count for something too. The main thing is that the old Lapp *noaidis* had their *Gan* flies and *Gan* boxes, with which they harmed people. *Gan* or *Gand* is an old Geatish word, which seems to have meant an ability to bring about something through witchcraft, or supernatural means; from this *gand* it is even thought that Gandviken, mentioned in the old Viking sagas, has gotten its name. v. Vesten thinks that Gandviken was the same as the White Sea; although he is not absolutely certain whether this could not be understood as Porsanger Fjord, which in later times is supposed to have been called Ganviken. (v. Vesten's treatise in Budstikken (newspaper).

§. 143.
We might conclude the Lapps' doctrine of gods with the worst of all mythological objects; I mean *Perkel*, which is known in all of Lappland and Finland. This name now means the same as the Devil or the principle of evil; but although we readily acknowledge that the Lapps as other nations were able to imagine an evil being as the origin of evil, we have nevertheless in *Sver[r]iges Stats Tidning* from June of 1836 included an article about the Lappmarks' borders, etc., in which we try to show that the name *Perkel* is not very old, since it does not occur in the Lapps' oldest tales. In the same place, we have stated the conjecture that this name stems from the *Birkarls* (cf. §. 27), who of course were hated by the Lapps because of their tyranny, about which history too attests. Though accordingly Birkarl was the worst evil for a while, which the Lapps forcibly knew, then it was natural that the name, originally designating the worst evil the Lapp knew in the material world, namely, a Birkarl,

eventually came to be transfered to the worst evil in the spiritual world, in the same way as *Ruotta*, according to what we have shown above, originally meant a tyranical king, but eventually came to mean the goddess of the abyss.

Whether the Lapps, before their contact with the Birkarls, had an idea about and even a name for an evil spiritual being, this name could even disappear in favor of the later one, since *Perkel* became the more general term. And thus it becomes quite probable that the Lapps' *Hin håle* "the Devil" inherited the Birkarls' name. Since Perkel thus really became at home among the Lapps, then it was natural too that the first pastors who came in contact with the Lapps had to apply the name to the Devil, especially as no more fitting name was found in the language. Roughly like that I imagine the origin of *Perkel*. As far as the Finns' *Perkele* is concerned, I can observe that it means exactly the same thing as the Lapps' *Perkel*, and it is possible the Finns adopted this name from the Lapps, or too the Lapps have inherited it from the Finns, in case the Finnish archaeologists can enlighten us that *Perkele* was known in Finland before the introduction of Christianity.

§. 144.
Some older authors, who necessarily wanted to have Finnish more closely related to Greek, have conjectured that the Finns' *Perkele* is derived from the Greek word περκνοω [perknos] 'black.' Ganander *Finnish Mythology*. Others have believed they found the Greek *Herkules* in the name *Perkel*. Högström, p. 187. All similar derivations we have to leave as is, as long as the cause can be found closer at hand. If it can possibly be shown that the Finns' *Perkele* is older than *Pirkala*, or Birkarl, then we will gladly acknowledge that the Lapps borrowed their *Perkel* from the Finns, and that the Birkarls nave no greater share in this name, than the new occasion they could give the Lapps through their tyranny to apply this name to themselves. I have already mentioned that the name *Perkel* does not occur among their oldest tales, and this provides me with the occasion for the guess that *Perkel* is not very old among the Lapps. Besides, *Perkel* has also in Lapp gotten many other names, as for example *Fuodno*, which I regard as borrowed from Swedish *Fan* or Danish *Fanden* and made closer to Lapp, which again probably was a relic of ancients' *Fenris ulfven* 'Fenris wolf.' Another Lapp name for *Hin-håle* 'the Devil' is *Nevre* 'the nasty one, the bad one' which is probably a translation of *Hin Slemme* 'the bad one.' The Lapps in Torneå Lappmark sometimes say *Huono*, from the Finnish word *huono* 'the poor one,' which also seems to be just a translation of *Hin slemme*, in case it is not thought to be a milder pronunciation of *Fuono*, genitive of *Fuodno*. Sometimes *Hin håle* can also be called *Tjapok* or *Tjappis ålmai* 'the black one,' which seems to be a translation of *Hin Svarte*. In Piteå as well as Luleå Lappmarks one sometimes says *Sjelwa*, from Swedish *sjelf* [själv] 'self,' since one presumably heard that the Swedes sometimes begin their swearwords with: *Sjelfva hin*, and *Sjelver Di[f]n*, etc. *Sattan* is nothing other than an imitation of Satan. v. Vesten has the word *Kieb ulmai*, which is also

Karajocki, first stop in Lappland, September 7, 1839

an imitation of *Djefvulen* 'the devil;' this *Kieb ulmai* is otherwise a misprint, and ought to be written *Tjebul-ålmai*. *Mubben ålmai* 'the other man,' is also one among the many names of *Hin håle*; this name occurs with the Norwegian authors. *Hilkat* is also a swearword used adverbially chiefly in Torneå Lappmark; but I do not know whether this word must be an imitation of Swedish *Hinken*, or whether it comes from Finnish *Helka* (cf. Ganander), or from Lapp *Hilket, Hilkem*, Finnish *Hylkän* 'reject, repudiate.'

§. 145.

About *Perkel's* power to create, harm and other tasks, we have already given some quotations from Högström (§§. 37-39). To even more precisely explain the Lapps' idea about this creature, it is probably necessary to cite some more of the authors just mentioned.

"As head of the good persons is Jubmel, so I have also become aware that they actually hold *Perkel* as a head of the evil ones. For though this name *Perkel* is a rather new word, but such that they also used before any of them got a taste of the Christian doctrine, nor have all Lapps up there gotten the same concept. Those who have some knowledge of Christianity, have the same thoughts about it as we have about the evil spirit. But the others up there as a matter of fact have had a concept like the old pagan nations about their evil *principio* 'beginning,' which they thought was just as everlasting as God. This I conclude from the tales I have to some extent mentioned in their places, namely, Perkel was in counsel with God or *Jubmel* when the world was going to be created, and that likewise he was the reason that not everything became as good as *Jubmel* would have had. And that he likewise competes with God for omnipotence, one has perceived from other of their stories. A certain Lapp has otherwise been known to speak about a time when *Perkel* made chains of iron, with which he bound *Jubmel*, and threw over him a large mountain, when *Jubmel* lay under the mountain without escaping from there. Then *Jubmel* bound *Perkel* and threw a mountain over him. But the evil one broke loose, so that rocks and dust shot sky-high etc.

And since they had dedicated such great power to the evil one alongside God, then one was not surprised that they like other pagans in all sorts of ways sought to placate this evil spirit, so that he would not cause them so much evil, which he otherwise was able to inflict on them." Högström, pp. 175-176.

Whether the Lapps actually sacrificed to *Perkel*, the author has not mentioned, and I would think it less likely.

§. 146.

"When upon my first arrival in Kaitum in Luleå Lappmark I offered to ascertain whether they had any stories which they had gotten as children from the children of their ancestors, about one thing or other, some started to tell what they heard from the old folks about the world's creation, and asked me whether it was true. They said that when God created the world, he conferred with *Perkel* or the evil one as to how everything should be arranged. God wanted all trees to consist of pith, all seas of milk, and on all grass, flowers and plants were to grow berries. But the evil one was opposed, which is how it remained." Högström, p. 57.

On *Perkel's* authority, the Norwegian authors have nothing special. His name though appears in several places. I have not heard anything further about *Perkel* either, except that for example the wolf is believed to have been created by *Perkel*. The horse, I trust, was created by God, but *Perkel* had spit on the legs, of which the stocking on the inner side of the horse's leg is thought to be a mark, etc.

End of *Gudalära* "Doctrine of the Gods."

Leonie d'Aunet

François Biard

"*This pastor was not a very pleasant acquaintance. In spite of our letter of recommendation and our miserable plight after the strenuous journey, he received us with a superior expression. With his cap on his head and pipe in his mouth he showed us to our room and didn't bother any more with us. I felt deeply offended.*"

A favorite Læstadius child had just died.

Painter, adventurer. Studied art as a young man, taught art on a French Navy ship. Biard won a gold medal in the Salon of Paris in 1828 for his painting The Teller of Good Fortune. The French king became his patron. Traveled with his young partner, Leonie d'Aunet, to Hammerfest to join the Recherche expedition in 1839.

Supplement

To the preface. In connection with *Pyhä ouda* 'a holy forest,' I remember that Ganander has under the articles *Ristikannot* 'holy stumps' and *Petäjät* 'pine barrens' the following: "*Ristikannot* and *Petäjät*, holy, sanctified stumps, pines and trees. That those were for a long time past in high esteem is seen in Pope Gregory IX's letter to Bishop Thomas in Åbo about their (the holy stumps) being gotten rid of. Such holy groves and trees the parish clerk Påhl Lydikäinen cut down in the year 1656 or so in Kuopio in Savolax. See the Åbo *Tidning* for the year 1772, Nº 14 page 3." Ganander, ibid. – If this information cannot be denied as being supported on real historical grounds, then too Dear Gottlund probably also has to concede that his wise and naturally poetic ancestors were not entirely free of idol worship. How could the Pope have forbidden these holy groves if such actually did not exist? Even more remarkable seems the circumstance that they existed as far as the year 1656. That Sjögren in his notes about Kemi Lappmark, pp. 4-5, brooded about the names *Outivaara* and *Outi tunturi* without getting them right, comes from his not knowing the Lapp word *Vuowde*, of which *ouda* is an imitation in Finnish. The Lapps' *Passe ruowde*, the Finns in Northern Finnland call *Pyhä onda*; the Lapps' *Passe vareh*, the Finns call *Pyhä tunturi*; *Outivaara* has thus been called *Vuowde vare* in Lapp; *Outi tunturi* Finnish *Vuowde Tuoddar* Lapp, etc.

§. 38. "Thunder ravaged trolls. When there was thunder, the trolls ran with dread into the woods, until they found a hollow tree. They crept into it, but lightning struck just then, and burned it up." Leem, p. 506.

§. 48. To everything that was of use or harm to them they dedicated a certain deity. Morning redness (*Iditis qvowso*) was a good one. Evening redness (*Ekkedes qvowso*) an evil deity. Therefore, morning redness was placed with *Radien* and the latter with *Ruta*." Jessen, p. 61. Cf. Högström, p. 179.

Yet we do not believe that these deities could be considered other than symbols.

§. 63. "A man does not want to go to *Passevare* with a woman's garment. He even does not want to go there with shoes that during tanning were in the same kettle as women's shoes." Leem, p. 443.

§. 79. A little black bird with a white ring around its neck, which is called in Lapp *Kuoik Garhek* (Cinchus sturnus) was thought to be a happy bird, and was kept like a shrine when it was captured. Leem, p. 504.

Ditto, the one who came under a tree where the cuckoo was cuckooing; also the one who found cuckoo eggs became happy. – Cuckoo eggs were eaten with an overturned kettle on the head. The one who shot a cuckoo became unsuccessful. The one who on an empty stomach heard the cuckoo the first time in the spring, became cold-hearted to his nearest. – The one who heard such, bit into the bark of a tree, and walked around it 3 times against the sun. Then the cuckoo's crowing had no harmful effect." Leem, p. 504.

"The one who on an empty stomach heard a diver for the first time in the spring, would come to grief that the milk from his livestock did not thicken or run." Leem, p. 505. One finds that belief in ill-omened birds is not alike in all places.

§. 96. In view of this, which Ganander alleges about *Maahinen*, I remember too that the Finns on Torneå River have the same belief about these underground creatures, namely that they cause certain outbreaks of rash, like virulent scabies, ringworms, *Elfblost* 'elf rash,' et al. Such an outbreak of illness is called *maa* (earth) and is believed can be remedied, if one daubs the places affected with soil from the churchyard. *Elfblost* is very familiar in Norrland; it is generally believed to be caused by a kind of underground being called *Elfvor* 'elves.' Very likely elf rash can sometimes appear from certain fumes rising from the ground; at any rate, I myself was once rapidly affected by elf rash, when after a swim in the river, I lay down naked on the ground. This actually ought to be the occasion for the common folk's notions about *Elfvor* 'elves' and *Elfblåst* 'elf rash.'

§. 101. "When a reindeer became ill in the milking pasture, an underground woman had milked it." Jessen, p. 66. The common folk in Norrland have the same belief about a cow that produces milk with blood in it.

§. 106. "Steel was put in a baby's cradle so that nothing evil would harm it." Leem, p. 493.

§. 107. Ganander writes *Painajainen*.

§. 108. Concerning the effect of *Para* [cat-shaped troll], Ganander cites Lencquist's thesis on the superstitions of the ancient Finns, (unknown to me). 100 years ago this creature was seen that in appearance was shaggy, black and white spotted, more round than oblong; (without a doubt a thieving neighbor cat) the feet slim like a crane's and 3 in number; resembled quite a bit an old-fashioned dragon-fly. When *Para* was squeezed in a door of a milk house and died, even the wife became ill and died immediately afterward. Ganander, ibid. article *Para*. One notices that the idea about *Para* is different in different provinces. Another story about *Baran's* effect I've heard in Luleå Lappmark. The old woman takes the bread of Communion out of her mouth, and puts this in the middle of the bundle described above, and proceeds as has been mentioned.

Paran vojta 'Troll-cat butter' is in fact a soft mushroom/fungus during the dog-days (Mucor unctuosus flavus Lin. Fl. Sv. 1282.) the superstitious usually boil in tar, salt, sulphur and whip with a withe when it's owner, the troll woman, is believed to be coming out of compassion, and is seen with the intercession of her servant. Ganander, ibidem. Even this information is different than what I heard in Norrland.

§. 120. Cf. Ganander article *Näkki*. Probably the Finns' näkki, at least the name, was borrowed from Swedish *Necken* 'evil spirit of the water.' "Here in Finland necken is described as having long hair hanging down and naked. It appears in water in sunshine on rocks in rapids, where it brushes and combs or arranges its light blond hair. Sometimes it is also heard singing (a siren song or crocodile tune) to entice children to the shore or swimmers to the water whom it embraces so they become blue with cold, sucks their blood, etc. (which as a matter of fact are cramps and pulled muscles)." Ganander under the article *Näkki*. It's correct name in Finnish ought to be *Veden haltia* 'water elf' or *Veden-Emmo*.

§. 132. "When the Lapp was going to explain why the legs of the sacrificed animals were gathered carefully and laid in a *Tamen kare* 'glue pot,' it was said to have happened because the deity to whom the sacrifice was made awakened in Saiwo the very animal that had been sacrificed to him in a more glorious form than it was previously, and were believed to be Saiwo's animals, who were occasionally seen, and were such as were sacrificed to the gods." Jessen, p. 52. "A trustworthy settler who saw how a certain Lapp sacrificed the head, feet and wings of a capercaillie at a well-known rock near *Sagga guoika,* not far from Gellevare [Gällivare], asked him to what end he did such? Then the Lapp is supposed to have answered, out of all this there will grow a profusion of other and newer birds, which he would get to shoot." Högström, p. 183. This notion about the renewal of animal bodies thus seems to have been common in all the Lappmarks. This is seen most clearly in the ceremonies after bear capture, about which more later.

§. 135. "At the Christmas moon's new appearance no woman dared spin, nor any man do any work that caused noise. When the moon rose for the first time, a ring was hung in *Kåta-reppan* 'smoke hole' (the so-called opening through which the smoke in the Lapps' tents goes out) through which its gleam would penetrate." Jessen, p. 81. I wonder whether this might be related to *Joulo Gadse* or *Julkusen* described above?

§. 136. Ganander states that *Kuowon päälliset* means bear funeral feast in Finnish, in connection with which one can ask whether the Lapps' *Kuowa* could have been borrowed from the Finnish *Kuowo*, or have the Finns who also usually held a feast for a slain bear with various ceremonies and songs, borrowed both the name and the funeral feast ceremony from the Lapps. In which case *Kuowa* would be one among the bear's old honorary titles, which he could have gotten from his characteristic of digging his winter lair in the ground (Finnish *kuopia*); and *Kuowa mano* would then come to mean bear month, as a result of the bear, which had been ringed in during the fall, was most easily captured in the month of February when the snow had already reached its proper thickness. This explanation of *Kuowa mano* can acquire a greater semblance of truth if the Finnish mythologists could give us the information that *Kuowa* really means bear. Renvall has not taken up this word. Nor have Lindahl and Öhrling been able to explain what *Kuowa* actually means. In the northernmost Lappmarks and Finnmark bear is called *Qvuowtja* (North Sámi *guovža*), which makes it likely that *kuowa* is just a dialectal variant or peculiar pronunciation.

§. 137. In certain climes *Tjappes olmak* (black people) lived and in others *Tjaba olmak* (good-looking people). Illnesses also had their deities. The pox were called *Sturen olmai*. Plague was called *Tjurre olmai*. Jessen, p. 66.

§. 109. In connection with what Faye says about *Qværn knurren*, ibid. p. 57, I remember that in Lappland one even has a notion about *Quarnkallen*, which the Finns on Torneå River call *Myllyn matti*, a gnome-like creature thought to reside at a mill. A settler in Karesuando says he was once awakened by *Myllyn matti*, when he had fallen asleep at the mill. *Myllan matti* had namely bumped into him and shouted: *jo pääsi*! 'it has fallen!' i.e. the mill is empty. As he awoke right away, he saw the last grain fall from the chute, and it was high time to dam up the mill. Another creature *Såg Gubben* 'the saw man,' whom the Finns call *Saha-matti*, is thought to reside by the saw.

§. 144. One among the Devil's many honorary titles is *Gammel Erik* 'Old Erik' whom even the Lapps copy (*Gambel-Erik*) and the Finns *Vanha Eriki* or *Vanherki*; another Norwegian name for the same man *Påkker*, also copies the Lapps (*Pååkkar*); *det var en Påckers fyr* 'that was a damn fellow,' the Norwegian says: *det var hin till karl* the Swede says; *The lii äska pååkar* the Lapp says. What sort of a remarkable person the Norwegian's *påcker* may have been, is unknown to me.

§. 112. Here one can read what Ganander says about *Saaris*. "Finnland itself, he says, is called *Suomen Saari*, i.e. Finnland's island!" I wonder whether this doesn't suggest a remote antiquity, when Finnland or perhaps all of Scandinavia was an island, as the Lapps even today imagine. That Östersjön 'the Baltic' and, above all, *Bottniska viken* 'the Gulf of Bothnia' annually fall is a well-known fact, but whether it is the water that falls or the land that rises, does not yet seem to have been completely investigated.

Remark. After the books' printing a register of all the mythological objects appearing in the work had to be added, whether in Swedish, Finnish or Lapp together with a brief résumé of their functions, which is particularly useful for the extensive research in general mythology of the Nations.

On the journey through Lappland a few ethnographic objects were collected; here a pair of "Lapp boots" of reindeer hide, given to the Ethnographic Museum in Stockholm by C. J. Sundevall. Ájtte, Swedish mountain and Sámi museum, Jokkmokk.

Visiting a Sámi house on the island of Seiland in Finnmark.

Further supplement to Lapp Mythology.

During the preparation of the forthcoming work, I did not have available Schefferus' *Lapponia*, which only later became available. It is probably necessary to make some excerpts from it, to the extent they concern the present subject. I have already previously remarked that Schefferus had access to good manuscripts, although he did not always draw the right conclusions from the facts correctly stated. The most reliable among Schefferus' informants were the following: *Samuel Rhe[e]n* has given a very good description of Luleå Lappmark, where as pastor he probably served a long time. *Olaus Petri Niurenius* has given an equally good description of Piteå Lappmark. *Erik* and *Zachar. Plantinus* seem to have been in Umeå Lappmark. Otherwise, I do not know for sure where these two lived, since [they] are not included in Series Pastorum in the Lappmarks. Presumably they were living at the mother churches in Vesterbotten, because the Lappmark congregations before 1640-50 were counted as an appendage to the rural parishes in Umeå, Piteå, Luleå, Torneå together with Kemi. Math. Steuchius seems to have been a son of Superintendent Steuchius in Hernösand [Härnösand], which at that time had to do with the Lappmarks; but his information is already less reliable. Even less reliability deserves Domianus à Goës, who had his information from Johannes Magnus; neither of them knew the Lapps' language or customs. The same thing can be said of all the other authors cited by Schefferus, of whom he does not know whether they ever saw the Lappmarks. They could well have gotten their information about the Lapps from persons who were there and seen the Lapps; but how reliable are those reports, when the reporter himself is not born Lapp, or grown up in the country? I have already previously remarked that one cannot rely on such persons' reports, who only as travelers or traders visited the land. One can even today hear various ridiculous reports about the Lapps in the vicinity of the actual Lappmarks. Thus, I have heard several estate persons in Västerbotten say that the Lapps spirit marrow away from marrow bones before they sell them. It has actually happened that marrow bones have come to the table entirely empty, i.e. without marrow. But this was not the fault of the Lapps but of the kitchen maid who boiled the bones so long that all the marrow melted. Marrow bones should not be boiled longer than 8 maximum 10 minutes. Zetterstedt has let himself believe several follies during his trips in the Lappmarks. As for example on his first trip, p. 209. "If they (the Lapps) can get hold of tallow candles, they eat them especially avidly." A Lapp in Vitangi Village at one time ate ½ pound of butter, without bread or the addition of other food. Thus what in older and more recent times has been reported by people who themselves did not know the Lapp language, customs and inner housekeeping, we must take at face value by adopting the reasonable and rejecting the unreasonable. Schefferus also cites an Anonymous manuscript. Which one this may have been, is quite unknown to me. The most reliable informants that Schefferus had, though he less often used their information, are without a doubt Spirzi Nils, a young Lapp student from Luleå Lappmark, together with Olof Sirma, a Lapp youth from Torneå Lappmark, who was studying at Up[p]sala Academi at the time when Schefferus was busy with his work *Lapponia*. This Sirma later became pastor in Enontekiö, and he is still fresh in his memories of the Lapps in this Lappmark.

These are the most essential and most reliable of Schefferus' sources. It is a shame I was unable to get to see the manuscripts cited, in case they are still intact. One would probably find there much interesting information which is not to be derived from the short excerpts in Schefferus. I must now cite the most important of these excerpts that belong to the Lapps' Doctrine of the Gods. Nevertheless, I have to remark beforehand that the authors mentioned above knew well the more important deities such as the Junkers, et al., but the lesser, for example *Saiwo akkerna*, et al. have quite escaped them, which seems to show that they were not so entirely at home in Lapp mythology as they should have been, if they had taken the trouble to consult the *noaidis*.

Addendum to §. 12. "They hold the sun as a mother of everything living. She would guard their reindeer young. The sun had no image." Olaus Magnus according to Schefferus. There is no doubt that the Lapps in times past honored the sun with some sort of worship, although the Swedish authors did not know so exactly what that worship consisted of. Schefferus thinks that the Lapps had no image of the sun, therefore, because she herself was visible. However, the sun seems to have had a definite sign on all the magic drums. Damianus à Goës had stated that the Lapps also worshiped fire, which information was nevertheless refuted by Torneus and Högström. Presumably, the information about the worship of fire was caused by the Lapps sacrificing some of their food and drink to Sarakka, who was thought to have her place by the fireplace. Even this year I have seen an old Lapp woman spill a little schnaps by the fireplace, before she put some in her mouth; and when asked why she did it, said it was a sacrifice to those underground.

§. 32. "So many reindeer the Lapp slaughters for sacrifice, so many idols will he set up in honor of Thor." Samuel Rheen. When one compares this with what was previously cited from Jessen about *Väärro-muor*, then one must assume that the Lapps really made idols for every sacrificial occasion, namely since the permanently standing idol was not so close that the offering could be carried there. But there were permanent idols too that were not renewed on every sacrificial occasion. Only those images made for the occasion were called *Väärro-muor*, i.e. the offer tree.

§. 35. Schefferus talks about Thor, Torden 'thunder,' etc. widely, but from Samuel Rheen's cited information, one finds that Thor is just a translation of the Lapps' *Aijek*, from which one can conclude that the name Thor was not known in the Lapps' language. From Samuel Rheen's cited information, one can conclude that *Tiermes* stems from Luleå Lappmark. This name is thus pure Lapp, and means *Backare* 'backer' or *Backgräfvare* 'hill digger,' as already earlier remarked in this §.

"This Thor they think has power over man's health and wholesomeness, life and death." Samuel Rheen. "Thor's idol should always be of birch." Same. "In the Thor idol's head they pound a steel nail or spike, plus a piece of flint, whereby Thor should strike fire." Anonymous in Schefferus. Schefferus thinks (but without reason) that *Seite* was the same entity as Thor, although also *Seite's* as well as Thor's image were of wood in Torneå Lappmark. Yet, one sees from the whole connection that *Seite* and *Aijek* or Thor were separate objects in the people's imagination. And although Seite's image was sometimes wooden in Torneå Lappmark, it was more often of stone in the other Lappmarks.

§. 37. The rainbow was called *Tors båge* 'Thor's bow,' in Lapp *Aijeke dauge* according to Schefferus. (Otherwise *Atja juoksa*) with which he would kill all trolls. According to Steuchii and Olof Sirma's information, Thor was depicted with a hammer, which was called *Aijeke wetschera* (more correctly *viettjer*). This last-mentioned epithet seems to have been borrowed.

§. 43. "Thor or Thordön the Lapps see as something alive which then rumbles in the sky." Rheen. I have also heard a few settlers in Karesuando be of the same mind.

§§. 41-47. Schefferus has (but without any reason) assumed that the Lapps, and especially the Bjarmians [Permians?}, were descended from the Finns, i.e. those Finns who were forced out of Finland by other Finnish tribes, should have retreated to the Lappmarks and there been Lappified, from which he further concludes that the Lapps' deities are originally Finnish. In connection with that, he also assumes that the Bjarmians' god Jumala was a Finnish deity.

I don't know whether any other historian holds this view; but for my part I see it more plausible that the Lapps were Lapps even though they occupied Finland. There are still many relics of the Lapps almost everywhere in Finland, and still 200 years ago Sodankylä, Kuusamo and Kemiträsk were counted as Lappmarks. The first reliable history we have of Finland, represents the Finns as a slash-and-burn using people. They thus stand on a higher rung of culture and civilization than the Lapps, who with the Finnish tribes' immigration had to give way, and head up toward Fen-

Sámi tent at Ovnene, Magerøya in Finnmark

no-Scandinavia. Now one knows that the people living along the east coast of the Arctic Ocean from Varanger fjord to the White Sea's shores, are Lapps who speak a broken Lapp or Lapp-Finnish with some Russian mixed in. Now if the Bjarmians had been Finns, then they would in later times have had to yield and abandon the land to the weaker Lapps, which is just the opposite of the usual state of affairs. That some so-called Russian Karelians later on, and perhaps early enough settled down in the vicinity of the White Sea, hardly prevents the Lapps from having been there earlier. Most geographers accept that Bjarmaland should be sought on the White Sea's shores. I have earlier shown above that that is not so certain. But even in the case that Bjarmaland's center, where Jumala was worshiped, is supposed to have been in those tracts where Archangel is now found, that people, whom the old Norwegians called Bjarmians, must have been more like Lapps than Finns, which assertion I wish to support on the following grounds:

1st The original Finns did not have any idols. 2nd v. Vesten affirms that there was a large Lapp village, or district that was called *Biarmiri* at the end of the Seve ridge's outermost steep mountaintop toward the east, *Nuorta tunturi*. See above. 3rd Lapps have been found as far away as the Gulf of Finland. Ge[i]jer's *Svenska Folkets Historie*, according to Petrus Læstadius. Journal. 2, p. 469. But if there were Lapps there, then they could also with greater reason have been at the White Sea, because one still finds, just on the other side of the White Sea, a people, *Samojeder* 'Samoyeds,' corresponding with the Lapps both in name and manner of living. But if, as I with greater reason conjecture, Bjarmaland's center was not situated at Archangel, but in the bay of the White Sea, which is on the opposite side and thus farther toward Fenno-Scandinavia, then it is more definite that the Bjarmians were Lapps, whose language nevertheless is more than any other Lapp dialect closer to Finnish, presumably because the Bjarmians were among the first Lapp tribes that entered Scandinavia, and one knows that Lapp and Finnish in times past were much closer to each other than they are now. One still finds in the central and southern Lappmarks names of the places that are more Finnish than Lapp, for example, *Pewrajaur*, from Finnish *Pewra*, et al. The Bjarmians' god was named *Jumala*. This sounds more Finnish than Lapp. But the Russian Lapps' *Jummel* instead of the Swedish Lapps' *Jubmel* and the Finnmark Lapps' *Ibmel* make the difference insignificant.

Since this Bjarmians' god by the name of *Jumala* became so famous in history, and it has now been shown that the Bjarmians belonged to the Lapp nation, then it ought not be out of the way to describe this idol in more detail. However, I must first admit in advance that I do not have the original works before me in which the old Norwegians' Viking journeys to Bjarmaland are fully described. I must thus be satisfied with the citations in Schefferus.

The most essential thing from these reports is that the *Jumala* idol stood in a deep forest; that it was sheltered by a grove or fence. The actual idol resembled a man in sitting position. It had a gold or silver bowl on its knee. The size of the bowl is described thus: 4 men could drink their fill from it, when it was full. This bowl, or as it is called in the saga, *Gullbolla*, was full of gold and silver coins. NB: According to *Herrod's Saga* [*Bósi and Herrauðr's saga*] both the bowl and its contents were gold, but in *St. Olaf's Saga* [*Óláfs saga helga*] it is described as having been of silver. Schefferus presumes that *Jumala* received several visits from Norwegians, which is not so unlikely. Accordingly, the contents (in Schefferus' opinion) of the *Jumala* idol would have consisted of gold, when it was plundered by Erik Blodoxe [Eric Bloodaxe], but when it was plundered by Thorer hund [Thorir Hound] and his companions, its contents should have consisted of silver. This at least sounds more likely. Presumably, the saga has over the course of time become somewhat embellished. The one who wrote the story likely did not have the opportunity to consult the actual eyewitnesses.

Beside the *Gullbollan* mentioned (NB: Today a bowl is still called in the dialect of the northern Lappmarks: Pållo), *Jumala* also had a chain or a clasp around the neck. Schefferus cannot decide for sure whether the Icelandic word *Mæn* [Old Icelandic *men*] means a chain (monile [necklace]) or a clasp (Torques [ringlike band around neck]). But to conclude from the word *Mæns*, etymology (måne [moon]), that it should have been a half-moon shaped neck clasp, which was never at all known to be used by Lapps, but from all of *Jumala's* outfit one sees clearly that *Jumala* was fabricated on a foreign model.

In the Lapp stories about *Staallo* [North Sámi *stállu*] there often appear no doubt such items that allude to the old Norwegians, for example, *Ruowdekapte* 'iron cloak.' One has even found within the area of the Lappmarks such neck clasps of silver, which clearly belonged to the ancient Geats or old Swedes. (Zetterstedt *Resa genom Södra Lappmarken* 'Travels through the southern Lappmarks,' p. 275). That *Jumala* was fabricated on a foreign model, becomes even clearer when one hears that he had a crown on his head, and that in the crown were 12 precious stones. This headdress cannot possibly be of Lapp invention. Among the Lapps there were no crowned heads; nevertheless, several stories about kings, princes and princesses circulate among them, which they heard from neighboring nations. The crown on *Jumala's* head can be compared to the brass crown that was found in *Rekkar-kajse* in Piteå Lappmark in the 1640's, and which is believed to have belonged to a Birkarl. The same crown now hangs in the Arjeplog church, and is furnished with 12 points. (Petrus Læstadius *Journal 2*, p. 500). In order to loosen the neck clasp from *Jumala's* neck, Thorer Hund's companion had to give *Jumala* so powerful a blow with the axe that the head fell off *Jumala*. For that reason, Schefferus concludes that the actual idol was of wood. If I remember correctly, Thorer Hund, in addition to his foster-brother, probably took the opportunity on a changing of the guard, during which they wrecked *Jumala*, and therefore they were in a big hurry. The guard drew near and at the same moment *Jumala* fell over. Then the robbers were pressed to hasten to their ship. Thus, *Jumala's* idol must have been near the sea. Thorer Hund had the malice later on to murder his companion on the return journey to be alone in the robbery.

This story about Jumala is so lengthy that it cannot have been invented. But from where did Jumala get all the finery and riches he had on? When one compares Jumala's idol with the unwieldy and formless stumps one later on found with the Lapps, then one is easily tempted to believe that the Bjarmians were an entirely different people than the Lapps and Finns. Even the latter, if one supposes that the Bjarmians were Finns, could not at this time have been so skillful that they would have been able to make coins, or make crowns and neck clasps? The twelve shimmering stones in Jumala's crown testify, more than other circumstances, that both the idea and attire on Jumala must have been borrowed, but from where? I wonder whether from the Norwegians who carried on trade in Bjarmaland? Or from the Russians? There is probably no one who knows how early the Russians began to visit the coasts of the White Sea, if their own chronicles do not contain anything about it.

§. 49. Samuel Rheen is of the opinion that the Lapps got the Junkar name from Norway, because the Norwegians in times past are supposed to have called their county administrators Junkare [Junkers].

§. 50. "*Stor Junkar* had power over all animals; he gave the Lapps good luck to catch them." Samuel Rheen, ibid. According to Rheen and the Anonymous in Schefferus the *Junkars'* idols were of stone. Högström has nevertheless shown that they were also of wood. The *Junkars'* idols were erected in several places. Samuel Rheen counts up no less than 30 known places of sacrifice in Luleå Lappmark; each and every such place of sacrifice was called *Passe vare*, i.e. a holy mountain. Some sacrificial places belonged to certain families, others belonged to an entire district. Every Junkar idol had a certain territory, within which area no grown woman could come. A few idols represented the Junkar himself, other idols represented the Junkar's wife and children. All according to Rheen and the Anonymous in Schefferus.

§. 60. On an island in *Tarrha*, (the first cataract that falls from Torneå Träsk) Torneus has seen stone idols sort of with hats on the head. No one knew how these stones got there. It is likely that the hats consisted of loose stones fastened onto the oblong stones that were supposed to represent the trunk or body. How the stones got there takes no skill to guess.

§. 92. "They think trolls are everywhere in the mountains and seas." Samuel Rheen. But the author has not indicated what these trolls were called in the Lapps' own language.

§. 129. "Præcipue terrentur et exagitantur a manibus post mortem." [especially frightened and tormented by his hands after death] Schefferus according to Peucer. "They sacrifice to Death or the dead." Anonymous in Schefferus, a confirmation of what was said before in this §.

§. 115. Samuel Rheen says the Lapps did not want to believe the resurrection of the dead; but that something remains after death, that they believe. What that something was the author has not found out. I have already previously mentioned that the Lapps had another idea about the resurrection of the dead.

§. 141. The Danish Petrus Claudi [Brun]/Per Klasson has the following remarkable story about *Ganflugorne* (Gand flies). It happened a few years ago that a farmer who still lives in Helgeland, went up onto a mountain to hunt bears. There he found in a cave a large, coarse idol, which was a *Finne Gud* (Finn god). There alongside stood the Finn's (the Lapp's) *Ganask* [gan box], and when he opened it, it was crawling with blue flies, which were the Finn's *Gan* and *Trolldom* (witchcraft), which he daily sends out. Further, according to the same Claudi: Finn (i.e. the Lapp) cannot live if he does not send out every day a *gan*, that is a fly or troll from his *Ganask* or *Gan-Ide*, that is, a leather bag, which he has them in. And when he doesn't have any person to destroy, or send his *Gan* into, then he releases it to weather and wind; then it may go into humans, livestock or other animals that it comes across. Sometimes he sends his *Gan* into the mountains, and blasts to pieces large mountains. Often they shoot their *Gan* into people and destroy them. Schefferus cites further according to the same author that a certain Asbjörn Gankonge, who did not have his equal in withcraft, was killed in this way, that another *noaidi* shot his *Gan* into a mountain under which the *Gan* king lay and slept, and from that the mountain collapsed and crushed the *Gan* king.

These and other wonders, which are alleged to have occurred through the *noaidis' Gan*, naturally belong to the fables.

But the circumstance that a box or bag was found with living insects in it, strikes me even more in the supposition that there existed a poisonous insect, which the old *noaidis* were aware of, although the authors did not learn the insect's Lapp name. – The eminent schoolmaster Kohlström has told me what he heard from the farmers in Råvaniemi Parish on the Kemi River. There it has often happened that horses and other livestock fell while they were grazing in a large marsh, for which reason the provincial doctor was sometimes ordered there to investigate the circumstances. But the farmers there in the district generally believe that it is an insect that causes the livestock's death. They even say they have seen how it shoots like an arrow toward the creature, whereafter the creature immediately begins to shake, and dies within 4 to 5 hours, or at the latest within a day. The matter really needs to be investigated, because this later information was gotten from the same district from which Linnæus got his information about *Furia infernalis*.

§. 108. At the end of Chapter XI Schefferus has sketched *Baran*, from a specimen from Dalarne, which he obtained from an Assessor Silfverström in Falun. He says it was made of fine wool or hair from some animal, hollow inside, smooth on the outside and of insignificant weight. Without citing the source, he declares that it is called in Lapp *Tyre*, a word I've not heard!

   To M. Gaimard
President of the so-called French North Pole Expedition, is presented this manuscript, by the undersigned and written in his own hand, containing *Fragments of Lapp Mythology* 1. Part Doctrine of the Gods, together with the following supplement, in return for the receipt of 100 riksdaler from the Bank, together with 10 copies of the printed book. Karesuando, the 4th of December 1842.
      Lars Levi Læstadius. Pastor in Karesuando.

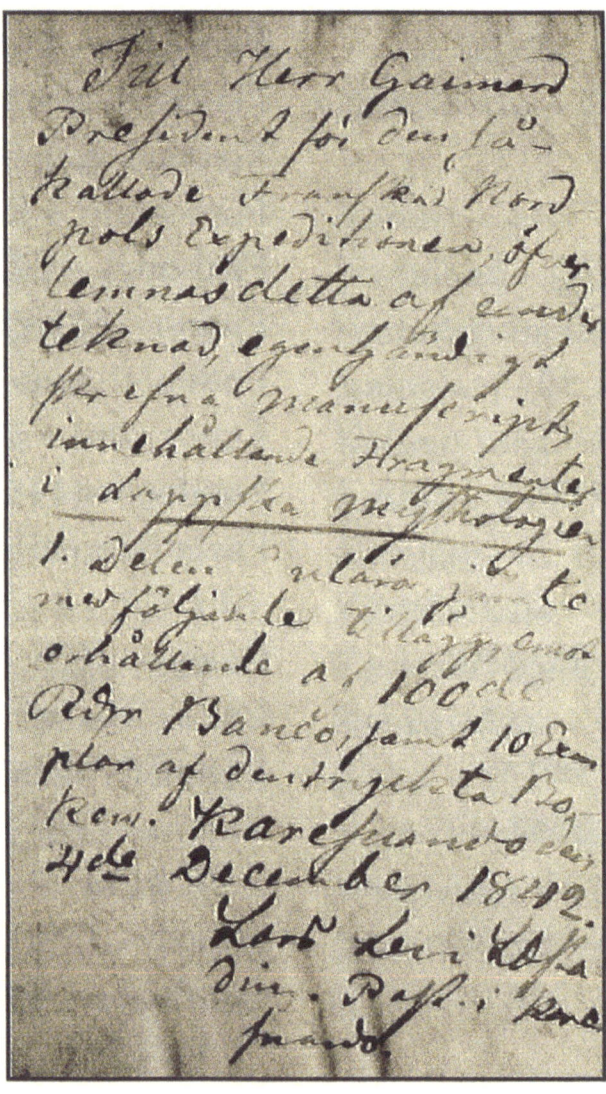

Index to Doctrine of the Gods

Abbreviations:
R. = Reminder to the reader
    (given with s. = page number)
S. = Supplement
S. Tp. = Supplement. To the preface
F. = Further supplement
F. I. = Further supplement. Introduction

Sámi gods, objects and concepts

Aija – §§36, 37
Aijek – §§36, 37, 38 F. §35
Aijeke dauge – F. §37
Aijeke wetschera – F. §37
Aileg – §14
Ailekis olmak – §§11, 13, 14
Aimoh – §114
Ajan joksa – §37
Aksjo – §56
Alakainio – R. p. 56
Alma-ulmuh – §113
Alpe – §76
Arka – §14
Atja juoksa – F. §37
Atjekatsch – §§36, 37, 41
Attje – §36
Attje-gadze – §§33, 34
Atzhie – §6

Baran – §108 T. §108 F. §108
Beiwe – §11
Beiwe labtje – §11
Biarmer – R. p. 56 F. §§41-47

Biegs galles – §48
Birkarlar – §§50, 143, 144 F. §§41-47
Bjeg olmai – §48
Bortbyting – §106
Brudnehark – §§76- 77
Burres – §13
B(j)äran – R. p. 52 §108
Bärardynga – §108
Byting – §106

Cadniha – §96
Cadniha Neidah – §94

Dal junkaren – §49
Draugen – §109
Druotta – §134
Dörakäringen – §23

Ekkedes gvowso – S. §48
Elfblåst (Elfblost) – S. §96
Elfvor – S. §96
Epparis – §§120, 121

Fan(den) – §144
Fenris ulfen – §144
Fietnaalegonum – §76
Finnekonst – R. pp. 55, 56, 57
Frid-ailek – §13
Fudno – §§18, 132
Fudno(s) aimo – §48, 110, 132
Funos aims – §48
Fuodno – §144
Furia infernalis – §142 Yt. §141

Gaasa – §§76, 77
Gadse (Gadze) – §138
Gammel Adam – R. p. 66
Gammel Erik – R. s. 66 §127 S. §144
Gan(d) – R. p. 55 §142 F. §141
Ganflugor – §§140, 141, 142 F. §141
Gast – §116
Geting – §84

Gierkits Gisa – §76
Gissen-olmai – §48
Gjase-almai – §54
Gullbolla – F. – §§41-47

Haavan katset – §138
Habik – §§76, 77
Helvit geune – §137
Helvit kiebne – §137
Helvit tarwe – §137
Helvit-tållå – §137
Hiita – §137
Hilkat – §144
Hin håle – §§109, 118, 143, 144 S. §144
Hin svarte – §144
Hora(n) Galles – §§16, 33, 34, 35, 40
Horan-Orias – §33
Horesgudsk – §33
Huono – §144
Hyden venet – §66

Ibmel – §44 Yt. §§41-47
Ibmel aimo – §§113, 114
Iditis qvowso – S. §48
Ilmarinen R. p. 66 §36
Immel – §44

Jabma aimo – §§71, 72, 81, 82, 110, 111,
          113, 114,115, 129, 132, 133
Jabma akko – §§110, 113, 129
Jamikiaiset – §§130, 131
Jap – §76
Jarnikahah – §113
Jaulo-herre – §135
Joik – R. p. 65 §§33, 71, 76, 81, 110
Juolo-gadze (gadse) – §§135, 139 S. §135
Juolo-peive-herra – §135
Jubma – §§41, 42, 43, 44, 46, 47
Jubmel – §§20, 41, 44, 45, 46, 47, 145 F. §§41-47
Jubmel ailes vuoigenis – §15
Jubmel attje – §15
Jubmel kare – §31

Jubmel pardne – §15
Jubtse – §11
Julkusen – §§135, 139, S. §135
Jumala – R. pp. 61, 66, 67, 68 §§44, 46, 65 F. §§41-47
Jumi(nä) – §47
Jummel – §44 F. §§41-47
Jumo – §47
Junkar – §§49, 50, 51 F. Tp., §49, 50
Ju(o)ks Akka – §§16, 17, 18, 20, 21, 22, 23, 24
Jåulå-herra – §135

Kabnja – §137
Kadnihah – §§93, 105
Kadniha-vuolle – §93
Kainolats – R. p. 56
Kainun maa – R. p. 56
Kaitne – §137
Karelere – R. p. 57 §§19, 56
Karjel-Skalo – §56
Kaskavakko – §14
Katse – §§138, 139
Katsem – §138
Keskiviiko – §14
Kiase-Olmai – §54
Kiebne – §56
Kiebulmai – §144
Kierkits – §77
Kiesse-olmai – §§48, 54
Kiöse-almai – §54
Kohtaus – §131
Kukkes-qwuolle – §82
Kumarta – R. p. 66
Kunka – §137
Kuoik garhek – S. 79
Kuowa – §136 S. §136
Knowa man(n)o – §136 S. §136
Kuowo – S. §136
Kuowon päälliset – S. §136
Kåta-reppan – S. §135

Labe tjeh (labtjeh) – §§13, 18
Lainöer – §76

Lappalainen – R. p. 56
Laudnje kååtte – R. p. 57
Lawa-ailek – §13
Leib-olmai – §§52, 53
Lempo – §137
Lill junkar – §§49, 51
Lista murit – §68
Lodde-pitta – §78
Loitimiset – R. p. 66
Luowe – §57
Luvut – R. p. 66
Läbbo – §137

Maa – S. §96
Maahinen – R. p. 63 §96, T. §96
Maahiset – §105
Maaka – §76
Maanala – §111
Maanalainen – §96
Maanalaiset – R. p. 63 §§113, 130, 131
Maanalan matti – §133
Maanhaldia – §109
Madder-akka – §§7, 16, 17, 18, 20, 21,
    22, 24, 26, 30, 33, 113
Madder-Attje – §§7, 9, 16, 17, 18, 30
Manu hiitui – §137
Maran – §107
Marmæler – §120
Molk – §76
Mubben aimo – §§110, 111, 113, 114
Mubben olmai – §18
Mubben ålmai – §144
Myllyn matti – S. §109
Myran – §73
Mæn(s) F. §§41-47
Målsotis – §106

Namma-quolle – §81
Necken – S. §§120, 109
Nevre – §144
Nibe – §56
Näkki – S. §120

Nåidat – §130
Nåide – R. pp. 52, 53, 55, 56, 63, 66,
    §§1, 3, 19, 20, 73, 75, 76, 77, 78,
    79, 81, 82, 84, 89, 91, 92, 105, 113,
    114, 129, 130, 138, 139, 140, 141
Nåide-gadse(h) – §§139, 140
Nåide lådde – §139

Oknytt – §99
Ormkung – §§83, 84
Ormskinn – §84
Ormsten – §§83, 84
Outitunturi (Outi tunturi) – S. Tp.
Outivaara – T. Tf.

Paha engel – §18
Paikatallam – §78
Paimatz (s) – §§76, 77
Paini(j)ainen – §107 S. §107
Paiwo – §76
Pajan – §36
Para – §108, S. §108
Paradne kuowa – §136
Paran vojta – S. §108
Pasatis – §70
Pasatis mano – §70
Passe(h) – R. p. 66 §§14, 15, 57, 58, 60,
    63, 64, 65, 67, 69, 70
Passe Peiwe – §§14, 70
Passse vare(h) – §§55, 57, 69, 71,
    112. T. Tf. §63. F. §50
Passe vuowde – §57 S. Tp.
Peiwe labtje – §13
Perjetag – §14
Perkel – §§37, 38, 143, 144, 145, 146
Perkele – §§143, 144
Perkel-gadse(h) – §139
Petäjät – S. Tp.
Piellokis – §105
Pirkala – §144
Puold-aija – §40
Puoreh gadseh – §139

Pyhä – R. p. 66
Pyhä tunturi – S. Tp.
Pyhä ouda – R. p. 66 S. Tp.
Pyhä unda – S. Tp.
Pädnak-Njunne – §§19, 109
Pådnje kuowa – §136
Påkker – S. §144
Pållo – Ft. §§41-47
Pårråm-gadseh – §139
Pååkkar – S. §144

Quarnkallen – S. §109
Qvuoddalvis – §79
Qvuowtja – S. §136
Qværn knurren – S. §109

Radien – §§4, 5, 6, 7, 10, 20, 21, 110, 113, 114, 132, 133 S. §48
Radien aimo – §110
Radien attje – §§6, 8, 9, 15
Radien atzhie – §84
Radien kiedde – §§4, 8, 9, 17, 18
Radien pardne – §15
Rananeid – §10
Ranom – §10
Ranot – §10
Rariet – §§9, 13
Ratskin – §113
Rauna – §10
Rauni – §10
Riggasah – §56
Rippo – §76
Rissja – §56
Ristikannot – S. Tp.
Rota – §133
Rot(a) aimo – §133
Rotalanda – §§133, 134
Rothamme – §133
Rucce – §66
Runa(n) (Runot) – R. pp. 56, 60, 62, 64, 65, 68
Ruonaneid – §140
Ruota-kiel – §134

Ruotalaiset – §134
Ruota landa – §134
Ruota ädnam – §134
Ruoti – §134
Ruotsi – §134
Ruotsin kieli – §134
Ruotta – §§133, 134, 137, 143
Ruott-aimo – §§113, 114, 115, 134
Ruottalatsch – §134
Ruott(a)-ekked – §§134, 135
Ruowdekapte – F. §§41-47
Ruta – S. §48
Rut-aimo – §110
Rutu – §§18, 133

Saha-matti – S. §109
Saiwo – §§71, 72, 73, 75, 75,78, 82, 85, 87, 88,
    89, 90, 91, 92, 110, 111, 114, 132 S. §132
Saiwo aimo – §§110, 111
Saiwo akka – F. I.
Saiwo gadse (gadze) – §§138, 139
Saiwo-guelle – §71
Saiwo-lodde(h) – §§71, 75, 76, 78, 79, 82
Saiwo-neid – §132
Saiwo-neid(ah) – §§71, 93, 105, 113, 132, 138
Saiwo ohmah – §§71, 73, 89, 91, 105, 113
Saiwo-quolle (qwuolle) – §§75, 81, 82, 85, 86, 92
Saiwo-sarwah – §§71, 74, 75, 91, 92
Saiwo-tjatse – §89
Saiwo-vesi – §88
Saiwo-vuoign(a) – §§74, 75
Samojeder – F. §§41-47
Saragads – §139
Sarag-Akka – §29
Sarakka – §§25, 27, 28, 29, 30, 31, 32, 139 F. §12
Sarakka-aimo – §§110, 114
Sarvah – §91
Sattan – §144
Saxan maa – R. p. 67
Saxa ädnam – R. p. 67
Seid – R. s. 55 §70
Seite (Säite) – R. p. 66 §§27, 37, 55, 58, 59 60, 61,

        62, 54, 65, 66, 67, 68, 69, 70, 71 Yt. §35
Seite kallo – §70
Seite tjålme – §70
Sergve-edne – §20
Shjort – §121
Sierg-Edne – §20
Silba – §56
Silmen vuoro – §141
Sjelfa hin – §144
Sjelwa – §144
Sjuda-qwuolle – §82
Själ – R. p. 62 §§109, 110, 114, 122, 125, 129
Sjörå – §109
Skalo – §56
Skogsrå – §109
Skratt – §116
Skridfinnar – R. p. 56
Sodna-peiwe-ailek – §13
Sola neid – §11
Solen peiwe – §11
Spåtrumma R. p. 55 §§1, 4, 5, 8, 11,12,
      13, 14, 16, 18, 29, 30, 33, 53, 71,
      15, 73, 75, 135, 137 F. §12
Stallo – F. §§41-47
Stank-Edne– §18
St(u)orjunkar – §§49, 50, 51, 60 F. §50
Stuoramus passe – §67
Sturen olmai – S. §137
Suolo-kårå – §112
Suolo-tjelke – §112
Suomen Saari – S. §112
Suorek – §76
Såg gubben – S. §109

Tamen kare – S. §132
The lii kaitne – §137
Thor – §§33, 37, 43 F. §35
Tor(de)n (Thordön) – §43 F. §§35, 43
Tiermes – §35, F. 35
Tjaba olmak – S. §137
Tjapok – §144
Tjappes aimo – §§110, 111, 113

Tjappes olmak – S. §137
Tjappis ålmai – §144
Tjatse olmai – §§52, 54
Tjebul-ålmai – §144
Tjerro-mubben-aimo – §132
Tjuder – R. p. 57 §19
Tjuolonis – §40
Tjurre olmai – S. §137
Tjåmotis – §95
Tjårwe radien – §§9, 17
Tomtegubbar – §109
Tomtorm – §82
Tonta – §109
Tonto – §138
Tors båge – F. §37
Trollkäring – R. p. 52 §§102, 104
Trollmessor – §13
Trollorm – §§82, 83
Trollsmör – §108
Tuoi ilmen – §111
Tuonan ilme – §§111, 114
Tuonela – §111
Tuoni – §133
Turaturos-podnje – §§33, 34
Tyre – F. §108
Täddalmis – §107
Täddatallat – §107

Udburrer – §121
Ukko – §10
Uks akka – §§16, 17, 18, 20, 21, 22, 23
Underboninga – R. p. 52 §§102, 105, 109
Utböling – §§116, 117, 119, 121

Vabda – §137
Vabda qwuolle – §137
Vanha eriki – S. §144
Vanherki – S. §144
Varrehanka – §76
Veden-emmo – S. §120
Veden haltia – §109 S. §120

Veralden olmai – §§9, 27
Vesi näkki – §120
Viran (Viron) akka – §§27, 58
Viran kannos – §27
Viros akka – §27
Vitterko – §101
Vittra – R. p. 52 §§101, 105, 109
Voi kattu – §108
Vuoja kattu – §108
Vuok(k)o – §§140, 141
Vuornis lådde (Vuornes-lodde) – §§76, 141
Vuoro – §141
Vuowde tuoddan – S. Tp.
Vuowde vare – S. Tp.
Väinämöinen – R. pp. 56, 66
Väros lodde – §140
Väärro-muor – §32, F. §32

Ylikainio – R. p. 56

Zarakka – §§7, 13, 16, 17, 18, 20, 21, 22, 25
Zhikkalaggah (Zhiggalaggah) – §120
Zhioaarve radien – §7
Zhiokkush – §§140, 142

Ädnam-halde – §109
Ädnam kåte – R. p. 57
Äppar – §§116, 118, 121, 122
Äppar-låkkusah – §121
Äpärä – R. p. 63 §§116, 117

Ådtjotalai – §131
Åskan – §43
Åsk-guden – §35

One of the mythological phenomena that Læstadius devotes much attention to in the newly discovered portion of *Gudalära* [*Doctrine of the Gods*], is *Utboren* – a murdered infant or an infant set out to die. In the Index above there are a number of words that characterize such a sobbing or crying infant: *Äppar, Epperis, Zhikkalaggah, Shjort* (Sámi); *Äpärä* (Finnish); *Utböling, Skratt, Gast* (Swedish) and *Udburr* (Norwegian).

The picture shows an exposed infant who has returned to get revenge. After having killed his mother and his father he comes into his aunt's turf hut while she is bathing her own son. She then says to the exposed infant: "Come my boy, I want to bathe you in your cousin's bath water," – in other words, she wants to baptize him. Such bath water that was both crossed and consecrated with steel, was considered by the Sámi in earlier times as holy. It stood for three days before it was thrown out, then under certain rocks such that exposed infants who were down in the earth could bathe in it.

Linocut by Emilie Demant Hatt from her book: *Ved ilden – eventyr og historier fra Lapland – By the fire – tales and stories from Lapland*. (København/Stockholm, 1922).

Jon Larsen Keino, Norwegian Sámi who was a travel guide on the expedition.

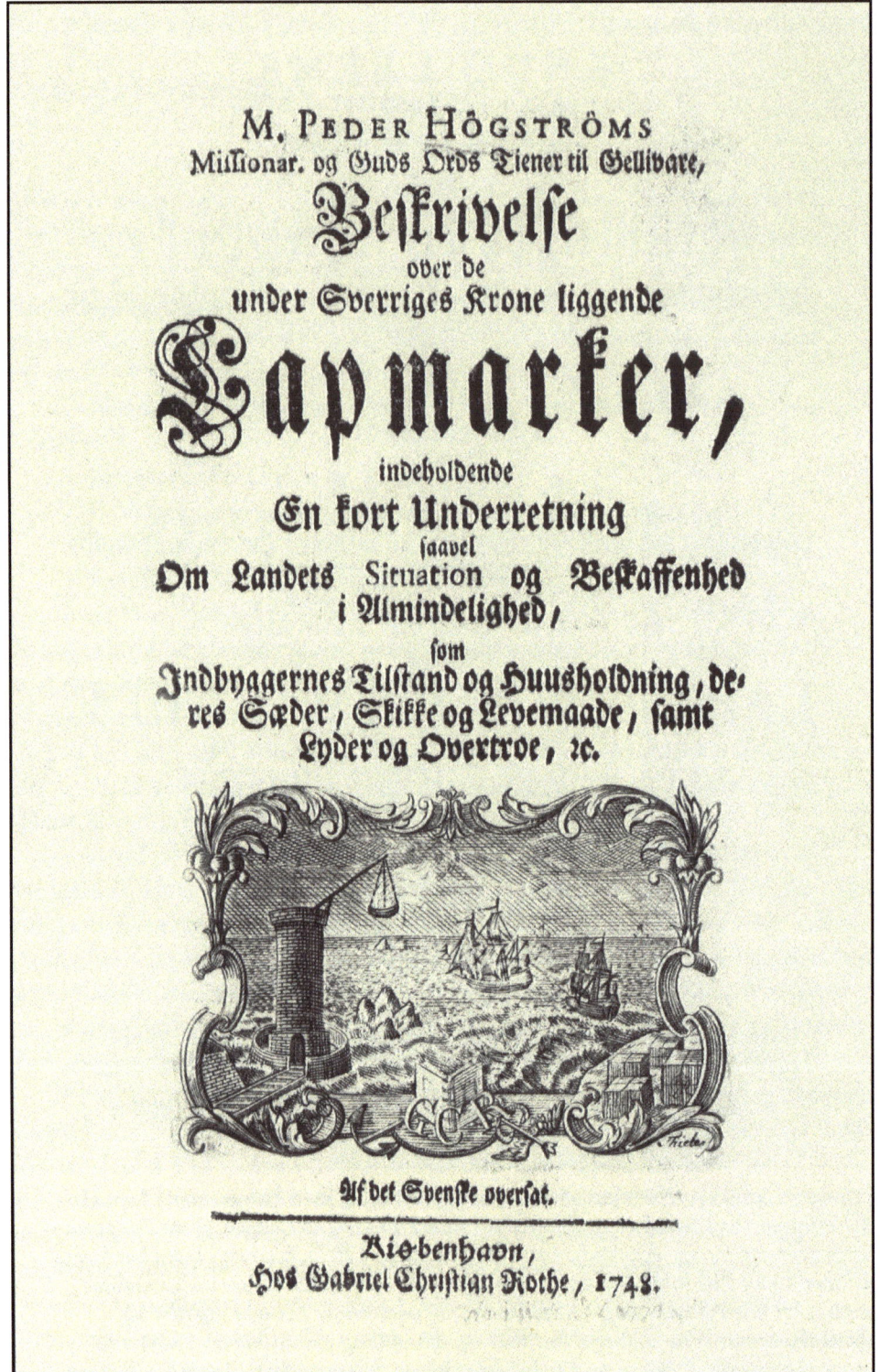

A very important source for Læstadius during work on *Fragmenter i Lappska Mythologien* was Pehr Högström: *Beskrifning öfver de til Sweriges Krona lydande Lapmarker*. The book was published in Stockholm in 1747 and was later translated into several languages. The illustration shows the title page of the Danish edition (København, 1748). Universitetsbiblioteket i Tromsø.

Læstadius' perhaps most important source during work on *Fragmenter i Lappska Mythologien* was Knud Leem: *Beskrivelse over Finmarkens Lapper, deres Tungemaal, Levemaade og forrige Afgudsdyrkelse* (København, 1767). At the back of the book Leem has included two of his sources both of which were also central sources for Læstadius, namely: *En liden Anmelding om en Deel af de uomvendte Finners Afguder og AfgudsDyrkelse* by an anonymous author and *Afhandling om de Norske Finners og Lappers hedenske Religion* by Erich Johan Jessen. Universitetsbiblioteket i Tromsø.

Authors cited or discussed in *Gudalära*

Anonymous in Leem	R. pp. 58, 59 §§3, 5, 7, 10, 11, 13, 17, 21, 22, 25, 35, 48,52, 54, 73, 81, 89, 91, 110, 114, 120, 129,133, 134, 139, 140, 142
Anonymous in Schefferus	F. I. §§35, 50, 129
Acerbi, Giuseppe	R. p. 59
Blom, Gustav Peter	R. pp. 53, 57, 59, 65
Brooke, Arthur de Capell	R. pp. 53, 59
Castrén, Mathias A.	R. p. 60
Damianus à Goës	F. I. §12
Engström, Jon	R. p. 55
Faye, Andreas	R. p. 60 §§96, 103, 120, 121 S. §109
Fellman, Jacob	R. p. 60
Fjellström, Pehr	R. p. 54
Ganander, Christfrid	R. pp. 59, 60, 61, 62, 64, 68 §§10, 11, 13, 22, 27, 35, 48, 49, 52, 76, 81, 91, 92, 110, 121, 133, 137, 144, T. Tf. §§96, 107,108, 112, 120, 136
Gottlund, Carl Axel	R. pp. 59, 60, 61, 62,63, 64, 66, 67 §§14, 46 S. Tp.
Gruber, Johann G.	R. p. 60
Gunnerus, Johan E.	§120
Hammond, Hans	R. p. 60
Holmström, Eric	R. p. 55
Högström, Pehr	R. pp. 54, 55, 58 §§5, 12, 25, 27, 37, 39, 46, 49, 51, 59, 60, 62, 63, 64, 65, 66, 67, 90, 105, 112, 121, 134, 135,136, 139, 144, 145, 146, S. §§48, 132, Yt. §§12, 50
Jessen, Erich Johan	R. pp. 56, 58 §§2, 3, 4, 6, 7, 8, 10, 11, 13, 15, 16, 17, 18, 19, 20, 22, 23, 24, 25, 29, 30, 31, 32, 33, 34, 40, 48, 52, 54, 69, 71, 72, 73, 74, 75, 76, 77, 81, 89, 91, 110, 114, 129, 132, 133,

	138, 140, S. §§48, 101, 132, 135, 137 F. §32
Kijhldal, Jöns	R. p. 59
Leem, Knud	R. pp. 56, 58, 59, 60, 68 §§4, 6, 16, 36, 55, 69, 77, 120, 121, 129, 135, 137, 139, 140, 141 S. §§38, 63, 79, 106
Lindahl & Öhrling	R. p. 55 §§5, 6, 7, 10, 14, 24, 25, 26, 34, 54, 70, 111, 121, 137 S. §136
Linné, Carl von	§§40, 142 F. §141
Lund, Morten	R. pp. 58, 59
Læstadius, Petrus	R. p. 55 §126 F. §§41-47
Lön[n]rot, Elias	R. p. 60
Niurenius, Olaus Petri	F. I.
Plantinus, Erik og Zachar.	F. I.
Renvall, Gustaf	§§34, 41, 138 S. §136
Rheen, Samuel	R. p. 54 F. I. §§32, 35, 43, 49, 50, 92, 115
Rosenvinge, Eiler H.	R. pp. 53, 59
Rühs, Christian F.	R. p. 61
Schefferus, Johannes	R. pp. 53, 54 §§12, 35, 47, 49, 65, 108 F. I §§12, 35, 37, 41, 47, 108, 129, 141
Sidenius, Lennart	R. p. 59 §§3, 5, 9, 10, 11, 13, 22, 25, 35, 48, 49, 52, 54, 76, 81, 114, 129
Sirma, Olof	F. I. §37
Sjögren, Andreas J.	R. p. 55 §64 S. Tf.
Spirri, Nils	F. I.
Steuchius, Math.	F. I. §37
Tacitus, P. C.	R. pp. 56, 57, 63, 66 §26
Torneus, Johannes	R. pp. 53, 54 §§27, 49, 50, 58, 59, 60, 62, 66 F. §§12, 60
Tuderus, Gabriel	R. p. 54 §§68, 70 F. §60
Westen, Thomas von	R. pp. 58, 67 §§4, 5, 8, 9, 10, 12, 25, 26, 27, 31, 48, 54, 114, 129, 132, 133, 142, 144 Ft. §41
Zetterstedt, Johan W.	R. pp. 53, 55, 59, 65 §§108, 109, 115 F. I. §41-47

Doctrine of the Gods in L. L. Læstadius' *Fragments in Lappish mythology*

By Roald E. Kristiansen

With the newly discovered handwritten manuscript from Læstadius' hand (§111b-146) that was discovered in France in the fall of 2001, his treatment of "the doctrine of the gods" in Sámi mythology is finally complete. It has long been suspected that the well-known manuscript was missing some sheets, partly because the previously known conclusion in §111 seems curt and unfinished, but also because the overall structure Læstadius gave the doctrine of the gods seemed to be unfinished.

The doctrine of the gods is in Læstadius' *Fragments* the first of in all four parts that consist of:

1. Doctrine of the gods (§1-111a + new §111b-146)
2, Doctrine of sacrifice [use of the drum as oracle and in sacrificial rites] (§1-71)
3. Doctrine of prophecy [about the noaidi's knowledge and activity] (§1-32) and
4. Doctrine of tales [Sámi storyteller tradition, legends and myths] (§1-40).

Læstadius' manuscript was finished in November of 1844. A few added commentaries were later made in May of the following year after he had read the manuscript of the parish pastor in Utsjok, Jacob Fellman (1795-1875). The further fate of the manuscript was treated by Grundström (1960) who published an excerpt of Læstadius' work, and by Kvideland (1997) who was responsible for editing the entire manuscript in Læstadius' hand as it was known up to that time. The last chapter in this story is treated elsewhere in this publication.

Læstadius' treatment of part 1: "the doctrine of the gods" in its main structure follows the depiction of Sámi ideas of faith in the divine forces as this was interpreted and laid out within the circle of Norwegian missionaries at the beginning of the 18th century. That he takes his point of departure in the original documents on the Norwegian side is connected partly to his thinking that the Norwegian missionaries had provided a more complete account of Sámi mythology than the Swedish pastors, and partly that the missionaries had gained a better knowledge of Sámi language.

Early on, the depiction of the doctrine of the gods acquired a classical formulation in an anonymous manuscript (hereafter called *Anonymous*) that possibly goes back to Thomas von Westen (1682-1727) or in any case from one of his close circle of missionaries.[21] This document was used, for one thing, by Knud Leem when he in 1767 published his great work on *Finmarkens Lapper* (pp. 409-419). Læstadius has had this book available during his work, and he says about Leem's treatment of the subject that he "with a thoroughness in inquiry, and a clarity in presentation that distinguishes him above all others (Læstadius 1997: 13). Læstadius' words of praise for Knud Leem have their background not least in Leem's familiarity with Sámi language, culture and daily life. Leem was a scholar who won Læstadius' confidence because he "not only verified, what others before him had written about the Lapps' superstitions, he himself also sought during his ten-year duties in Finmarken, to penetrate the Lapps' mysteries, and can therefore be considered a classic author of his kind" (ibid.). Læstadius has therefore largely chosen to follow the presentation of the Sámi doctrine of the gods as it appears in Leem.

Anonymous is an "Account of the Lapps' idols" that divides the doctrine of the gods into five sections. The account begins as follows: "The Lapps have imagined gods in various places.

1. Some live uppermost in the starry sky.
2. Some farther down in the air.
3. Some down on earth.
4. Some a bit down in the earth.
5. Some very deep down in the earth."

It is accordingly this structure that lies at the bottom of Læstadius' account. For the concrete treatment of the material however, he also makes use of Erik J. Jessen's monograph, printed as a supplement to Leem's book, and a manuscript from 1726 written by the Swedish missionary Lennart Sidenius.[22] This text was accessible to Læstadius in Ganander's mythological lexicon (1789).

Sidenius divided the Sámi notions of gods into four "classes" (upper celestial, lower celestial, terrestrial and subterranean) while Jessen divided the powers into three classes (upper celestial, celestial and terrestrial). Læstadius operates with a synthesis of *Anonymous*', Sidenius' and Jessen's into a five-fold scheme that encompasses upper celestial, celestial, lower celestial, terrestrial and subterranean powers. Moreover, he believes that the subterranean powers ought to be divided into different categories (as Anonymous does in points 4-5).

The Sámi spelling in Læstadius' manuscript follows in the main the Lule Sámi dialect even if he is not entirely consistent in his orthography. He must be regarded as a pioneer in the development of the Lule Sámi written language (cf. Rydving 2000).

Læstadius begins his account by claiming that the Sámi's mythological notions must be considered as equivalent to other peoples' mythological traditions. The systematization of Sámi mythology as well as ascribing the gods rank and dividing

---

[21] Læstadius himself finds it likely that the original document was composed by von Westen (Læstadius 1997: 12).

[22] Lennart (Leonhard) Sidenius (1702-1763), born in Jemtland in Sweden. Theological exam from København 1724. Missionary to Senja and Vesterålen 1725-28, pastor in Buksnes 1728-1763.

them into classes, does not however have a Sámi origin, but is something that was done by the missionaries themselves to get a perspective on their material. Læstadius nevertheless chooses to follow this classification in his account since the missionaries' systematization in spite of everything was done on the basis of the noaidis' own information such that one can put one's trust in them. At the same time one needs to be aware that the noaidis themselves hardly made such a classification of the gods, and that there can also be large local variations in the ideas about the gods' status and roles: "The Lapps' deities were different in particular Lappmarks" (Læstadius 1997: 23).

Celestial Powers

Læstadius treats the "upper celestial" powers in §§4-10. *Radien* or *Veralden olmai* is referred to as the sovereign with absolute power, not just over heaven and earth, but also over the other gods. He also draws attention to these names being typical for the Sámi of Helgeland, and that they are short of material from the North Sámi areas (Finnmark). Læstadius then touches upon *Madder Akko* and her daughters who create the people's souls and bodies (§7), as well as *Rananeida* who lives uppermost in the starry sky near *Radien* and are associated with the renewal of nature and the maintenance of living conditions for all life on earth (§11).

Among the "celestial" powers belong the sun god *Beiwe* and the sun's daughter, *Sola Neid*, as well as the so-called "holiday men," *Ailekes Olmak*, who are guardians of powerful holy time (holy days) and which Læstadius thinks are influenced by Catholicism. These powers are treated in §§11-15.

The "lower celestial" powers who deal with the origin and conditions for growth of life is the subject of §§16-32. Here Læstadius discusses both the holy progenitor, *Madder Attje* who lives highest up in the sky right below the sun, and his feminine companion *Madder Akka*, the primordial mother in the middle air province. The primordial mother's daughters, *Sarakka*, *Uksakka* and *Juksakka* also belong to this sphere, but their residence is in the lower air layer just above the earth (§§16-32). Among other powers who are grouped in the lower celestial sphere and who serve "the father of power," are the god of thunder Horagalles, who among other things can undo what has been bewitched and that harms people (§§33-40), as well as the god of wind *Bjegs olmai* who rules over weather and wind, sea and water, and who according to Læstadius' understanding was probably mostly worshiped by the sea Sámi since none of the Swedish sources know anything about him (§48). Since *jubma* in Sámi can mean thunder, Læstadius also has a lengthy discussion of the meaning of the designation *Jumala* (Finnish) and *Ipmil* (Sámi) as designation for the deity (§§41-47).

Terrestrial Powers

The "terrestrial" gods are powers who have their haunt on earth and are treated in §§49-70. Here Læstadius discusses the notions about (*Big-*)*Junkars* as idols one sacrifices to (§§49-51) and launches a theory as to whether this idea is historically tied to the Birkarls' activity as tax collectors. Of other powers with a "terrestrial" connection Læstadius mentions *Leib Olmai* who rules over animals and hunting areas (§§52-53), and *Tjatse Olmai* who rules over the fish and who sends fish to the hook or seine (§54). Sacred places in nature are also classified in the terrestrial sphere. These encompass *passe varre* (sacred mountains), *passe vuowde* (sacred forests) and *seite* (sacrificial stones).

Subterranean Powers

The "subterranean" powers are apparently Læstadius' favorite subject and take up most of the space in the doctrine of the gods. This category has several subcategories. Among other things, he discusses the designation *Saiwo* in those places where the subterranean powers stayed and discusses the different creatures that live there in a state Læstadius characterizes as half spiritual and half material. These creatures could be used by especially skilled people to carry out different kinds of services, as well as to bring success in fishing, hunting and other activities. In the realm of the dead under earth, *Jabma-aimo*, lived the souls of the deceased as "virtual" spirits. The treatment of the *Saiwo-* and realm-of-the-dead ideas is very extensive (§§71-105) and includes stories Læstadius himself has heard about the subterranean creatures. Of other types of subterranean powers Læstadius mentions changelings (§106), the nightmare (§107), the butter cat (§108), as well as other creatures in Scandinavian popular belief who only to some extent have counterparts in Sámi tradition (§109).

Mention of the subterranean creatures then gives Læstadius the opportunity to discuss the Sámi's view of the soul's immortality and life after this one. It is in the middle of this section that the manuscript as known up to now stops – in the middle of §111. According to Læstadius' understanding, the Sámi have not only always believed in the soul's immortality, but also in the resurrection of the dead or the body's renewal after death. In the presentation as it continues in the new part of the manuscript, he discusses the difference between a happy and an unhappy state and their different designations, e.g. *Saiwo-aimo* or *Jabma-aimo* for the happy state, and *Mubben-aimo* or *Ruott-aimo* for the unhappy. Læstadius then goes through an etymological discussion of the various *aimo*-designations in order to gain an understanding of the cosmology that characterizes the older period's Sámi conception of the world. He also connects to a story from Högström (1747) about the world being an island floating on a large sea, which continues with an account of the fall of man where God in a distant antiquity let the lakes and rivers rise up and drown all people but for a pair of siblings. These God placed on a high, holy mountain, a *Passe vare*, until the water was gone. It was these two who after that became the origin of the human family.

The main reason for this somewhat complicated presentation examining concepts is for Læstadius to explain that the older Sámi conception of man's fate after death implied two types of *aimok*, i.e. subterranean worlds where the souls of the dead could come. In the first *aimo* the dead would get a new body. Then those who had lived correctly on earth were moved to *Radien* or *Ibmel-aimo* in the starry sky to enjoy eternal bliss. Those who had lived immorally would however sink even deeper beneath the earth and end down in *Ruott-aimo* there to be plagued for all eternity.

Læstadius is open to some of the ideas in the Sámi notions of life after death possibly being influenced by Christian thinking. But more interesting for Læstadius than discussing possible loan hypotheses (this was important for research on Sámi religion from the 1870's and a long time afterward), is to show that the Sámi are not behind other peoples with regard to mythological ideas (§115). This matter has its background in his thinking that Carl Axel Gottlund, that era's greatest authority on Finnish mythology, reduces these notions to no more than a form of nature poetry.[23] He thus finds parallels to *aimo*-conceptions in the Hebrews, Greeks and Romans, and does not at all feel that the Sámi ideas represent a form of "primitive" nature poetic view. Læstadius rather considers Sámi mythology as a form of a Sámi "old testament" that confirms or at least reflects the Christian teaching in its own way. Authenticity in the Sámi ideas Læstadius finds confirmed in that the resurrection of the dead also includes the animals – their bodies too would be renewed in the coming world. In the fact that the idea of the resurrection of the dead is actually a genuine part of Sámi mythology from an earlier epoch, Læstadius finds support for the hypothesis that the Sámi in fact stand on a higher level than the Greeks and the Romans since such an idea did not exist with these people.[24]

After the extensive discussion of the ideas of the coming world, Læstadius continues his presentation by accounting for individual figures who according to popular belief are tied to the deceased. Here (§§116-121) we first meet ideas connected to murdered children who have been put out in forest and field and whom one can meet in the form of what one calls in Norwegian *utbor* (äppar / äpärä), accompanied by a number of stories Læstadius knows about meetings people have had with such beings. He also discusses what Knud Leem called in his book *Zhikka-laggah* and which represents a form of "water ghosts" in child-like form (§120), as well as this creature's relationship to the Norwegian *marmæl* of popular belief and the Tornedalers' *vesi näkki* (water sprite). Læstadius shows himself to be here a pronounced rationalist and considers all such notions as highly problematic with

---

[23] In the foreword "Reminder to the Reader" Læstadius has a clear refutation of Gottlund's argumentation.

[24] To be sure, Læstadius has reservations in the last part of §115 in that he perhaps feels he is claiming a little more than he can purely scientifically defend. That he nevertheless thinks the matter is such as he first proposes it, is on the other hand apparent from his own interpretation of how someone with a Christian temperament ought to judge Sámi mythology.

regard to whether they actually exist. He chooses to be sceptical until someone has managed to catch such a childlike "water creature" and submit it to public scrutiny.

The human soul's immortality and the spiritual beings' existence are the themes for §§122-128. Here Læstadius repeats four tales: about sheriff Granström in Jokkmokk (§§122-125), coffin maker Olof Alstadius in Kvikkjokk (§126), an unpleasant meeting with a revenant in Karesuando in February of 1840 (§127), and about presentiments about visitors (§128). The stories serve as an introduction to observations about Sámi notions about the dead in *Jabma aimo* and their relationship to the living (§§129-132). *Jabma akko*, the mother of death, one thought had designs on the living. If someone became ill, it could be because *Jabma akko* wanted the living down with her. To restrain her she could be satisfied with sacrifices. Læstadius illustrates the ideas about the mother of death with quotations from original Norwegian documents (§§129, 132) and reports from dwellers on the Torne River (§130). That such conceptions are not only found among a "primitive" people on the fringe of the world, is illustrated by corresponding reports from both Jews and Christians at the time of Jesus (§131).

After having treated the "near" subterranean powers (§§110-132), Læstadius then comes to the powers that stay deep down in the earth (§§133-146). These are the evil powers who are harmful to people and other life. Foremost among them is *Ruotta* (or *Rutu / Rota*) (§§133-134). To him come those who do not live according to the gods' will. The living too can meet up with *Ruotta's* wrath, for it is he who sends illnesses and plagues both to humans and reindeer. The remedy is to offer him a horse so he can ride away and not bother anyone any more. Læstadius discusses the etymological background for the word *Ruotta* and has interesting observations about the theme where he connects *Ruotta* both to the Swedes' tyrannical ruler (Drott) and the goddess of the abyss itself.

"The Yule man" – *Jåulå/Jaulo-Herra* – is for Læstadius a somewhat obscure figure (§135). In Leem he has noticed a sketch of a "Yule day man" on a drum and that Yule spirits are spoken about too (*Joulo-Gadze*). What these sketches aim at, however, remains unclear. Læstadius is satisfied with suggesting that the idea about a Yule day man may be of relatively recent date and have a Scandinavian origin. The word's constituents ("jul" and "herre") seem to suggest that such is the case.

In sections §§136-137 Læstadius discusses a number of words that have been or could be characterized as words with mythological background (*kuowa, kaitne, vabda, kabnja, kunka, hiida, läbbo, helvit*). Some of these words must be regarded as pure swear words, while others have a more neutral meaning in their daily usage. Such words may nevertheless at earlier times have had a pithier meaning with direct references to the effect of spiritual powers on life in this world. From the Norwegian sources Læstadius brings forth in §§138-139 *gadsene* (or *katse*) which he understands as sorts of demons or subterranean beings the *noaidis* have much to do with, because they are their teachers in the art of prophecy and dutiful servants to promote both health and harm.

Gan flies are the subject of §§140-142, and Jessen and Leem are the sources for Læstadius' discussion of them. He himself interprets the gan flies as real insects and alleges (§142) that there are no doubt such poisonous insects in the Lappmarks and that they are well known by the Sámi, even if not identified by natural science yet. It is however possible that Linné himself once had a highly unpleasant encounter with such a "gan fly" in Kemi Lappmark and named it *Furia infernalis*.

The last chapters in Læstadius' presentation (§§143-146) discuss "the worst of all mythological objects" – the Devil himself under the names *Perkele* and *Fudno*. The first word Læstadius had already treated in an article in 1836 where he claimed that the word was relatively new and that it had a historical background in the Sámi's reference to the Birkarls (cf. his interpretation of the *junker* designation). The Birkarls were people who were feared and hated by the Sámi for their tyrranical conduct. The evil they were connected to in the material world was so serious and extensive that it got its counterpart in the spiritual world too, and became a designation for absolute evil. As to the word *Fudno*, Læstadius thinks that this word was borrowed from the Swedes' *Fan* or the Danish *Fanden*. He suggests too that this word can be traced back to *Fenris wolf*.

Læstadius also discusses several other designations for personified evil, in part words with obvious Sámi background, but also loanwords from Scandinavian languages that have been adapted to a Sámi context. It is for that matter worth noting that Læstadius finds it little believable that the Sámi have ever sacrificed to *Perkel* (§145).

Supplementary Sections

In the section "Supplement" Læstadius has added a few quotations and some commentary based on the knowledge he himself had concerning Sámi religion and popular belief. The quotations were gotten from Leem (1767), Jessen (1767), Högström (1747) and Ganander (1789) all of whom belonged to Læstadius' most important sources of written information, together with Faye (1833) and Sjögren (1828).

During work on the doctrine of the gods he hadn't had access to Johan Scheffer's (Johannes Schefferus) famous work *Lapponia* from 1673. The book came in several languages in the years that followed (but not in Swedish until 1955). When he finally got hold of a copy of *Lapponia*, he therefore wrote in a "Further supplement to Lapp Mythology" a few commented excerpts from this book. In spite of Schefferus having good sources, he didn't always know how to use them well, Læstadius alleges, and identifies himself who should be seen as Schefferus' most trustworthy sources. His criterion is the insight the authors can be thought to have gotten about the Sámi's life and influence based on how long they served in the Lappmarks and to what extent they mastered the Sámi language. Among the best sources is Samuel Rheen (ca. 1615-1680), preacher in Jokkmokk ca. 1666-1671 and thereafter parish pastor in Råneå to 1680), and Olaus Petri Niurenius (1590-1645 who was parish pastor in Umeå in the period 1619-1645 and the one who founded the first school for the Sámi in 1632). Both have copious descriptions of the areas where they worked. Læstadius also calls attention to the contributions Scheffer got from Spirri Nils (Lule Sámi, wrote for one thing about Sámi sacrificial practice) and Olof Sirma (pastor in Enontekiö 1675-1719). Both were young Sámi who were studying at Uppsala Academy at the time Schefferus was working on his book. In the introduction to *Fragments* Læstadius has besides also called attention to Johannes Torneus (1772), Gabriel Tuderus (1773) and Pehr Fjellström (1755) as useful sources for his work.

Accounts from people who only on occasion visited the Lappmarks, e.g. Damianus à Goës (16th century), Giuseppe Acerbi (1802), Gustav P. Blom (1830), Arthur de Capell Brooke (1823), Eiler H. Rosenwinge (1824) and Johan W. Zetterstedt (1833), are seen by Læstadius as very dubious: about them "they are not worth speaking about" (Læstadius 1997: 13).

In connection with §§41-47 about the Sámi designation for the god *Jubmel* (which for Læstadius is originally Sámi and presumably the oldest Sámi for the deity), he touches on theories of the Sámi's origin as a people. He has his own well-founded points of view on this matter – for one thing, that the so-called Bjarmians on the White Sea were really Sámi. Læstadius builds several of his standpoints on observations of language. These probably can hardly be said to be well founded linguistically; linguistics was after all not a subject he had studied (one might wish he had been better schooled in linguistics as he was in botany!), but he makes use of common sense which by virtue of his knowledge of Sámi, Finnish and Swedish in spite of everything puts him in a position to make interesting arguments.

In the chapter on the Gan flies (§141) Læstadius has included the story Peder Claussøn Friis (by Læstadius called "Petr. Claudi") wrote about in his manuscript from 1632: "Norriges Oc Omliggende øers sandfærdige Bescriffuelse." Læstadius source for this story however is not the original, but a retelling of the story as it appears in Scheffer.[25]

---

[25] (Next page) A complete list of Læstadius' sources for all parts of *Fragmenter*, is found in Læstadius 1997: 230 ff. Note that this list's reference to von Westen's writing is incorrect and should be replaced by the work that is here referred to. Another mistake is that Hans Hammond, *Den Nordiske Missions-Historie* (København, 1787) is cited as a source for Læstadius; he draws express attention to the fact that he has not read this book (Læstadius 1997: 14).

Literary References:[25]

Acerbi, Giuseppe. 1802. *Travels through Sweden, Finland and Lapland, to the North Cape in the years 1798-1799*. Vol. 1-2. London.

Blom, Gustav P. *Bemærkninger paa en reise i Nordlandene og igjennem lapland til Stockholm i Aaret 1827*. Christiania 1830.

Brooke, Arthur de Capell. *Travels through Sweden, Norway, and Finnmark, to the North Cape in the summer of 1820*. London 1823.

Faye, Andreas. 1833. *Norske sagn*. Arendal.

Fellman, Jacob. *Anteckningar under min vistelse i Lappmarken I-IV*. Helsingfors 1906 [only accessible to Læstadius in manuscript copy after he had finished his work].

Fjällström, Pehr. 1755. *Kort berättelse, om lapparnas björna-fänge, samt deras der wid brukade widskeppelser*. Stockholm 1755.

Ganander, Christfried. 1789. *Mythologia fennica*. Åbo.

Goës, Damianus à. 1540. *Deploratio Lappianiae gentis et Lappiae Descriptio*. Lovanii.

Gottlund, Carl Axel. *Försök att förklara Caj. Corn. Taciti omdömen öfver Finnarne*. Stockholm 1834. Cf. also letter from Gottlund to Læstadius (Kuopio, 4. August 1839), cited in "Erinran till Läsaren" (foreword to *Doctrine of the Gods*) in Læstadius 1997: 14-16.

Grundström, Harald. 1960. "Inledning: Fragmenter i lappska mythologien av Lars Levi Læstadius" in *Fragmenter i lappska mythologien*. Stockholm, pp. 5-17.

Högström, Pehr. *Beskrifning öfver de til Sweriges Krona lydande Lapmarker*. Stockholm 1747.

Jessen [Schardeböll], Erik. "Afhandling om de Norrske Finners och Hedenske Religion." Included in Leem 1767.

Kvideland, Reimund. 1997. "Læstadius' lapska mytologi – manuskriptet och dess öden" in *Fragmenter i lappska mytologien*. Åbo, pp. 233-236.

Leem, Knud. *Beskrivelse over Finmarkens Lapper, deres Tungemaal, Levemaade og forrige Afgudsdyrkelse*. Kiøbenhavn 1767.

Linné, Carl von. 1737. *Flora Lapponica*. Amsterdam.

Læstadius, Lars Levi. 1960. *Fragmenter i lappska mythologien*. Redigert av Harald Grundström. Vol. 61, Serie B. Svenska landsmål och svenskt folkliv. Stockholm.

Læstadius, Lars Levi. 1960. *Fragmenter i lappska mythologien*. Reimund Kvideland, red. Med etterord av Juha Pentikäinen. Åbo.

Læstadius, Petrus. 1831-33. *Journal I-II*. Stockholm.

Rosenwinge, Eiler Hagerup. 1824. "Noget om Norlandene, især om Saltens Fogderi, skrevet i 1790" i *Budstikken* 5: 753-816.

Rydving, Håkan. 2000. "Lars Levi Læstadius og det første lulesamiske skriftspråket" i *Lars Levi Læstadius: botaniker, lingvist, etnograf, teolog*, ed. Bengt Jonsell, Inger Nordal, Håkan Rydving. Oslo: Det Norske Videnskaps-Akademi og Kungl. Svenska Vetenskapsakademien. Novus forlag.

Schefferus, Johannes. *Lapponia*. Frankfurt 1673 (Latin), Oxford 1674 (English and German). [Used only as background for "Additional supplement" in the newly discovered manuscript.]

Sidenius, Lennart. [1726] "Lennart Sidenius' bref till Joh. Tornberg med en 'Fortäknelse på een deel oomvendta Lappars Afguderij.'" In Ganander 1789. [Later published in E. Reuterskiöld, *Källskrifter till lapparnas mytologi*. Stockholm 1910.]

Sjögren, Anders Johan. 1828. *Anteckningar om församlingarne i Kemi Lappmark*. Helsingfors.

Tornæus, Johannes. 1772. *Beskrifning, öfwer Torneå och Kemi lappmarker – författad år 1672* in S. S. Loenbom *Historiska Märkwärdigheter, till Uplysning af swenska Häfder* 1767.

Tuderus, Gabriel. [ca. 1670] 1773. "En Kort Berättelse genom hvad tilfälle Sodankyle, Sombio, Kuolajerfvi, Kittka och Mansälke Lappars, i Kiemi Lappmark, Afgudadyrkan, Widskeppelse och skrymtaktige Gudstjenest […]" in S. S. Loenbom, ed. *Twå Berättelser om Lapparnes Omwändelse ifrån Deras fordna Widskeppelser, och Afguderi*. Stockholm, pp. 9-62.

Westen, Thomas von. [1717]. "Topographica arctarchiæ Danicæ ecclesiastica" in *Budstikken* 7 (1826) pp. 8-56. Christiania.

––– [1723] "Danske Missionariens til Lappmarken, Thomas von Westens Berättelse on Norska Lapparnas widskepelser, uti Bref til Swenska presterskapet i Jämteland," Skrifwit år 1723" in S. S. Loenbom, ed. *Twå Berättelser om Lapparnes Omwändelse ifrån Deras fordna Widskeppelser, och Afguderi*. Stockholm, pp. 62-72. [Later published in E. Reuterskiöld, *Källskrifter till lapparnas mytologi*. Stockholm 1910.]

Zetterstedt, Johan Wilhelm. 1833. *Resa genom Umeå Lappmarker i Vesterbottens län*, förrättad år 1832. Örebro.

www.ingramcontent.com/pod-product-compliance
Lightning Source LLC
Chambersburg PA
CBHW040903020526
44114CB00037B/45